Charles M. Schulz

Conversations

Conversations with Comic Artists
M. Thomas Inge, General Editor

Charles M. Schulz
CONVERSATIONS

Edited by

M. Thomas Inge

University Press of Mississippi
Jackson

www.upress.state.ms.us

08 07 06 05 04 03 02 01 00   4 3 2 1
∞
Library of Congress Cataloging-in-Publication Data

Charles M. Schulz : conversations / edited by M. Thomas Inge.
    p.   cm.—(Conversations with comic artists)
Includes index.
ISBN 1-57806-304-3 (cloth : alk. paper)—ISBN 1-57806-305-1
(paper : alk. paper)
    1. Schulz, Charles M.—Interviews.   2. Cartoonists—United States—
Interviews.   3. Schulz, Charles M. Peanuts.   I. Inge, M. Thomas.
II. Series.

PN6727.S3 Z4625 2000
741.5'092—dc21   00-027339

British Library Cataloging-in-Publication Data available

Contents

Introduction

Charles Monroe Schulz is a seminal figure in American cultural history. Whether it is the times that produce the man, or the man that shapes the times, Schulz came along at exactly the right moment in the middle of the twentieth century with *Peanuts* on October 2, 1950. The nation had just emerged from a devastating World War with a sense that justice had been done in a victory over destructive political forces and ideologies, but the very power of those ideologies had revealed a growing sense of alienation and despair in human history.

Perhaps it began with the Enlightenment when scientific rationalism discovered that the earth and human beings were not at the center of the universe. Or perhaps Charles Darwin is responsible when he demonstrated that life seemed dependent on a struggle for survival from which only the most fit or adaptable emerged. Karl Marx also revealed economic man, engaged in a bloody revolution between the haves and the have-nots, all trapped in an inevitable cycle of history which was supposed to lead to a more just society. Sigmund Freud turned inward to examine neurotic man, responding to repressions and psychological conflicts only intense therapy could resolve. Then Albert Einstein delivered the final blow when he found that speed and direction exist only in relation to where we stand. What we once believed were constants have been found to be relative in the scheme of things.

All of these discoveries were seeming products of progress and advancement, yet they also served to illustrate how little control we have over our destinies. The resulting philosophy of existentialism, the horrors of the Holocaust, or the God is dead movement in theology suggested that humans are ineffective creatures responding to political, economic, social, scientific, and psychological influences that we cannot control and barely understand. Thus enter Charles Schulz and his comic strip *Peanuts*, which provided a safe haven for his readers from the uncertainties and insecurities of the last century. His gift was the saving grace of comedy, a laugh or two on a daily basis for fifty years, itself a singular record in the history of the comic strip.

While some have considered *Peanuts* a chronicle of defeat in which Charlie Brown always loses, Schulz put it differently, as he said to *Penthouse* in 1971: "If *Peanuts* chronicles defeat it is probably because defeat is a lot funnier than victory. Most of us know what it is like to lose some kind of contest, and we can identify with the loser."

There is also a larger heroic folk tradition to which Charlie Brown belongs—the figure of the little man, the timid soul, or what Charlie Chaplin called the Little Fellow. This seemingly inadequate hero has come about in response to the overwhelming anxieties of the technological society of the Industrial Revolution. This tradition includes such figures as the heroes of James Thurber's fables and cartoons, Chaplin's Tramp, Buster Keaton's screen persona, George Herriman's Krazy Kat, Chic Young's Dagwood Bumstead, and characters in the writings of Robert Benchley, Dorothy Parker, S. J. Perelman, E. B. White, Ring Lardner, Langston Hughes, and Art Buchwald. Like Woody Allen, who belongs as well, Charlie Brown is a particularly appropriate little soul for the past five decades because of his preoccupation with what has possessed us all—anxiety over our neurotic behavior, the need to establish our identities, the relationship of the self to society, and the overwhelming need to regain control of our destinies. The power of Charlie Brown, and the timid souls who preceded him, lies in his resilience, his ability to accept and humanize the dehumanizing forces around him, and his eternal hope for improving himself and his options in life. In his insecurities and defeats, Charlie is someone with whom we can identify, and through him we experience a revival of spirit and a healing of the psyche. I'm O.K. if you're O.K., Charlie Brown.

The interviews gathered in this volume provide engaging insights into the distinctive genius of Charles Schulz—his ideas, his working habits, and the kind of thought that went into his work as an accomplished humorist and practicing comic artist. Schulz would have been the last person to admit that there was any "art" in what he did. Over and over in these interviews, he acceded to the opinion that the comic strip occupies a position of little consequence in American culture. As he put it in an interview with Stan Isaacs for *Newsday* in 1977, "Comic strips aren't art, they never will be art. They are too transient. Art is something so good it speaks to succeeding generations. . . . Comic strips are not made to last; they are made to be funny today in the paper, thrown away." Partly this attitude had to do with the personal humility characteristic of Schulz himself, who added to the above comment, "I didn't want to be accused of thinking I was better than I really was" (although he just as quickly told Hugh Morrow in his earliest interview for the *Saturday Evening Post*, "You know, I suppose I'm the worst kind of egotist—the kind who pretends to be humble").

In any case, there is plenty of reason to find Schulz wrong on this score. A truly significant piece of art—be it visual, plastic, verbal, or musical—is one that draws from the cumulative traditions that have preceded it, at the same time that it reshapes the traditional form so as to revive and renew it for the future. *Peanuts* perfectly fits this definition. Schulz's comic strip drew on a rich American tradition of creative accomplishments in graphic humor that preceded it and ultimately revived the comic strip for the remainder of the century by demonstrating its versatility in dealing with the social, psychological, and philosophical tensions of the modern world. Arguably without *Peanuts* there might not have been a *Far Side* by Gary Larson, a *Calvin and Hobbes* by Bill Watterson, a *Bloom County* by Berke Breathed, or a *Mutts* by Patrick McDonnell.

Schulz said repeatedly that he drew neither for fame nor fortune but for the pure love of it. He told film critic Leonard Maltin in 1984: "I think cartooning has a certain quality and a certain charm unlike any other medium, . . . a bringing of joy, a bringing of happiness without being too pompous about it. I simply like to draw something that is fun." This is why he holds an unusual if not unmatched record in the fraternity of comic artists for never having used an assistant to either write, draw, ink, or letter *Peanuts*, while most popular cartoonists have sought such help while they turned their attentions to managing merchandising or other careers. Therein lies the distinctive thing about *Peanuts*, perhaps one of the most widely merchandised properties outside those of the Disney Studios. The integrity and staying power of

Peanuts has nothing to do with commercial marketing but rather with the daily strips produced to meet a deadline yet always held to the highest standards of the humorous and artistic skills of a master talent. Commerce can neither detract from nor influence that substantial body of work.

A part of the marketing of *Peanuts* has involved the reprinting of the daily and Sunday strips in countless series of books that have sold millions and millions of copies and remain in print. Schulz has said that only a creation that speaks to succeeding generations can truly be called art. Since these books obviously continue to speak to generation after generation of readers, under his own definition *Peanuts* qualifies as art.

In a recent survey of critics and comic artists, *Peanuts* was selected, second only to the undisputed masterpiece by George Herriman, Krazy Kat, as best comic strip of the century. Schulz was the major pop philosopher, theologian, and psychologist for the second half of the twentieth century in America, but more importantly, he combined these concerns in an eloquent and enduring art form, the comic strip. Now that *Peanuts* has reached fifty, we can see even more clearly the genuine power and brilliance of his artistry.

These interviews have been selected from approximately 300 that were reviewed by the editor, thanks to the faithful and generous help of Edna Poehner who maintains excellent records at Creative Associates. It seems that Schulz seldom said no to a request for an interview, a sign of his generous spirit, although he told Gary Groth that he found them "relaxing." My student research assistant, Kathryn Evered, was invaluable in seeing this book into print. Numerous others have helped in various ways or supported my endeavors in things comical: Seetha Srinivasan at the University Press of Mississippi, and at Randolph-Macon College Susan Timberlake, President Roger H. Martin, Dean Robert Holyer, and former President Ladell Payne.

M. Thomas Inge

Chronology

1922   Charles Monroe Schulz, the only child of German born barber Carl Schulz and his wife Dena Halverson Schulz, is born on November 26 in Flat No. 2 at 919 Chicago Avenue, South in Minneapolis, Minnesota. An uncle nicknames Charles "Sparky" after the horse Sparkplug in the comic strip *Barney Google*.

1928   The family resides on James Avenue in St. Paul; Charles attends kindergarten at Mattocks School where a teacher encourages his first drawings.

1934   The Schulz family acquires a black and white mutt named Spike, later an inspiration for Snoopy.

1936   The family resides at 473 Macalester Street in St. Paul; Charles enters St. Paul Central High School and works as a caddie at Highland Park Golf Club.

1937   Schulz's first published drawing is a sketch of Spike contributed to the February 22 panel of the newspaper comics feature *Believe It or Not* by Robert Ripley.

1940   Schulz graduates from high school, and although he contributes drawings to the senior yearbook, they are not published.

1941   Schulz signs up for a correspondence course in cartooning offered by Federal Schools (later known as Art Instruction, Inc.) of Minneapolis.

1943   Dena Schulz, his mother, dies of cancer. Drafted into the Army during World War II, Schulz serves with the Twentieth Armored Division in France and Germany as an infantryman, staff sergeant, and machine gunner.

1945   Discharged by the Army, he returns to St. Paul, is hired to letter comic book pages for the Roman Catholic publication *Timeless Topix*, and becomes an instructor for Art Instruction, Inc. Schulz lives with his father in an apartment above his barbershop on the corner of Snelling and Selby Avenues.

1947   He begins to contribute a cartoon feature called *Li'l Folks* to the St. Paul *Pioneer Press* where it runs weekly for two years.

1948   Schulz sells a panel cartoon to *The Saturday Evening Post*, where sixteen more of them would appear through 1950.

1950   Assembling a group of his *Li'l Folks* cartoons, Schulz sends them to United Features Syndicate, who invites him to New York where he signs a contract to develop a comic strip. On October 2, the first *Peanuts* daily strip appears in seven newspapers. He lives at 5521 Oliver Avenue, North in Minneapolis.

1951   Schulz marries Joyce Halverson (no relation to his mother's family) on April 18; they would have five children: Meredith, Charles Monroe, Craig, Amy, and Jill. His father Carl marries his second wife, Annabelle. Schulz moves his family to Colorado Springs, Colorado, but returns the following year to Minneapolis.

1952   A *Peanuts* Sunday page begins on January 6, the strip appears in over 40 U.S. papers, and the first anthology, *Peanuts*, is published by Rinehart.

1955   Schulz is awarded the profession's highest honor, the Reuben (named after Rube Goldberg), by the National Cartoonists Society.

1958   With *Peanuts* in 355 U.S. papers and 40 foreign dailies, he is declared Humorist of the Year by Yale University. The Schulz family moves to 2162 Coffee Lane, Sebastopol, California.

1960   The National Education Association gives Schulz the School Bell Award. The first Hallmark greeting cards featuring *Peanuts* characters are released.

1962   *Happiness Is a Warm Puppy* by Schulz is published by Determined Productions. The National Cartoonists Society names *Peanuts* the Best Humor Strip of the Year.

1963   Anderson College in Anderson, Indiana, awards Schulz an honorary LHD degree.

1964   Robert L. Short's *The Gospel According to Peanuts* is published by John Knox Press. A second Reuben is awarded to Schulz by the National Cartoonists Society.

1965   *Peanuts* appears on the front cover of the April 9 issue of *Time* magazine. *A Charlie Brown Christmas*, a television special, wins both Emmy and Peabody awards.

1966   Schulz receives an honorary Doctor of Human Letters degree from St. Mary's College in Moraga, California. Carl, his father, dies from a heart attack while visiting in California from Minnesota. The Schulz family residence burns to the ground, as did Snoopy's doghouse in *Peanuts*.

1967   The Art Directors Club of New York awards Schulz a Certificate of Merit. *Peanuts* appears on the cover of the March 17 issue of *Life* magazine. The musical *You're a Good Man, Charlie Brown* opens off-Broadway on March 7 for a four-year run; it would become the most frequently performed musical in American theatrical history. Governor Ronald Reagan of California declares May 24 Charles Schulz Day.

1968   Robert L. Short's *The Parables of Peanuts* is published by John Knox Press. Snoopy is assigned to the Manned Flight Awareness Program.

1969   The astronauts on Apollo X carry Snoopy and Charlie
              Brown into space with them. *Peanuts* appears on the cover
              of the April 12 issue of *The Saturday Review*. The Redwood
              Ice Arena in Santa Rosa, California, is built by his wife,
              Joyce, and opens on April 28.

1970   *Charlie Brown and Charlie Schulz* by Lee Mendelson and
              Schulz is published by World Publishing Company.

1971   June 17 is declared *Peanuts* Day in San Diego and Schulz is
              given the Key to the City. Snoopy publishes *It Was a Dark
              and Stormy Night* with Holt, Rinehart, and Winston.
              Peanuts appears on the cover of the December 27 issue of
              Newsweek, and Snoopy joins the Holiday on Ice show.
              Peanuts appears in more than 1,100 newspapers reaching
              a daily reading audience of over 100 million people.

1972   Schulz is divorced from Joyce Halverson.

1973   Schulz marries Jean Forsyth on September 23. He builds a
              studio complex at 1 Snoopy Place in Santa Rosa, California,
              adjacent to the Redwood Ice Arena. He receives the Big
              Brother of the Year Award. *A Charlie Brown Thanksgiving*,
              a television special, brings an Emmy Award to Schulz as the
              writer.

1974   Schulz is named Grand Marshal of the Tournament of
              Roses Parade in Pasadena.

1975   *Peanuts* appears in 1,480 newspapers in the U.S. and
              another 175 throughout the world. *Peanuts Jubilee: My
              Life and Art with Charlie Brown and Others* by Schulz is
              published by Holt, Rinehart and Winston. *You're a Good
              Sport, Charlie Brown*, a television special, wins an Emmy
              Award.

1976   *Happy Anniversary, Charlie Brown*, a television special,
              wins an Emmy Award.

1978   Schulz is named Cartoonist of the Year by the International
              Pavilion of Humor in Montreal.

1979   *Happy Birthday, Charlie Brown*, by Lee Mendelson and
              Schulz is published by Ballantine Books.

1980   Schulz himself receives the Charles M. Schulz Award from United Feature Syndicate for contributions to the field of cartooning. *Charlie Brown, Snoopy, and Me* by Schulz and R. Smith Kiliper is published by Doubleday. *Life Is a Circus, Charlie Brown*, a television special, receives an Emmy Award.

1983   *What Have We Learned, Charlie Brown?*, a television special, wins a Peabody Award. Camp Snoopy opens at Knott's Berry Farm in Buena Park, California.

1984   *Peanuts* is sold to its 2,000th newspaper and achieves a place in the *Guiness Book of World Records*.

1985   *You Don't Look 35, Charlie Brown* by Schulz is published by Holt, Rinehart and Winston. The Oakland Museum in California opens an anniversary exhibition, *The Graphic Art of Charles Schulz*, and publishes the catalog.

1986   He is inducted into the Cartoonist Hall of Fame by the Museum of Cartoon Art and given its "Golden Brick" award for lifetime achievement.

1989   A biography, *Good Grief: The Story of Charles M. Schulz* by Rheta Grimsley Johnson, written with the cooperation of Schulz, is published by Pharos Books.

1990   The French Ministry of Culture awards Schulz the *Ordre des Arts et des Lettres* in Paris, and the Louvre opens its exhibition *Snoopy in Fashion*. The National Museum of History in Washington, D.C., opens its exhibition, *This Is Your Childhood, Charlie Brown—Children in American Culture*.

1992   The Montreal Museum of Fine Art opens an exhibition, *Snoopy, the Masterpiece*. The Italian Minister of Culture awards Schulz the Order of Merit.

1994   *Around the World in 45 Years: Charlie Brown's Anniversary Celebration* by Schulz is published by Andrews and McMeel.

1995   *Around the Moon and Home Again: A Tribute to the Art of Charles M. Schultz* is held at the Space Center in Houston in celebration of the 45th anniversary of *Peanuts*. An A & E television biography is devoted to *Charles Schultz— A Charlie Brown Life*.

1996   A star is placed in honor of Schulz on the Hollywood Walk of Fame.

1997   The world premiere of *Peanuts Gallery* by composer Ellen Taaffe Zwilich is held at Carnegie Hall.

1999   In a survey of critics and comic artists by the *Comics Journal*, *Peanuts* is selected second only to George Herriman's *Krazy Kat* as the best comic strip of the century. *Peanuts: A Golden Celebration* by Schulz is published by Harper Collins. *You're a Good Man, Charlie Brown* opens in a new production on Broadway. The International Museum of Cartoon Art in Boca Raton, Florida, opens a year-long celebration of the comic strip with an exhibition, *Fifty Years of Peanuts: The Art of Charles M. Schultz*. *Peanuts* appears in more than 2,600 newspapers in seventy-five countries. Because of health problems, on December 14 Schulz announces his retirement.

2000   Last *Peanuts* daily appears on January 3 and the last Sunday on February 13. On the evening of February 12, Schulz dies at his home in Santa Rosa. The Milton Caniff Lifetime Achievement Award is presented to Schulz posthumously by the National Cartoonists Society. Schulz is posthumously awarded the Congressional Gold Medal, the body's highest civilian honor.

© 1999 United Feature Syndicate, Inc.

Dear Friends,
I have been fortunate to draw Charlie Brown and his friends for almost 50 years. It has been the fulfillment of my childhood ambition.
Unfortunately, I am no longer able to maintain the schedule demanded by a daily comic strip, therefore I am announcing my retirement.

I have been grateful over the years for the loyalty of our editors and the wonderful support and love expressed to me by fans of the comic strip.
Charlie Brown, Snoopy, Linus, Lucy...how can I ever forget them....

Charles M. Schulz

1-3-00

Charles M. Schulz
Conversations

The Success of an Utter Failure

HUGH MORROW / 1956

Charles Monroe Schulz started his rise to success at an early age by
flunking every subject in the eighth grade. Schulz is the creator of
Peanuts, a comic strip in which children talk and act like unvarnished
adults. This libel on childhood appears in newspapers of some 230
American and fifteen foreign cities, and thus far has pushed Schulz's
income up to $50,000 a year. It has also won him millions of fans,
many of whom have given him an undeserved reputation as a superin-
tellectual. Professional recognition was added last April when the
National Cartoonists Society selected Schulz as Cartoonist of the Year.
Schulz was then thirty-three years of age.

All this might never have come to pass if Schulz hadn't been such a
miserable failure in the public schools of St. Paul, Minnesota. His
advancement toward a successful career received a minor setback

during the second year he attended the eighth grade, for he passed that time. But Schulz showed his mettle once again when he reached St. Paul's Central High School. There he triumphantly flunked freshman algebra, sophomore Latin and English, and junior-year physics, the last with a grade of flat zero. This, he recalls contentedly, won him the honor of being the worst physics student in the history of the school.

Socially, his high-school career was equally distinguished. His presence in the school was an occasion of universal apathy. He never dreamed of asking a girl for a date, for he was confident the answer would be negative. While he did make the golf team, he lost his only important match—and then lost the consolation round as well. Life was one grand snub; Schulz was astonished if anyone from the school said hello to him outside school hours. Even his natural early talent at drawing was ignored, for all of the cartoons he prepared for his class graduation annual were rejected.

"I wasn't actually hated," Schulz reminisces. "Nobody cared that much."

Ten years later, Charlie Schulz's memories of his days as a schoolboy failure shaped the personality of Charlie Brown, the round-headed little boy who heads the cast of remarkable small fry in *Peanuts*. Charlie Brown is the epitome of nonachievement, the boy who strikes out at the crucial moment of the crucial baseball game. His chief claim to distinction is that nobody else ever lost 10,000 checker games in a row. His contemporaries in the Schulzian world plan parties solely for the privilege of not inviting Charlie Brown. Two of the little girls in the comic strip find they have something in common—they dislike the same things about Charlie Brown.

"We should wear uniforms," they agree.

Charlie Brown has brought Charlie Schulz such fame that he now must travel from his home in Minneapolis to New York City to be snubbed properly, such fortune that he worries about the income tax. Charlie Brown has become a national symbol of the little man who defeats life's comic outrages simply by surviving them, who solves his insurmountable problems by determined inactivity. As such, he is a comforting and popular figure.

By all external appearances, Charlie Schulz himself is anything but a Charlie Brown. Schulz is half an inch under six feet tall, carries a well-distributed one hundred and seventy-five pounds, has blue eyes and dark blond hair. He is personable, entertaining and gregarious within the bounds of reason. Everyone laughs at the right places when he makes a speech at a women's club or similar gathering—though they still haven't invited him back to talk at Central High School in St. Paul.

His home is a large, solid white stucco with red trim, standing on a fashionable, tree-lined Minneapolis street with the sound of laughter in its name, for the address is 112 West Minnehaha Parkway. His wife, Joyce, is an attractive blonde, and she has borne him four healthy, happy children who hardly ever give him any ideas for his comic strip—

contrary to the popular snap guess. Schulz gets practically all his ideas while doodling at the drawing board. There are two new cars in the driveway, though Schulz won't ride in his wife's predominantly pink convertible.

"It makes me feel silly," he says.

The house within is a showcase of upper-middle-class comfort, from air conditioner in the bedroom to baby grand piano in the living room to pool table in the basement—not to mention an electrical-appliance-manufacturer's dream of a kitchen and breakfast room. From his home it is a short, easy drive to his penthouse studio in downtown Minneapolis—supplied free of charge by Art Instruction, Inc., the correspondence school from which he received his only formal art training, and for which he served five years as a member of the staff. There he works about twenty-five hours a week, at a task, which he finds fascinating. Schulz has never wanted to be anything but a cartoonist.

He is as well disciplined personally as he is professionally. Schulz does not smoke, drink, or swear. "Good grief" and "rats" are his entire expletive vocabulary, and he uses both of these in his comic strip. He is also deeply religious. A member of a fundamentalist congregation in Minneapolis in which everyone tithes, Schulz teaches Sunday school, is president of the board of trustees, serves on the board of Christian education, and sometimes preaches the Sunday sermon.

Schulz sleeps well. Once, however, some months ago, he woke in the middle of the night with a disturbing thought.

Good grief, he said to himself, *who are all these little people? Must I live with them for the rest of my life?*

These were sobering questions, for the little people born of Schulz's off-beat imagination are not to be lightly dismissed. There is, for example, Lucy, the female critic incarnate, the disturber of mental peace. *I Was a Fuss-Budget for the FBI* is among the titles in Lucy's library. Lucy, of course, is the one who defeated Charlie Brown at checkers 10,000 times in a row.

Then there is Schroeder, the musical prodigy, who keeps a bust of Beethoven on his toy piano, stays home from school on Beethoven's birthday, and would lay down his life if it would do Beethoven any good.

How does Schroeder perform classical works when the black keys are only painted on his piano?

"I practice a lot," says Schroeder.

Schroeder told Lucy she might be able to play, too, if she practiced.

"You mean you have to practice to play the piano?" sniffed Lucy. "I thought it was just fool luck."

Schulz, a classical-music addict himself, heard recently that a music school in Florida had hung three portraits on the wall—Beethoven on one side, Brahms on the other, and Schroeder in the middle.

Another contemporary of Charlie Brown is known as Pigpen. He is an incredibly dirty child, though he "thinks clean thoughts." The question arises as to whether Pigpen is a product of heredity or environment; the decision is that it must be environment because he "is covered with it."

"I have affixed to me the dust of countless ages," Pigpen announces. "Who am I to disturb history?"

Linus, Lucy's baby brother, finds security most of the time by sucking his thumb and holding a blanket against his face. Every now and then, however, Linus displays an astounding flash of competence. Charlie Brown tries to explain basketball to him. Linus takes the ball, dribbles it smartly, then shoots a basket in the nearest waste can without even getting up off his diaper. Or, playing outfield, he will spot a fly, remove his thumb from his mouth, fold his blanket neatly and place it on the ground, catch the fly, rifle the ball to the infield, then go back to thumb and blanket.

Snoopy, a Walter Mitty type of dog that likes to pretend he is a cobra, or a lion, or an alligator, zips idiotically in and out of the panel, frequently coming a cropper—as when he zooms through a series of croquet wickets and finally crashes head-on into the goal stick. But Snoopy of late has taken to dancing on his hind legs, thereby achieving a certain superiority over the children because he is able, while dancing, to ignore them.

"Floods, fire and famine!" cries Lucy, while Snoopy dances. "Doom, defeat and despair!" But Snoopy dances on.

"I guess it's no use," Lucy sighs. "Nothing seems to disturb him."

Four days later, Charlie Brown watches Lucy dancing in an imitation of Snoopy.

"If you can't lick 'em, join 'em," Lucy advises.

Patty and Violet, two little girls who team up with Lucy in making Charlie Brown do penance for existing, and Shermy, a little boy who appears when Schulz needs an extra little boy, complete Schulz's cast.

The fact that such an assemblage has waked Schulz only once is an indicator that here is a remarkably stable, well-adjusted human being.

Yet there is a strange loneliness in Schulz, an eagerness for approval that suggests the Charlie Brown in his system hasn't been entirely worked off onto the strips of white paper on which he neatly inks his characters.

"I'm more interested in praise than money," he told me at one point during a recent visit to his home in Minneapolis. Later, while we were shooting pool in his recreation room, he sank the eight ball in the side pocket, chalked his cue and said reflectively, "You know, I suppose I'm the worst kind of egotist—the kind who pretends to be humble."

Schulz is, in fact, a rather complex young man, though not nearly so complex as his fans seem to be trying to make him. In the six years he has been on the national scene in the person of Charlie Brown, Schulz has acquired enough misconceptions about himself to last him a lifetime. He has become philosophical about it.

"Cartoonists don't live anywhere," he observes. "They aren't real people."

Prior to my Minneapolis visit, I was chatting with Schulz in the New York office of the syndicate—United Feature Syndicate—which distributes his work. Schulz was still in a mild state of shock from his appearance the previous evening on Tonight, an NBC television network show. First he had been brusquely denied admission to the theater from which the show originates; no New York theater usher could believe that anyone as mild in manner as Schulz was scheduled to go on the air. With that straightened out, Schulz was admitted, only to find his time on the air reduced to about thirty embarrassing seconds.

"It was good for me," Schulz observed, "Made me realize that I'm only a semi-celebrity."

At this point Schulz received a telephone call from a young woman representing the Democratic National Committee. She was obviously an egghead-for-Adlai, for she told the baffled Schulz that he was "the youngest existentialist," that she was sure he must be for Mr. Stevenson, and wouldn't he do some cartoons to help the cause along?

Schulz responded that cartoonists had no business getting involved in politics, in his opinion, but he thanked the young lady politely and observed that he was flattered by her opinion that he could help shape the course of history.

"Besides," he told me later, "I'm an Eisenhower Republican." At the moment, however, he was more concerned with another question.

"What," he inquired, "is an existentialist?"

I mentioned Jean Paul Sartre, the French intellectual who is the leading light of existential philosophy.

"Oh, yes," said Schulz. "I read about him in *The New York Times,* where he said it was very difficult just to be a human being, and the only way to fight against it is to live an active life—that's very true." That, he added, was all he had read of Sartre. So much for existentialism.

Recently, too, the New York Society for General Semantics asked permission to use some *Peanuts* strips in a textbook on semantics. Schulz is an inveterate fusser over the words he uses in the dialogue he puts in the mouths of his babes. While he will yield to editorial supervision from the syndicate on matters involving commas and dashes, he regards himself as a precisionist in the selection of words. It is a subject on which he stands his ground. "Nobody tells Hemingway," says Schulz. Nevertheless, he had to look up "semantics" in the dictionary.

Schulz fans have written him to suggest that he must have been psychoanalyzed. He has not, and a less likely candidate for the confessional couch would be hard to find. He has yielded, slightly, to what would appear to be a conspiracy to make an egghead out of Charlie Brown, in that he tried to read Toynbee. He soon discovered he was a man who knew when he was licked, and gave up. When

CHARLES SCHULZ

THE SATURDAY EVENING POST

I visited him in Minneapolis, he was yawning his way through Proust. He did read all of Tolstoy's *War and Peace,* even before he saw the movie.

The speculation among followers of *Peanuts* as to what Schulz is really like has caused Schulz to do some thinking on the subject himself.

"I've been trying to figure out whether I'm smart or dumb," he told me, "and I've about come to the conclusion that I'm just sharp. It doesn't really require intelligence to do the strip, but it does take a certain sharpness."

The real Charlie Schulz doesn't like to be called Sparky, given him when he was an infant, after Sparkplug, the horse in the *Barney Google* comic strip. He could draw a recognizable Popeye when he was in the first grade, and dates his ambition to be a cartoonist from that time. He was known in later school years, to his distress, as *The Timid Soul,* after yet another cartoon character.

But Schulz is at a loss to explain where he acquired his dedication to the lively art of cartooning.

"There were no artists in the family, but there were a lot of funny people," is as close as he can come to it. "My grandmother had a sly sense of humor; so did my mother and my aunts. That was the Norwegian side of the family. Dad's side, the German, was more serious."

Schulz's mother died in 1943, shortly after he entered the Army for World War II duty as a machine gunner. His father, Carl, is a handsome, white-haired, senatorial-appearing individual who has operated the Family Barber Shop at the same corner in St. Paul for thirty-nine years. He is enormously proud of his only child's success, though dubious about the way he has achieved it.

"It is a peculiar way to make a living," the son agrees.

Dad Schulz is also somewhat miffed that he must spend ninety cents every two weeks for a Minneapolis paper if he wants to read *Peanuts,* for the strip does not appear in the St. Paul paper he is used to reading.

"Dad's a conservative," Charlie Schulz observes. "It took him twenty years to have a telephone installed in his home, and he still doesn't have one in the barbershop. I sure wish I could be as popular as he is, though. Friends are always telling him he should run for mayor of St. Paul, or something like that."

Dad Schulz, however, is quite content to go on cutting hair, including free haircuts for his son. Charlie sometimes brings along one of his fat monthly pay checks, and the two of them just stand there in the barbershop, staring at the $4000-plus figures on the check and laughing at the delightful joke fate seems to have played, while the other barber in the shop clips away at a customer and pretends not to notice.

Charlie Schulz's feeling that his father, or practically anyone else, is more popular than he, appears to stem from his schoolboy experiences. These, in turn, resulted from the fact that he was too good at his studies in his early school years. He skipped two and one half grades in his early bouts with learning, and the result was that he was, later on, the youngest and smallest boy in his class. Thus his spectacularly bad showing in the eighth grade and in high school, scholastically and socially, occurred because he had been pushed along too fast.

Not that it bothered him too much, as Schulz recalls it. "I just waited for three o'clock to arrive and got on back to my own neighborhood where things were better," he says.

Something somewhat parallel occurred several months ago in Charlie Brown's now-famous comic-strip battle with the kite. Schulz had Charlie Brown get his kite caught in a tree. Charlie Brown's solution of the dilemma was to resolve that he would stand there for the rest of his life, holding onto the string of the immobilized kite. For eight straight days, Charlie Brown did just that, while tension mounted among the fans of *Peanuts*. How would Charlie Brown ever be extricated from this fix?

Finally, in the comic strip, it started to rain. Charlie Brown was advised to come indoors because he was getting soaked. Charlie Brown asked whether the kite was getting wet too. He was told that it was. Whereupon, he smiled, dropped the kite string and walked away, victorious.

This sequence raised editorial eyebrows from coast to coast, for no cartoonist had ever before dared to have absolutely nothing happen in his comic strip for eight days. It also moved one cleric to sermonize on "first-rate dedication to second-rate causes." But to Schulz, it symbolized the little fellow with a problem who can't do anything about it but just hold onto it and wait for something to happen. As such, it was an expression of Schulz's personal philosophy.

"You've just got to let things go along," says Schulz, "ride them out and see how they turn out in the end. There's no use swinging right and left and trying to solve all your problems in one day. It's a policy of moderation."

All through his school days, Schulz was spending much of his spare time drawing, and later, before he entered the Army, he took the correspondence course in cartooning. He was living in St. Paul and the school was just across the Mississippi River in Minneapolis, but Schulz was too ashamed of his work to visit the school in person. He mailed in his lessons and waited for the postman to bring back the critique.

Two weeks after Schulz was drafted into the Army, his mother passed away. The clergyman who preached his mother's funeral sermon whetted Schulz's interest in religion. Prior to that, the Schulzes had been "what you might call drifted Lutherans," in Schulz's own phrase.

In any event, Schulz looked up the preacher again when he returned from the war and became a devoted church worker.

He had, in the meantime, grown up in the Army. He gained twenty-five pounds during basic training, drank his first and only bottle of beer one hot day, became fascinated with machine guns and interested in being a good soldier, and finally reached the front with the 20th Armored Division in Bavaria shortly before the war ended. Schulz was a staff sergeant leading a light-machine-gun squad. As he and his men were mopping up in a German village, he was about to arm a concussion grenade and toss it into an artillery emplacement which still harbored enemy troops, for all he knew, when he saw a little dog wandering into the emplacement.

Schulz stayed his hand. He wasn't going to kill a little dog just on the chance that there might be men there who would kill him. And, fortunately, there were no German soldiers in the emplacement.

"I guess I fought a pretty civilized war," he recalls.

When he returned to St. Paul, however, Schulz returned to a lonely and unsatisfactory life. For a time he was a member of the "52-20 Club," the ex-GIs who got twenty dollars a week while they were job-hunting. He spent most of his time playing golf. Then he went to work for a while lettering the comic pages of a religious magazine published in St. Paul. Finally, one day, and much to his astonishment, he was summoned to Art Instruction, Inc., and asked whether he would like to work on the staff, criticizing the work of other would-be cartoonists.

The cartoons he had been so abashed about, in his prewar days as a student, evidently showed more promise than he realized. In any event, a new world opened up for him. While he still lived in St. Paul with his father, over a liquor store in an apartment into which the liquor store's electric sign flashed dismay until eleven o'clock every night, and while he sometimes had whole weekends with nothing to do but sleep, he did find congenial friends at the art school.

Through them he became interested in classical music, and with them spent enjoyable evenings playing hearts and listening to recordings. Through them, also, he met Miss Joyce Halverson, sister of a member of the school staff, and they were married in 1949 when Schulz's pay had risen to sixty-five dollars a week.

Not long after he was married, Schulz began doing a once-a-week cartoon for a St. Paul newspaper and then, to his surprise, started selling an occasional cartoon to *The Saturday Evening Post.* Finally, when he had assembled about eight cartoons which had been published in this magazine, and some of his strips from the St. Paul paper, he bundled them together and prayerfully mailed them off to the United Feature Syndicate.

The odds against him were as high as 1000 to 1, for the syndicate receives around twenty ideas for comic strips a week, and can take on only about one new one a year. Something about Schulz's work struck a spark at the syndicate, and in October of 1950 *Peanuts* ventured forth into the world in eight daily newspapers. It has grown steadily in circulation since, a Sunday panel has been added, and three book collections of *Peanuts* strips have been published.

Schulz hates the title, *Peanuts,* but the syndicate found that *Li'l' Folks,* the title Schulz had suggested, already was copyrighted by another cartoonist. As Schulz warned at the time, *Peanuts* has caused confusion ever since among new readers who think there must be a character by that name in the strip—until they learn otherwise.

This confusion is as nothing compared with the confusion that has come into the life of a Minneapolis artist friend of Schulz whose name actually is Charlie Brown. He admires Schulz so much that he can't be annoyed at the theft of his name. Besides, he has to admit that he rather gets a kick out of having people at parties ask him how come he was invited, or "Where's your kite, Charlie Brown?"

Some weeks ago, though, Charlie Brown decided to try for a job as a social worker. The man who interviewed him, unfortunately, was a *Peanuts* fan.

"So Charlie Brown wants to work, heh-heh," the interviewer said. "Well, well, well."

All that Charlie (For Real) Brown could do was hang on to that old kite string and wait. Sure enough, the man finally did get around to asking what his qualifications were. And if the flesh-and-blood Brown does get a little tired of having people burst out laughing when he is introduced, or of having them say, "Yeah, and my name's Lucy," he does feel that it is at least making strangers care about who or what he is.

Charlie (The Comic Strip) Brown got to worrying in one recent strip about the fact that nobody cared about him when he had a sudden inspirational thought that "I'll bet Doctor Spock cares about me." Sure enough, not long afterward, Schulz received a letter from Dr. Benjamin Spock, the famous pediatrician whose book on child care is a must for so many young mothers.

"You can tell Charlie Brown that I care about him very much," said Doctor Spock. And, somehow, Schulz has made millions of others feel the same way. Just why, Schulz himself is not too sure, but without too much arm twisting he would be willing to settle for the opinion expressed in an anonymous letter he received from Columbus, Ohio.

"Hey, Schulz," the letter went. "You're a damn genius. A Fan."

You're a Good Man, Charlie Schulz

BARNABY CONRAD / 1967

From *The New York Times Magazine,*
April 16, 1967, pp. 32–35, 42, 44, 46,
49, 52, 54. Reprinted by permission.

"Cartooning is a *fairly* sort of a proposition," said Charlie Brown's
creator recently. "You have to be fairly intelligent—if you were really
intelligent you'd be doing something else; you have to draw fairly
well—if you drew really well you'd be a painter; you have to write fairly well—if you wrote really well you'd be writing books. It's great for a
fairly person like me."

For an only *fairly* person, Charles (Sparky) Schulz bids fair to becoming the most successful newspaper cartoonist of all time. *Peanuts,*
which appears in some 900 newspapers in the U.S. and Canada, plus
100 abroad, has endeared the characters of Charlie, Lucy, Linus,
Schroeder, and Snoopy to an estimated 90 million readers. Records,
films, advertisements, sweatshirts, dolls, books, cocktail napkins, and
other *Peanuts* paraphernalia have capitalized on the craze to make it a

$20-million-a-year industry. The statistics of the triumphs of the strip and its various offshoots are so staggering that its millions of fans—and even its creator—are wondering how the original quality and simplicity of the product can be maintained. As I was interviewing him in his studio—an unexpectedly overdecorated and plush office—near Sebastopol, Calif. (an hour north of San Francisco), the telephone interrupted constantly: A Hollywood producer wanted to talk about a big *Peanuts* musical movie; a caller wanted to know something about the London opening of the hit play *You're a Good Man, Charlie Brown,* (now running Off Broadway in New York), another wanted information on his new paperback, *The Unsinkable Charlie Brown.* And then there were all the calls from people who wanted him to paint posters for charities, make personal appearances or donate money to this or that cause. Each time Schulz—who, with his crew cut and serious boyishness looks like every freshman's senior adviser—hung up the phone with a sigh. It was not a sigh of exasperation, but rather regret—regret that he was not always able to do the many things that people demand of him.

"I usually get between 400 and 500 letters a week and for years I've managed to answer all of them personally, but I don't know." He leafed through some of the letters. "Most of them are so nice and their requests are so polite and worthwhile—a drawing for a crippled kid, a poster for a special high-school dance. 'Just do a quick sketch of Snoopy,' they ask; 'it'll only take five minutes.' And they're right—it *would* only take five minutes. But they think their letter is the only one on my desk. The five minutes have to be multiplied by hundreds." He looked mournfully at the heap of mail. "Thousands. They forget that I not only have to do some drawing, I occasionally have to do some thinking."

He looked out of his studio window and studied a clump of trees beyond an artificial pond. "It's hard to convince people when you're just staring out of the window that you're doing your hardest work of the day. In fact, many times when I'm just sitting here thinking and therefore working like heck I hear the door open and I quickly grab the pen and a piece of paper and start drawing something so that people won't think I'm just goofing off and anxious to have a little chat. But I like visitors when I'm drawing. It gets lonely up here all day, not like an office or a dentist or somebody who has company around him all the time." Schulz has been termed a recluse but he says: "Oh, we go to San Francisco about once a month, see friends, go to a play. But we aren't nightclubbers or cocktail types. Neither of us drink, never have, just isn't part of our life and our friends just have to accept us like that."

He picked up some more letters. "Lots of people write in ideas. Some are good, but I don't seem to be able to use other people's sugges- tions. Here's a pretty good one—'Why not make Snoopy pretend he's a Grand Prix racing driver?' Now that's not a bad idea, and I guess it would work. But first of all, I didn't think of it, and secondly I'd be imitating myself—

CHARLES M. SCHULZ   THE SATURDAY EVENING POST

"We're close enough. . . . Let's try for a field goal!"

sort of copying the Snoopy and the Red baron business. It's always dangerous to copy yourself. Al Capp had a great success with the Shmoos, so then he had to try to repeat with the Kigmies and it wasn't as good. The Red Baron was a good idea but let's not imitate it. My son says he gave me the idea for that—he was working on a World War I model and claims he suggested the Red Baron business, but I don't remember. People think I'm a World War I nut and send me these"—he gestured at shelves of flying books.

I asked him about the hit record "Snoopy and the Red Baron," based on the dog's flights of fancy and aerial encounters with The Red Baron, the king of World War I skies. "I based the Baron on Richtofen because he's sort of the Beethoven of flying. Incidentally, I never heard about this record by the Royal Guardsmen until a friend said, 'Great song you wrote.' I checked with my lawyer the next day and we put a stop to that right away. Or rather we threatened to put a stop until we were included in the success. I understand they've sold two and a half million copies of it already." (Schulz gets a varying percentage of two other hit records as well—Vince Guaraldi's "Jazz Impressions of Charlie Brown" and "Charlie Brown's Christmas," put out by Fantasy Records.)

"Speaking of records, have you heard this?" He picked up the album of You're a Good Man, Charlie Brown, and played the overture. "I'd like to see the show, but haven't really had time. Maybe next

month we'll get to New York, but fist I'm taking my wife and four of our five kids and four kids of friends of ours to Sun Valley for our first real vacation in two years. I hear it's a good show—love the music."

The Off Broadway play, made up of prose taken from Peanuts strips, opened on March 7 at Theater 80 St. Marks. In his ecstatic review Walter Kerr wrote: "They [the people of Peanuts] have marched clean off that page of pure white light . . . and into forthright, fuming, explosively funny conversation without losing a drop of the ink that made their lifelines so human."

When Schulz talks he is every bit as modest and unassuming as one could want the progenitor of Peanuts to be, yet there is a pride of profession in his voice. "Hollywood wants to make a movie of the play and I guess some day we'll do something. There was a nice fellow up here recently who produced To Kill a Mockingbird, and we talked pleasantly. But the moment they start talking about 'their writers' I kind of get chills. I want it to be my words in everything I do. Just as I guess I'm the only cartoonist who doesn't have a helper to do the Sunday strip or fill in backgrounds and stuff. I even do my own lettering. I've thought of it—hiring someone to help. Sometimes I think it would be nice. But then—what would be the point? I don't do this for the money"—he gestured at his big drafting table with several half-inked-in strips on it. "People think I do, but I don't. I do it because I love to draw.

"The things I like to do best are drawing cartoons and hitting golf balls. Now if I hire someone to do my work for me what fun would I get? It'd be like getting someone to hit the golf ball for me. But maybe I'll have to." He glanced balefully at his secretary as she brought in a new stack of mail. "*Life* magazine said I was a multimillionaire—heck, no cartoonist can become a millionaire—but that's what the magazine said and now I'm getting requests for money from all over the world."

Whether or not he is in the millionaire bracket yet, Schulz lives like one. On his 28-acre estate, Coffee Grounds (on Coffee Lane), he has two elegant houses besides his big studio. Then there are stables, a cat, dog and horse per child, a tennis court, a baseball diamond and a four-hole golf course. He is an excellent golfer, 5 handicap, and shoots consistently in the 70's The highlight of his year is the coveted invitation to the Crosby golf tournament in Monterey. He tries to play golf once a week, but as his success mounts and the work load increases he has to forgo more and more games.

Schulz begins his day at 9:30 by walking the quarter mile from his sprawling one-level house across the lawns of his golf holes, past the big swimming pool to his studio. With a secretary in the outer office and a plush living room before you arrive at the place where he actually draws, it could very well be the office of a successful real-estate broker or a preneed cemetery-lot salesman.

Clinically neat and organized, Schulz sits at the drawing board and begins by playing around on a scratch pad with a pencil, doodling situations and ideas. He tries to conceive of the week's work as a whole; six separate days' drawings which will somehow make a unity. When he has the ideas fairly well set in his mind he takes a 28-inch illustration board, which has the margins of the four panels printed on it already, and inks in the dialogue. When he has all six days' strips "dialogued in," he begins to draw the figures and the action, preferring to draw directly with the pen with a minimum of penciled guidelines.

One day's strip takes him about an hour to draw. He is required by the syndicate to be five weeks ahead on the daily and eleven weeks ahead on the Sunday. When I called on him he was just finishing up

the strips for the week of May 8 to May 13, the theme being "Be Kind
to Animals Week." (In one sequence, Snoopy is holding a sign with
that legend on it, and as Lucy goes by he shuts his eyes and puckers up
for a kiss. "Not on your life!" bellows the dear girl bowling the dog
and his sign over backward. Another day ends with Snoopy's saying:
"This was a good week—I didn't get kicked.")

Right now Schulz is also busy preparing an hour-and-a-half film,
plus another TV special. (He writes every word, and supervised the animation of the other three TV specials.)

The books are a further drain on his time. Since the first one, called
plain *Peanuts,* Holt has published some 4,493,000 copies, and they are
all in print. After Holt has had a year or two to sell a *Peanuts* book at
$1, the rights are turned over to Fawcett, which takes the Holt vol-
ume, splits it in two, and sells each copy for 40 cents. To date Fawcett
has sold 12 titles to the tune of 10 million copies. But the publishing
doesn't end there. A few years ago an enterprising San Francisco
woman named Connie Boucher persuaded Schulz to do a book for her
Determined Productions company. It turned out to be *Happiness Is a
Warm Puppy,* and it was on *The New York Times* best-seller list for 45
weeks in 1962 and 1963. This was followed by more "Happiness Is—"
books, plus a Peanuts Date Book, totaling around three million copies
in all. In 1965 the John Knox Press published *The Gospel According to
Peanuts,* being the theological thoughts extracted from the strip,
which has been that firm's best seller of all time at more than 635,000
copies.

Which brings one to another consuming interest of Charles Schulz:
religion. A member of a Scripture-oriented Protestant nondenomina-
tional organization called the Church of God, he keeps 12 Bibles, plus a
set of the dozen volumes of the Interpreters' Bible, in his studio. On
Sundays he teaches Sunday School in Sebastopol ("to adults only—I
could never teach other people's children"). A pushover for charities
and organizations designed to help people, he recently consented to
accept the chairmanship of the National Aid to the Visually Handi-
capped and set about organizing a huge golf tourney, to be known as
the "Charlie Brown-Lucy Tournament," the proceeds of which will go
to the aid of partly blind children. He brooded for weeks over a request
to do a poster for Aid for Retarded Children, tried dozens of ideas, and
finally had to give up. "There was simply no way to do it without the
danger of seeming to mock them."

LUCY—"Little girls of that age are smarter than little boys and she knows it better than most little girls. But she's not as smart as she thinks she is. Beneath the surface there's something tender. But perhaps if you scratched deeper you'd find she's even worse than she seems."

CHARLIE BROWN — "Sure he's wishy-washy but I like him. I didn't mean to give him a failure face in the beginning—I just wanted him to have an anonymous bland round face while the others had more character in theirs."

SNOOPY—"He has his origins in Spike, my dog that I had when I was a kid. White with black spots. He was the wildest and the smartest dog I've ever encountered. Smart? Why, he had a vocabulary of at least 50 words . . ."

So this is the hectic world that was created by Charlie Brown/Schulz (he confesses that they are one and the same person). How did it come about and how did it snowball into these proportions?

Charles Monroe Schulz, as every good *Peanuts* aficionado knows, was born 44 years ago in Minneapolis, Minn. When he was two days old, he was nicknamed "Sparky" by his family for Barney Google's horse Sparkplug, and is still called that by his family and friends. From almost the beginning he wanted to become a cartoonist, thinking it among the noblest of the artistic professions.

"It's a great art," he says now. "I'm convinced it's much harder and more important than illustration. Look at that"—he points to a framed original cartoon page of "Krazy Kat" by George Herriman—"that's art. It was done around 1912 and its humor is every bit as fresh today as then."

Sparky's early life was very Charlie Brownish. "People read a lot into the strip, and I guess what people see in it, that's what's in it. But actually the strip is just about all the dumb things I did when I was little."

In fine Charlie Brown fashion he was the goat on the baseball field, once losing a game 40 to nothing, and even his drawings were turned down by the high school yearbook. In the Army he was similarly unsuccessful. After being trained as a machine gunner, he discovered he had

forgotten to load his weapon the one and only time he was confronted by members of the enemy forces.

"It was the last week of the war and we were going along a road in Southern Germany in a halftrack and somebody said, 'Hey—look over there, there's somebody in that hole over there in the field, shoot him.' So I swung the gun around—50-caliber—pressed the butterfly trigger, and nothing happened. Before I could load he came out with his hands up and I was sure glad I hadn't been able to shoot him."

After the war he got a job lettering a comic magazine, then taught in a Minneapolis art school of the "Draw-me-and-win-a-scholarship" mail-order variety. A fellow instructor was named Charlie Brown, and later unwittingly lent his name to posterity. Another had a pretty blue-eyed sister named Joyce Halverson, and Schulz married her. In 1948 he sold his first cartoon, to *The Saturday Evening Post.* Then he did a weekly cartoon for The St. Paul Pioneer Press called *Li'l Folks.* Within a year it was dropped. After many rejections from other syndicates, it was picked up by United Features in Manhattan. Over Schulz's protests it was renamed *Peanuts.* To this day he is still indignant.

"What an ugly word it is," he says disgustedly. "Say it: *Peanuts!* I can't stand to even write it. And it's a terrible title. Now 'Peppermint Patty' is a good title for a strip. I introduced a character named that into the strip to keep someone else from using it. Funny, people don't tell you how to draw or write but *everybody*'s an expert on titles."

The first month Schulz made $90 with his newly titled strip. A few months later it was up to $1,000 a month. Now, 17 years later, it is close to $1,000 a day.

"Funny," Sparky muses, "I never set out to do a cartoon about kids. I just wanted to be a good cartoonist, like, say, Herriman or my boyhood idol, Roy Crane, who draws *Buz Sawyer*—a fine cartoonist. I always dreamed of some day coming up with some permanent idea or phrase that would pass into the language, like Snuffy Smith's 'bodacious' or some of Al Capp's gimmicks. I guess maybe 'Good grief' has made it. And perhaps the Great Pumpkin. And the 'Happiness Is . . .' title.

"There are a lot of good cartoonists around. I read all of 'em. Capp, Caniff, *Miss Peach.* It pleases me that my children seem to like *Peanuts* as well as any of the others. They know all the books by heart and have favorite strips on their walls and play the records. It's all very gratifying."

When asked about Snoopy, who is my family's favorite character in the strip, he said, "Snoopy's not a real dog, of course—he's an image of what people would like a dog to be. But he has his origins in Spike, my dog that I had when I was a kid. White with black spots. He was the wildest and smartest dog I've ever encountered. Smart? Why, he had a vocabulary of at least 50 words. I mean it. I'd tell him to go down to the basement and bring up a potato and he'd do it. I used to chip tennis balls at him and he'd catch and retrieve 'em." Schulz's sensitive face clouds at the memory. "Had him for years before he died."

Many psychiatrists who charge a good deal more than Lucy van Pelt's 5-cent consultation fee have tried to analyze the special appeal of *Peanuts.* My pedestrian conclusion is that Charles Schulz feels the loss of his dog Spike today as deeply as—or more deeply than—he did a quarter of a century ago, just as he feels the loss of his childhood. Happily for the readers, he is able to translate this long memory and deep feeling into words and pictures. It seems to be universal, either because we had a childhood like that, or wish we had. There's a little Charlie Brown in all of us males and, Lord knows, we've all known, and maybe even married, a Lucy van Pelt, a girl who shouts: "I don't want any downs—I just want ups and ups and ups." Certainly there's been *someone* in each one of our lives ready and eager to pull away the football just as we're about to kick it.

So very often the strip touches chords that remind us of things and homely events we thought we had forgotten. As the catalogue for the recent Whitney exhibition of Andrew Wyeth (Schulz's favorite painter, along with Picasso) stated: "But art arises in the human spirit beyond the reach of words from the levels of deepest memories. We are creatures who need the near and the familiar as well as the exotic."

Emerson wrote in 1838: "A man must have aunts and cousins, must buy carrots and turnips, must have barn and woodshed, must go to market and to the blacksmith's shop, must saunter and sleep and be inferior and silly."

Another factor in the strip's popularity with all ages in his sublime handling of how far the fantasy should go. For example, Snoopy's dog house is always shown in profile; we never see it three-quarters view or

actually go inside it. We just accept the fact when it is said that Snoopy has a Wyeth and a Van Gogh and a pool table in there, but if we actually saw inside and discovered an unbelievable dog house we would cease to believe in Snoopy as a dog and his relationship with the children. Another all-important factor in Schulz's astonishingly good batting average is his unfailing sense of what is subtly funny.

"I get letters all the time," he told me, "from optometrists saying, 'How come you're always talking about ophthalmologists'—Linus wore glasses, you know—'why not give us a break?' It's hard to tell them that ophthalmology is somehow funny and the word optometry just isn't. Like Beethoven. My favorite composer is Brahms—I could listen to him all day—but Brahms isn't a funny word. Beethoven is, so I gave him to Schroeder. Like names: Linus is a good name. I borrowed that from a friend, Linus Maurer. Funny, the other night I was trying to think of a good last name for Pigpen—he hasn't got one—and I felt asleep and I dreamed of a new character named José Peterson. That's a good name, isn't it? But I only put him in the strip for a week—he was a baseball player—but he just didn't belong, so out he went, along with some others I've gotten rid of. My strip is not like the kind that depends on variety or new characters. I've got pretty much the same characters and basic idea that I had 17 years ago. I want to keep the strip simple. I like it, for example, when Charlie Brown watches the first leaf of fall float down and then walks over and just says, 'Did you have a good summer?' That's the kind of strip that gives me pleasure to do.

"I liked one I did that I got from one of my children—the only idea I've ever gotten right from something they did or said. We were at the dinner table and Amy was talking away on a real talking streak and finally I said, 'Can't you *please* be quiet?' and she was silent for a moment and then picked up a slice of bread and began to butter it, saying, 'Am I buttering too loud for you?'

"I gave the line to Charlie Brown after Lucy yelled at him. And I like the violent action ones, kids getting bowled over and such things that cartoons were born to do. Too many of these new strips are not car-toons—they're imitations of films, and the movies can do it so much better, beat them at their own game. But I like the quiet ones too. I like it when Linus says, simply: 'Sucking your thumb without a blanket is like eating a cone without ice cream.' I like it when Charlie Brown gets all excited about a big spelling bee and then goes out on the first word because they say, 'Spell "maze,"' and, being the good baseball fan he is, he spells it 'Mays.' I like to keep it all simple. For instance, it seems to me that Snoopy's been getting pretty fantastical lately. I think I'll simplify him, let him just be a dog for a while.

"Incidentally, Snoopy wasn't in the most popular strip I ever did, the one I've had the most mail on. That was the one where the kids are looking at the clouds and Linus says, 'See that one cloud over there? It sort of looks like the profile of Thomas Eakins, the famous portrait painter. And that other group over there—that looks as though it could be a map of British Honduras. And then do you see that large group of clouds up there? I see the stoning of Stephen. Over to the side I can see the figure of the apostle Paul standing.' Then Lucy says, 'That's very good, Linus. It shows you have quite a good imagination. What do you see in the clouds, Charlie Brown?' And Charlie says, 'Well, I was going to say I saw a ducky and a horsey, but I've changed my mind.'"

The phone rang and he talked for a while. When he hung up he said, "That was something about having a helicopter be attacked by the Red Baron. Over Chicago. They've got a real German World War I plane. Publicity stunt of some kind." He shook his head incredulously, and a little sheepishly, at the world he had created. "Where's it all going to end?"

Where, indeed, is it all going to end? Last Thursday I came home from work, hungry for dinner, to find the entire kitchen given over to the making of a two-foot birthday cake for my daughter. It was in the shape and color of Snoopy. Like any other red-blooded male of this generation, I could only look straight out of the panel at the reader and say, "Good grief!"

A Visit with Charles Schulz

KENNETH L. WILSON / 1967

From *Christian Herald,* September,
1967, pp. 14–15, 59–66, 79, 81.

The creator of Charlie Brown, Linus, Lucy, Schroeder, Snoopy and
friends had given me precise directions for reaching his home, an hour's
drive north of San Francisco's Golden Gate Bridge. On the telephone,
Charles Schulz reeled off the turns from Sebastopol—left at the traffic
signal, "exactly" two miles to the next turn, "approximately" another
two miles to Coffee Lane. Obviously, he had given the same directions
to a lot of people.

I had no trouble at all until I rounded the last turn and saw the curv-
ing buff-brick entrance marked with the street number I was hunting
and the name "Coffee Grounds," the puckishness of which convinced
me that I had indeed arrived. Then my problems began.

A gate barred the driveway that swung off among the trees somewhere. There was no attendant and no discernible way to get the gate

open. Well, I thought, the least I can do is angle my Avis Special in as close as possible and decide what to do next—take a first step of faith, so to speak. As I approached and ran over a hose, behold, the gate opened of itself before me. When I charged on through and ran over another hose, the gate closed behind the car. There was a moral in this somewhere, I was sure; perhaps enough to justify a brand-new best-seller, *The Gospel According to Gateposts.*

"Once you get in, ask somebody where you can find me," Schulz had said, though he had not thought to mention the gate. So I started looking for somebody. As it turned out, there were twenty-seven acres of looking space.

Stopping at what seemed to be an office or reception center, I knocked, but couldn't raise anyone. An overalled workman said, "I think Mr. Schulz went down to the house." Briefcase in hand, I headed toward what I decided must be the house—long, low-slung and homey. On the way I caught up with a blue-shirted delivery man who was also seeking signs of life. A couple of immense, non-Snoopy type dogs exhibited mild interest as we walked up on the patio and rang the doorbell. Inside, we could hear a record player going full blast, and I caught a flash of movement that looked to my professional father-eye like a teen-age daughter gyrating barefoot on the carpet. Either the Tijuana Brass, or whatever, drowned out the doorbell or took precedence over it, for we got no takers. The man with me muttered something I translated as, "If they don't want their gas, it's up to them," and we walked away. Then he had an idea. "I'll radio the office from the truck, and they can telephone him that I'm here." I had no radio, and all I could do was wander back to where the men were working and try somebody else.

"I think Mr. Schulz is at his studio up at the golf course," this one said. "You can't miss it."

He didn't know me. I have an unerring ability to miss things, even golf courses. Back in the car, I headed it in the general direction he had pointed, saw a yellow sign reading, "Charlie Brown Boulevard" and decided this offered greater likelihood than the fork with no name. Soon a couple of greens hove into view. On a knoll to the right I saw a chalet-type structure and pulled up and parked in the carport. There was a newness about the place—not a raw newness, but the kind of finished newness you can get when tasteful and expensive landscaping is a part of the contract. Two wings jutted out from the part of the building that connected them. I tried the nearer entrance, tentatively rattling the wrought iron knocker on a green door. No response. I looked through the glass wall beside it. Nobody home, as far as I could tell. By the other glass-fronted wing, a fountain splashed into a reflecting pool. I tried to look in. It was one-way glass.

Beginning to feel as frustrated as Charlie Brown, I went back to the green door. Somewhere about then a tall, slender, youngish-looking man in shirtsleeves materialized. "Come on in!" said Charlie Schulz. "My secretary is away today." We went into his studio through a sliding door in the glass wall. He settled down at his drawing board where he had been working on a Sunday *Peanuts* strip, and I sat in a comfortable chair. From inside the studio, the view was idyllic. Tall trees, green leaves, the fountain, the play of light and shadow—this was what I saw. Charles Schulz didn't have this distraction; he worked with his back to the glass wall, so that the light would fall on his drawing board.

I admired the room and the building.

"The old studio burned last year," he explained. He was shy and had a quiet but carefully articulated way of talking. He not only looked but sounded the way Charles Lindbergh did when he was younger. I began to feel better. Charlie Schulz wouldn't have barged through that green door, either, I decided.

"I was thinking on the way up here," I said, "how these characters of yours have taken over the country. My younger boy has a white mouse that he calls Snoopy, and he had a little gray mouse that he named Linus, but Linus died. There are your comic strip, daily and Sunday, your Charlie Brown books, the television programs, the off-Broadway play, sweatshirts, all the rest. This leads me to wonder what you are trying to do with *Peanuts*. When you sit down at your drawing board—and I guess you were just doing that when I arrived—to turn out the strip, what do you say to yourself?"

"The thing that interests me mainly is the strip I am working on *today*," he said. "My main job is to draw funny comic strips for the newspapers. The side items which you mention have sprung from the ambitions of other people who came up with ideas which were related. Now, I have nothing against ideas like that. In fact, I have had many wonderful associations with many very nice people. I think our television associations have been especially nice. The privilege of being able to turn out books like *Happiness Is a Warm Puppy* and some of the related items has also been good. I don't think any of these things have detracted from the quality of the feature. But we are accused now and then of having gone commercial. I think this is because people feel so strongly about the characters they fear that someone is going to do something to destroy them. I have always contended that as long as I continued to do all the drawing on the newspaper feature myself, we do not have to worry too much about this. Features of this kind go downhill when they become too big for one man to handle and he begins to have other people do the work for him. Barring ill health or something like that, I see no reason why the strip cannot grow if I as a person continue to grow."

HERE'S THE WORLD WAR I FLYING ACE POSING BESIDE HIS SOPWITH CAMEL... UNFORTUNATELY, THIS HAS NO THEOLOGICAL SIGNIFICANCE!

SCHULZ

© by United Feature Syndicate, Inc.

I said, "You are pointing out that this is something that has to be funny—which brings up the whole business of humor. What is humor?"

Schulz thought about it. "I think that any humor which is really worthwhile is humor which comments upon some aspect of life. This is what I am trying to do most of the time, although there are certain times in the drawing of comics that you do not necessarily have to make a strong social statement; you can make a drawing which in itself is simply a funny little drawing. Maybe no more than a little rubber ball bouncing through the strip and the dog watching the ball go bouncing by and then showing his reaction. This, in itself, can be funny for one day. The thing which you must try to do is to develop a change of pace so that your ideas are not too heavily weighted along certain lines. I like to have a simple idea one day and then go for something profound the next."

I made sure the tape recorder was working. "I guess that another aspect of humor is that it has to be something people can identify with in some way or other. I was looking through one of your books today and I had the feeling that you must have been brought up in the town I was, because that was the way *we* did things. I suppose 'identifying' is not something you can do deliberately. Either you have it or you don't have it."

"I think this is very true," Charles Schulz replied. "One of the advantages I had was being brought up in the Midwest where my interests were not too sophisticated and yet not too bland. I think it is an actual drawback if you were to know only what is going on in New York City or San Francisco. These are too extreme in their cultures. This is why I think it was an advantage to me to be brought up in a place as relatively calm as St. Paul, Minnesota."

I asked, "Do your wife and family think that you're funny?"

Charles Schulz smiled. "I don't really know! They've never actually said so. I do think that our family has a pretty good sense of humor. We have five children. The youngest is Jill who is 9; Amy is 11, Craig is 14, Monte is 16, and Meredith is 17. Monte is the only one of the group who was born in Colorado Springs, which is kind of a standing joke in the family. My wife and I were married and lived in Minneapolis. Then we lived in Colorado Springs for a year. All the other children were born in Minneapolis, but Monte just happened to be born while we were living in Colorado Springs.

"Joyce, my wife, has a fine sense of humor and laughs a lot and I find our children are quite the same. I don't consider myself an especially cheerful person. I don't even consider myself intelligent. I think that I would be what you might call quick-witted. I can think of funny things to say very easily."

I said, "It seems to me that nobody can really be very funny if he takes himself terribly seriously. The fact that your family sees humor in all sorts of situations is an indication that humor is not necessarily a now-I-am-going-to-tell-a-joke sort of thing but the whole process of living."

He agreed. "I am convinced that one of the things which has helped man to survive has been his sense of humor. This is apparent when you look at the high humor found among American soldiers. They have always been men who could laugh at themselves and at each other in the most miserable surroundings."

I asked, "Can humor and faith go together?"

"It's almost a necessity! Those who find no humor in faith are probably those who find the church a refuge for their own black way of looking at life, although I think many of us find the church a refuge for a lot of our personality faults. Those of us, for example, who never learned how to dance feel that the church is an ideal place for us if we can find a church that doesn't believe in dancing. Then we can get away with never having learned how to dance. You can carry this in all sorts of directions and see that the church is a refuge for what is really a 'flaw' in your own makeup. Faith is positive. Humor is a proof of faith, proof that everything is going to be all right with God, nevertheless. There is humor in the Bible. I myself have wished many times that I could read Hebrew so I could catch the humor written between the lines in the Old Testament. The ancient Jewish storytellers must have had humor. The Jewish people must have sat there around the campfire, listening to their teachers tell the stories of how their nation tricked other nations, and laughed mightily. This is all part of the humor of the Bible."

I observed, "When you stop to think of it—and I never really did think especially about it before—it's disturbing that although many people feel that the Bible represents the sum total of all meaningful experience, there is no recognition of any humor in this anywhere or that humor has any part in faith. You were talking about dancing, which makes me think of the legalisms that we've been drawn into. If there was anybody who blew up legalisms, it was Jesus."

"There's no doubt about it," said Charles Schulz. "I think that we have distorted many of the things which he said, so much so in the church that we have lost these things. We are surrounded by scribes and Pharisees who insist upon worshiping on certain days, upon having certain ceremonies and holidays and that people go to certain rituals. We find certain groups among us declaring that they are the true church. You could think of six separate groups right now without putting your mind to it, each of which declares that it has the complete truth and has absolutely no tolerance for anything that any other group is teaching. This is to me the most frightening aspect of what is going on in Christianity today. While we are trying desperately to draw near to each other, there are groups doing exactly the opposite. They are not simply groups to which we can't pay any attention but ones that are gaining ground amazingly each day, gaining adherents. Of course, all you have to do is get yourself a little bit criticized or a little bit persecuted and then this is all you need to convince yourself that you must be part of the true church because somebody hates you. If you can just be obnoxious enough so that somebody will dislike you or criticize you, then obviously you must be right! This, then, is a perfect excuse to withdraw from the rest of the world."

I said, "I have wondered whether the religious implications in

Peanuts are something that people like Robert Short have read into it, as you could read theology into a baseball game or anything else, whether you deliberately put them in, or whether they simply get in because this is a part of the way you are."

"I think it is a combination of these things," said Schulz. "When a person has to turn out something funny every day of every week of every month of every year, and this goes on year after year after year, you obviously have to draw upon every thought which comes to your mind! Everything that you know becomes part of this comic strip. Of course, I do have an interest in spiritual things. I do like to study the Bible. It is fun to throw in some of these items now and then, which was what prompted Robert Short to examine the strip more carefully than perhaps the average reader does. He combined this with his own theory, which is that you can take works of art, of what we might call the lively or contemporary arts, and you can use them to teach Christian lessons. He does not maintain that there are deep hidden meanings in *Peanuts* which I have put in. He has never really said that. So he has combined these two things and has been able to come up with this most useful book, *The Gospel According to Peanuts.* I say 'useful' because it has enabled Robert to go to all sorts of campuses throughout this country, and recently even overseas, to talk to people who normally might not listen to the average speaker or the average preacher."

"Last night just before I went to sleep, I prayed that if I asked you for a date, you'd accept...sort of puts you on the spot, doesn't it?"

"There are many things, incidentally, that have come from this feature, which please me. You mentioned the Broadway show. Through it, *Peanuts* has had an influence on cleanness of entertainment. Now,

we've never had to worry too much about the comic strip because the comic strip itself is a very strongly 'censored' form of entertainment. Probably more people read the comic strips each day than take part in any other form of entertainment. Therefore, we know right away that there are a lot of people who are part of this entertainment medium. But I am strongly disturbed by the trends that are taking place in other forms of entertainment, so when this opportunity to do an off-Broadway show came up I asked the producer to retain the innocent quality which *Peanuts* has, and I told him he would be pleased then at the reaction he'd get. I said, 'You will find that mothers and fathers will be only too happy to bring their children to see something like this, because where else these days can you go to the theater and take your children?' It has become almost impossible to find a movie to go to as a family, anymore. So they did this and the results were amazing. We now find entire families going to the theater in New York. Was this happening before? I am not so sure that it was. Out here in San Francisco the producer of the theater, which is right in the heart of the North Beach district, volunteered to suspend the liquor license in his theater for the entire run of the show, *You're a Good Man, Charlie Brown.* This is an amazing thing to have happen in this area!"

"Where is the play expected to run this year?" I asked.

"It opened on June 1 at the Little Fox Theater in San Francisco. It is still in its run in New York City and it will very soon, I think, open in London and possibly several other cities in Europe. The producer probably will eventually have it running in maybe four or five cities in the United States and also have a touring company."

I wondered, "How does an artist like yourself work? How long does it take to do a strip?"

He replied, "I can do a daily strip in about an hour, sometimes less, if it is a very simple one. I have been known, on two or three occasions, to draw as many as six daily strips in one day."

I said, "Do you ever have days when you sit there and nothing happens?"

"Quite often!" He sighed. "I sit there and two or three magazines which happen to have come in the mail that day become extra-tempting. I find myself flipping through the magazines, kidding myself into thinking that what I am really doing is looking for something which will prompt a thought. And, of course, this does happen. And then I get sleepy and my head nods and I find myself falling asleep. I suppose what I really should do is just forget the whole thing and go off and do something else, but I know I can't, because I've got to get something going. Finally the whole day has passed and I not only haven't accomplished anything but have fallen one day further behind. I try not to let it get me down because I've experienced it enough not to let it really bother me, to know that this is all a part of it."

I had been looking around at the studio, which was clearly not one of the major battlegrounds of the war on poverty. "I suppose one never necessarily thinks of himself as a success, but it's obvious that you are successful in your chosen field. What does success do to one's concepts?"

He slowed down on that one. "It's really more of a disturbing element in my life than anything else, I think, especially because of my Christian belief. I've never quite been able to resolve this. I cannot *help* that the comic strip brings in a good deal of money. I do not draw the comic strip to make money. I draw it because it is the one thing which I feel I do best, and I can see no reason why I should give up drawing the comic strip in order to go to the mission field, for instance, and

become a terrible missionary or to study for the ministry and become a
terrible minister, merely because the ministry would seem to be closer
to spiritual things. I think it's much better to be a good cartoonist than
a terrible minister. But I find this always difficult to resolve. I'm not sure
I have resolved it completely. This is why I suppose I shy away from
thinking of myself as a success, and I always think of myself as a success, and I always think of the admonition to beware when people
speak well of you."

"Perhaps there are too many people these days speaking well of me
and I should begin to beware. I enjoy, of course, knowing that what I
draw is liked by so many people. I enjoy knowing that other cartoonists
regard it fairly highly. I enjoy having received the 'Outstanding Cartoonist of the Year Award' a couple of times, because to know that
other people in your own craft admire what you do is a wonderful
thing. I enjoy being recognized by people when I go into stores. I enjoy
the little extra-nice treatment that you get merely because someone
likes what you draw. These are all nice things and I try never to let
them turn me into an obnoxious sort of person. The more I think about
it and try to define it, I see nothing wrong with my drawing a comic
strip, although a way back, years ago when I was first getting started, I
am certain there were people in the church who thought that it was a
useless endeavor and that I could have been doing something more
worthwhile. But I think I've reached a lot of people this way and have
given a lot of people some cheerful moments and I'm quite happy
because of this."

We drank coffee a Girl Friday brought from the studio kitchenette.
"I asked about your success in your chosen field," I said. "How 'chosen' was this field? How did you get interested in drawing?"

"It all started when I was about six years old," he reminisced. "I've
been drawing practically all my life. I've always enjoyed drawing—cartoon characters, especially. But I don't draw as a hobby. For instance, I
don't do watercolors or paint. I simply enjoy drawing cartoons, this is
all, and I always have. This was the one ambition I had in life and it
simply worked out, that's all. It's that simple."

He made it sound embarrassingly easy, but I knew that it never is.
"How did you break into print?"

"To cut through the years rather rapidly, when I was very young, I
copied 'Mickey Mouse' and 'Popeye' and 'The Three Little Pigs' and
other things. Then in my early teens I began to create comic strips of my

own, but as a progression toward what I wanted to do some day. It was a struggle because I had no one, really, to show me how to do it. When I was about eighteen years old, after I was graduated from high school, I sent out a lot of cartoons and tried to sell them, but I didn't even come close because I had such a long way to go. It wasn't until I had returned from World War II that I began seriously to attempt to sell things. I finally got a job with Art Instruction Schools in Minneapolis—the correspondence school—and while working for them for a period of five years I was able to develop my cartooning style, my drawing improved, I was surrounded by lively conversation and imaginative people throughout the day. While working there, I was able to have time to submit cartoons to magazines and eventually to break through."

"How did these particular *Peanuts* characters evolve?" I asked.

"They grew out of gag cartoons which I had sold to the *Saturday Evening Post* and the Sunday St. Paul *Pioneer Press.* When I finally collected the best of all these cartoons and submitted them to the United Features Syndicate in New York, United Features decided they would rather have a comic strip than a series of gag panels with just an anonymous character each day in them. They suggested that I create some specific characters. I took the faces which I had drawn in these anonymous panels and blended together faces which I knew I wanted to draw every day. Charlie Brown's face was the round simple one. For it I borrowed the name of a very close friend. I went over to the desk where we both worked at Art Instruction and I asked, 'Charlie Brown, do you care if I use your name in a comic strip?' He said no. I was working on a strip when he came over to look at it. 'Is *that* the character you're going to put my name to?' he said. I used the name 'Patty' from a cousin of mine. I used 'Snoopy' because my mother used to think that this would be a good name for a dog, even though at that time we had a dog named Spike."

"Where did Linus come from?" I asked. "He's one of my favorites."

"Linus didn't come along for several years. He came because one day I was doodling on a piece of paper and I drew this little character with some wild hair straggling down from the top of his head and I showed it to a friend of mine who also was working at Art Instruction Schools and whose name was Linus Maurer. For no reason at all I had written his name under it. He looked at it and we both kind of chuckled. Then I thought, why not put this character in the strip and make him Lucy's brother?"

The telephone rang—Schulz answered several calls during our talk. It was nine-year-old Jill asking for a ride home from school. Her mother couldn't pick her up, he explained to her, but he would meet her at the bus stop at the main road and bring her home. "It's not good for a little girl to walk home by herself," he said to me, and we both watched the time so that he could keep his date. Presently he excused himself, promising to return after his errand. I put in the fifteen minutes or so looking at the books on his shelves and at other *Peanuts* artifacts. There was a framed cover of *Life,* featuring Charlie Brown and his friends. Nearby on the wall hung the copper plate from which a *Peanuts* cover of *Time* had been printed.

© by United Feature Syndicate, Inc.

On the shelves was a set of *The Interpreter's Bible,* a book of Thurber's drawings, and such varied authors as Trueblood, Fosdick, Phillips, Glenn Clark and four volumes of Laurence Durrell. There were also two volumes of the Anchor Bible, and numerous specially bound copies of *Peanuts* books, together with a whole row of *Peanuts* paperbacks.

When Charles Schulz returned, mission accomplished, he commented on the paperbacks. "The publisher tells me they expect to sell eight million this year."

My reaction to that was "Wow!" I said, "I noticed the religious books on your shelves. How do you feel about religion?"

He said, "I have always regarded religion as gratitude. We live on an earth which is not ours but belongs to God. We are his creatures. We worship him out of a feeling of gratitude for what he has done for us and for his guidance, his protection, his leading. Maybe gratitude is not the perfect word. In fact, I don't think we ever find a perfect word for all these things. I tend to lean toward the primitive church, toward a basic church which is merely a gathering together of believers.

"I do not like a high-organized church. I think that as soon as the congregation reaches a level of one hundred or so people, it is time to build a new church. As soon as the congregation gets to the point where you are not on fairly intimate terms with every other person in that church, then you have become too big, you are no longer a gathering of believers, but have become a theater where people can attend services. I do not think you can attend a church service. *Service* is not something which is there to be viewed as if it were a play or a movie. You should be part of this because you are part of the people who have gathered together because you belong to God. I certainly believe that a church has to grow and has to be organized in its work to accomplish things, but I am fearful of an overly organized church and I am *very* fearful of a church which equates itself with Americanism. This is a frightening trend: people who regard Christianity and Americanism as being virtually the same thing."

"For you," I asked, "is religion something that happens primarily inside a church or something that happens primarily outside?"

"I think it's a perfect combination of the two. Religion happens first inside the person. I think that at some time in everybody's life he feels some sort of calling by the Holy Spirit or whatever we wish to call it—I am certainly more flexible along these lines in my thinking than some might be. Some would say you have to be called by the Holy Spirit and put it just that way. I would want to qualify it more than that. I don't know theologically what it is or who it is that speaks to us, but I think we all have a time when we become aware of something and it is at this point that some react by what Jesus called being born again. Now, being born again may be going to the altar at a Sunday evening service and it may merely be a turning around spiritually in your life, just facing toward more mature things. It doesn't matter what you call it, but there is some kind of experience which happens to those who then decide that they want to do something for God or want to be closer to him.

"I try to be very flexible," he went on. "I hate to use the word 'tolerant,' and I don't really know what word to use to talk about these things. But I want to leave it open enough not to give the impression of excluding anyone from the Kingdom of God. I think the Kingdom of

God is a very broad Kingdom. The church is much more narrow. The church is composed of Christians who turn toward Christ and then operate within this church to accomplish things of a Christian nature, but I think the Kingdom of God is much larger. But the more I talk about it the more difficult it gets for me to express it and it just simply gets away from me!"

"When did this turning about, or whatever you want to call it, happen to you in your own life?"

"I think one of the first feelings I got was when I was about eighteen. I was riding a streetcar home from a job I had in downtown St. Paul and I noticed one of the car cards, which read, *Come unto me all ye who labor and are heavy laden and I will give you rest.* I was quite impressed by this Scripture verse. Even though I had attended Sunday school a little as a child I really didn't have too much knowledge of the Scriptures, and this impressed me quite a bit. But it was not until I came home from World War II that I began attending any church with regularity. This was the Church of God in St. Paul. I was much impressed, too, by the book *Caesar and Christ* by Will Durant. A section on Jesus and the Apostle Paul impressed me greatly. Also, a couple of other things which I had read began to make me lean in this direction."

I asked, "How involved are you in church now? I take it you are a member of a church here in town."

"No, I really am not. We've never joined the Methodist Church here in Sebastopol and my only involvement is teaching the adult Sunday school class. I was most involved for a period of a few years right after World War II, in St. Paul, in the young people's group. My wife and I also took part in helping to build a new Church of God in Minneapolis. When we moved out here to Sebastopol—where there was no Church of God congregation—I was invited to attend the Methodist Church and I was much impressed by the Sunday school class."

"Just a couple more questions," I promised. "Do any of the new ideas—religious ideas, things that are happening today, long hair on boys, miniskirts—do any of these disturb you?"

"Well, you have put a couple of questions together, and I don't know that they belong together. Long hair on boys: our boys have sort of gone for this British style, but this doesn't mean that they let it grow long like a girl. I don't see anything wrong with miniskirts. If a girl can wear one well, then I think it looks very nice. I am all for experimental changes in fashion if they make a person have a nice appearance, make

them feel good. I remember back about 1948, the church was crying out against 'the new look' and that was when the skirts had dropped down to about six inches off the floor. The girls who took on the new look were being criticized for following modern fashion. So it really doesn't matter what you do, you are going to be criticized by somebody. I'm not really up enough on the latest theological developments to be able to discuss them well. I don't think I have the mind for it. I have tried to read Bonhoeffer's writings, Harvey Cox and Tillich, but I just am not well enough educated to be able to follow them. My mind doesn't work well in these areas, much to my own disappointment."

"What would you wish most for young people today?" I asked.

"I would wish them to be tied strongly to some kind of family tradition. I think that today we are bursting so many bonds we are becoming a country with no traditions. And yet I would wish, also, for a young person to be well enough adjusted to be able to go off and make a life for himself without clinging too much to his family and his old ties. This is a paradox, of course, but I think it is necessary to strike a proper balance here. I would wish also for a young person the freedom to be able to choose what he wants to be in life and the opportunity to know that the only satisfactions he's going to get from life are those satisfactions which come from contributing; to know early in life what he wants to do and to realize that he is going to have to contribute and not wait to find this out until it is too late so that he spends the last forty years of his life wishing he could have done something a little more constructive. It is a terrible thing to have to spend your working days looking forward to the weekends and to think that it is only on the weekends and your days off that life is any fun, and to spend your whole year waiting for your vacation. Every working day should be just as enjoyable, if not more enjoyable, than vacation days.

"I would urge parents and teachers and friends to be more tolerant of young people who happen to have an ambition which is a little bit offbeat."

"What would you say to ministers if you had the chance?" I asked. "Some laymen have said, 'If I could preach a sermon to preachers, there are several things I would tell them.' Do you have anything you'd like to tell ministers?"

Charles Schulz replied, "I've always felt that they should allow themselves to be more flexible. I see no reason why church services have to be standard. I've discussed this with the man who used to be the pastor here at the Methodist Church in Sebastopol. I told him I saw no reason why, on a certain Sunday morning, if a minister has felt during the week the burden of a topic upon his heart and he knows that it is going to take more than the standard twenty minutes to discuss this thing, why he can't rise at the beginning of the service and say, 'I have something of special importance this morning so let's sing just one song, and if you'll forgive me, I think I'm going to need about an hour to explain it to you.' I think the congregation would appreciate his candor and give him their attention. If, on the other hand, he does not feel that a definite message has been given him, why not admit it from the pulpit and say, 'This morning, I'm not going to try to make up something to fill the time. We'll sing a few extra hymns and go home!' Why do the services have to begin and end at the same time, and why does everything have to be so rigid?"

"There is a great deal of inflexibility in all of us," I agreed.

"There are all kinds of ideas to be thought about," Charles Schulz mused. "Did you ever wonder whether Jesus knew that at his birth other children were killed because of him? If he did know, how did he carry that burden? I read something about that once."

"It never occurred to me," I had to admit.

"I've got an idea I want to try to work into the strip sometime," he said, shuffling through some notes on his desk. "One of the characters will say something about the 'patience of Job.' And Linus will say, 'Scholars point out, Charlie Brown, that the Book of Job is not concerned with patience but with the problem of human suffering.' I like to work in something like that once in a while!"

I stood up to go. "I noticed a good sermon illustration as I came into your place," I said. "I saw the road with the gate and I thought, well, now how do you get the gate open? And I sort of started over in that direction and the gate opened as I went."

Charles Schulz laughed. "When we first moved out here we had to install some sort of gate because as you come down the road to our place there is a strange turn. People came up into our property either because they mistook our driveway for an extension of the road or else they wanted to see what our property looked like. Because our children were quite small and we also had animals running loose, this was dangerous. We thought it was best to have a gate, and so we installed this hose running across the driveway and the gate is operated electronically. Run over the hose and the gate opens."

Sure enough again, for me, on the way out, it did.

I drove back to San Francisco feeling good about having met a very nice, unassuming, non-omniscient human being. He's the kind of person I would enjoy knowing better, I decided. That might be difficult, what with the price of plane fares and rented cars and all. But, I consoled myself, I could read, regularly, maybe even now religiously, *Peanuts.* For I was developing the strong suspicion that Charlie Schulz *was* Charlie Brown. Maybe a little more successful, that's all.

A Conversation with Charles Schulz

or The Psychology of Simplicity

MARY HARRINGTON HALL / 1967

Mary Harrington Hall: Why is Lucy so mean? It just breaks my heart every year when I know that Charlie Brown is going to try to kick that football, and I know she's going to take it away from him.
Charles Schulz: She's always going to do that, you know. He's never going to get to kick that football.

Hall: But he will keep hoping?
Schulz: Oh, yes. Charlie Brown will always keep hoping. Now about Lucy being so mean. She is mean first because it is funny, and because it just follows the standard comic-strip pattern—that the supposedly weak people in the world are funny when they dominate the supposedly strong people. There is nothing funny about a little boy being mean to a little girl. That is simply not funny! But there is something funny about a little girl being able to be mean to a little boy.

45

Hall: Wasn't that the old *Maggie and Jiggs* formula, the start of the comic strip theme of women dominating men?

Schulz: Maggie started it, yes. And it's a true thing. Little girls *do* dominate little boys of their own age, and if you want to carry it further, the family generally goes in whichever direction the wife wants. Don't you think so?

Hall: Do you like women?

Schulz: Oh, yes, I like women very much.

Hall: Do you think families get run by women because men are kinder people than women are, or because women are raising the children, or what . . . ?

Schulz: I don't know. I only draw pictures.

Hall: Does your wife, Joyce, mind because people compare her to your heroine or whatever you'd call Lucy?

Schulz: Oh, my wife is a very nice person. But I'm afraid that generally women never find the man who is ideal enough in their estimation so that they can continue to be dominated by him and accept his decisions and his leading all the time . . . which is, after all, only human because no one is ever going to find anyone just perfect anyhow. Plus the mere fact that women are not this much—in fact, not at all inferior. I think in many ways women are superior to men. But it is quite obvious that women would prefer some sort of leading and domination, and when they don't get it, then they have to compensate for it in some way. And in their struggles to try to get their husbands to be stronger, they probably end up making him even worse than ever.

This is a self-defeating thing which in most problems of this kind ends up being tragically depressing as the years go on.

Hall: I remember once when Lucy and Snoopy had a terrible fight. Snoopy won because he kept kissing her, and she surrendered. I don't suppose that's apropos of much, but I remember the fight was because "he was standing where I wanted to walk." She could have walked around that problem, you know.

Schulz: There are little thoughts people can take out of my cartoons if they want. I think there is nothing more depressing than to see a married couple out in public where the wife is cutting the husband down all evening. She is ashamed of him and of everything that he says. You know, you don't see men doing this to women very often. Men are so gentlemanly.

Hall: I knew a man once who was ungentlemanly. I didn't know him well, of course. But you are a very gentle man. And you know, Charles Schulz, you sound exactly like the people in *Peanuts* when you talk.

Schulz: Nobody will believe this, but all the things that are said in the strip are things that I would normally say, and you would find out if you were around me for a week that this is just the way I talk all the time when I am with people that I know very well or with whom I feel comfortable.

I have to watch myself, of course, so that I am not Lucy-ish and sarcastic. This strip gives me an outlet because there was a time in my life when I didn't know that sarcasm was not a good trait to have, and I have overcome this. Having a comic strip is a marvelous outlet for the various frustrations in one's life.

Hall: I wish I had a comic strip. Who are your favorite people in *Peanuts*?

Schulz: Snoopy, Linus, and Charlie Brown. Lucy is not a favorite, because I don't especially like her, that's all. But she *works*, and a central comic-strip character is not only one who fills his role very well, but who will provide ideas by the very nature of his personality. This is why Charlie Brown, Linus, and Snoopy and Lucy appear more than the others. Their personalities are so broad and flexible that they provide more ideas.

"LUCY IS NOT A FAVORITE, BECAUSE I DON'T ESPECIALLY LIKE HER, THAT'S ALL."

© by United Feature Syndicate, Inc.

Hall: Linus could carry a strip of his own, and so could Snoopy, couldn't they?

Schulz: I really think so, yes. Linus has a way of saying pompous things and then being brought down quickly. Life has a way of slapping you down. And I'm very glad you like Snoopy's funny face, Mary. Expression is so much in these things. Schroeder provides a few situations, and then the other characters are there merely to fill roles when they are needed. Except for Peppermint Patty. I put her in because that's a great name, and I didn't want to lose it, because another cartoonist might think of it.

Hall: I haven't seen Schroeder lately. Where has he been? Lucy hasn't had any chance for love, or for rejection.

Schulz: Well, you see, I don't listen to music as much as I used to. When I go to a symphony or a concert, though, I'll be inspired to do something about Schroeder. I kind of like Schroeder. He's fairly down to earth, but he has his problems, too. He has to play on painted black piano keys, and he thinks Beethoven was the first President of the United States.

Hall: Then, actually, some ideas for the strip come from things you are interested in at the moment. You must be interested in ice skating right now, because those strips over on the desk show that great Snoopy, and he is skating just gorgeously.

Schulz: We're building an ice skating rink in Sebastopol (California) here where we live. The rink in town was condemned, and everybody in the area likes to skate. Our kids *really* like it. So Joyce started planning a community rink. It's gotten to be pretty big. You'll have to come up here and skate when it's finished. There'll be lots of room.

Hall: Is that where Snoopy is practicing, in this week's panels?

Schulz: Oh, no! Snoopy is a figure skater, you know, and he has dreams of skating in the Olympics in February. Well, all of a sudden, we find that Lucy is yelling at him, and in this one strip she is saying to Charlie Brown: "Do you know that silly dog of yours thinks he is going to Grenoble, in France, and skate in the Olympics?" And she says: "Why you stupid dog. What makes you think you can skate in the Olympics?"

I think this is sort of an interesting point if you look at this a little deeper. It is none of her business. Why should she be bothered by the thought that somebody else's dog thinks he is going to skate in the Olympics? But there are people who are bothered by what *other* people think they *can* or *cannot* do. So here we are touching on something else which is a little extra to the main story.

Hall: How did you happen to have Snoopy decide to go to Grenoble?

Schulz: I can tell you why I have drawn certain things, but I don't really think about points all that strongly before I draw. I am governed mainly by getting something done for that particular day. I am governed by

my ability—by what I hate to think of as a gag line or a punch line, but which I guess is the only way in which I can describe it in the technical and professional language.

At the start, I don't know what direction the story is going to take. I don't even know if I am going to tell a story. I started this thing off with Snoopy doing some figure skating. And I have some figure-skating books here by some authorities. And I have some photographs and very authentic figure-skating poses. I think everything in the strip should be authentic and should instruct. When Tolstoy took his characters on a bear hunt, you learned about bear hunting even though the information was not relevant to the story.

Hall: But that silly little dog isn't wearing any skates!

Schulz: Isn't he a silly little dog? But you will note that his moves are very authentic. When he is practicing a forward outside roll, he is doing it exactly the way skaters do. So I am giving you a little bit extra, and this is what raises the strip's quality, I hope.

And this is why the people in the strip are talking about him going to a specific town—Grenoble, in France—to a specific Olympics.

Hall: But, good grief, what's going to happen to him? Will he be all right? He can't go to the Olympics. The Olympics are real, and he's part of a fantasy.

Schulz: I have it all figured out. The last panel will show Charlie Brown leaping around Snoopy's doghouse saying that Snoopy has come home, and it is going to be a Merry Christmas after all. Snoopy is lying up on the roof of his doghouse, and he says: "Well, you see, there was this ocean . . ."

Snoopy and these kids aren't the brightest, but this dog knows about the Olympics and that they are in Grenoble, in France, but he doesn't even know how to get there. He doesn't even know that an ocean exists. This again ties the fantasy to the real world and keeps him always a bit of a real dog, and yet not a real dog. It is treading a very thin line, which is what makes these things successful when they *are* successful. Are we getting anyplace for *Psychology Today*? A fantasy world can become very real, as I'm sure you know.

Hall: Well, if it isn't real, it isn't successful, is it?

Schulz: Someone can set out to do something which he is going to call real and end up not being real at all; while something carried off successfully in a fantasy can become very real to people. That's why people worry about various comic-strip characters.

Hall: You know who's very real? The Red Baron! And he doesn't even appear in person. How did you ever happen to think of the dreaded Red Baron?

Schulz: Well, it was just because Snoopy looks so funny with goggles. It all started as one week's take-off on World War I movies. You know the great line: "Captain, you can't send men up in crates like these to die."

Hall: "Get hold of yourself, Lieutenant. Our duty is clear."

Schulz: Then I discovered I had something good going, and I let Snoopy's imagination go wild. Snoopy is funny. He leads his little life out of his doghouse.

Hall: You have to do something special if you live in a doghouse. Will you tell me a Red Baron story that shows that wonderful and strange connection between Snoopy's Red Baron fantasy and the ability Charlie Brown has somehow to know about it.

Schulz: Well, I think the latest one. It is Christmas Eve, and Snoopy is overseas. And he is sitting in this little French cafe drinking root beer. He is depressed, and he thinks: "I'll take a bottle of root beer over to the barracks and cheer up the men. It is good for the officers to cheer up the enlisted men." When he gets there, he hears the enlisted men singing Christmas carols, and he feels that they don't need him. In the next to the last panel, Charlie Brown and his sister, Sally, are sitting by the Christmas tree, singing Christmas carols. Charlie Brown says: "Let's not sing anymore. It is sometimes very depressing when you are alone and away from home to hear Christmas carols being sung." Sally is puzzled and says: "Sometimes I don't understand what he is talking about." You see, Charlie and Snoopy have this rapport—he understands what Snoopy is thinking. This is fantasy connection.

Hall: But very real. And so are the men overseas. Were you a flyer during World War II?
Schulz: That's nice of you to make it the Second World War. People keep asking me if I was a pilot in World War I. I'm only 44 years old! And I wasn't a pilot; I was a foot soldier.

Hall: Where?
Schulz: In Germany, where the war was. And that story about my machine gun not being loaded the first time I faced the enemy in battle is not true. My machine gun was loaded. It just didn't shoot. It was about five days before the war ended. We had never seen any enemies, except a few captured men. I was the squad leader, and one of my men in the half-track called my attention to a movement in a field. Rifle fire came from the spot. I swung my gun around. I was a pretty good marksman, too. I just forgot that a 50-calibre machine gun has to be pulled not once, but twice, before it will fire. But it was just as well. The fellow threw his hands up and surrendered before I was ready to fire.

Hall: I think that's a kind of Charlie Brown story.
Schulz: Charlie Brown wouldn't have been able to pass the draft board.

Hall: Did you have any other great war experiences? Did you ever meet anyone like the Red Baron?
Schulz: No, but I met a little dog. We went into a little German village and stopped to take care of a German soldier who had been wounded and somehow left behind when his troops were evacuated. There at the edge of the village was a huge artillery emplacement, with stairs

going down to a dark building, painted all black. It must have been barracks. There wasn't a soul around, and I thought if I went down there, I might even find a Luger.

Hall: I'd have been scared.
Schulz: I thought: I'm all by myself, and if there's anyone in that building, I'll get shot. So I thought I'd just roll a concussion grenade down the steps to knock out anyone who was around. Just then this nondescript little dog trotted down the steps and into the building. I couldn't hurt that little dog. He didn't even know what was going on. So I didn't get the Luger.

© by United Feature Syndicate, Inc.

Hall: I still think that sounds like Charlie Brown. He would never want to hurt anyone. Charlie Brown's a good man, and I find it distressing that his friends call him "wishy-washy."
Schulz: But you can understand why the others get annoyed with him. He bores them because he wants so much to be liked. I think they are justified sometimes in their treatment of him. Charlie Brown is too vulnerable. He is full of hope and misdirected faith. Lucy is too sharp for him, and she is full of misdirected confidence. You have to give her credit, though; she has a way of cutting right down to the truth. This is one of her good points. She can cut through a lot of the sham and she can really feel what is wrong with Charlie Brown which he can't see himself.

Hall: That's why she's so great when she put up her sign: *The doctor is in.* The theme of loneliness is there always in *Peanuts*. And that gets to all of us. The lonely memories we have. You know, when suddenly the wispy fragrance of a particular day will bring a memory that sears the throat. You describe loneliness as being like eating a peanut butter sandwich all by yourself at night and the peanut butter sticks to the roof of your mouth.

Schulz: Well, I know about loneliness. I won't talk about it, but I was very lonely after the war. I know what it feels like to spend a whole weekend all by yourself and no one wants you at all. How do *you* solve the problem of loneliness, Mary?

Hall: By working hard and caring deeply about the precious handful of people I care about.

Schulz: And that works for you?

Hall: I keep working at it. All the articles I've read about you saying you were afraid to go to art school after you graduated from high school, and that you sort of flunked a lot. Is that true?

Schulz: The first indication of trouble came when I was in the seventh grade. On my final report card, I got an E in arithmetic, which was failing. I was just stunned, because my report cards had always been quite good. I remember one girl looking at it and saying: "Hah! Charles got an E." And laughing with this other girl. Then, one year I failed everything. I failed English. I failed Latin completely—I didn't even come close. I failed algebra, and I think I failed history. Al Capp says he failed algebra nine times.

At any rate, I was so glad when I graduated from high school. The whole experience was miserable, and I was just glad to get out. I hated being made a fool of, and I hated not knowing what was going on. But it was my own fault. I didn't work hard enough. I hated homework, and I was extremely immature. All I was interested in were art and golf.

Neither my mother nor my father, who was a barber in St. Paul, had any education themselves so it was difficult for them to understand all that was going on and to help me in any way.

Hall: How did they feel about your school problems?

Schulz: I never really knew. They are both dead now, and it would be interesting to know. They never said anything to me. They were very nice people. They never got mad at me, and they never punished me for getting bad grades.

The first time I was interviewed by *The Saturday Evening Post*, the writer and my father and I were sitting in a restaurant booth, and the writer asked how my Dad felt about my failing all those grades. And my Dad said: "What do you mean? I always thought he did pretty well."

Hall: Now about your being afraid to go to art school.
Schulz: I would have liked to go to art school, but I was afraid. I was never good at art classes. I hated them. In art classes, the teacher had to see what you were going to plan, and the project went on and on, and it just drove me crazy. That is another reason why I draw comics. I pick out a clean piece of paper, and a half-hour later I am done. I don't have to size canvas. I don't have to make a host of preliminary sketches and plan for months.

At any rate, I was afraid to go to art school because I'd be right back where I was in high school—in a class with a lot of people who could draw better than I could. And I'd be a nobody again. With a correspondence course I could stay home, and nobody would ever know the difference. So that is what I did. Now, if that isn't immature, what is?

Hall: And you really went to correspondence school.
Schulz: It was called the Federal Art School. People always think correspondence courses are rackets. But resident schools aren't so holy either. I don't see them grinding out perfect students. I think that any time a person criticizes a correspondence school, he'd better be talking from a very good school himself.

Hall: How did correspondence school work for you?
Schulz: I didn't even do the correspondence course especially well. But I enjoyed it. What I gained was an appreciation of good cartooning. You can't really learn to draw in a correspondence course. I don't know if you can learn to draw anyplace, expect perhaps with lots of practice and a master teacher and thousands of life sketches.

It all depends upon what level you are after. This is a profound subject, and it is really not important to what I do. Good cartooning requires drawing ability, but it also requires an innate sense of design, and it requires common sense. And you should be able to handle the pen fairly well. I think I am a good pen-and-ink artist. I don't think I could earn my living as a commercial artist or as an illustrator. I don't think I could earn my living drawing in any other way than in cartooning.

Hall: Well, thank goodness for us all. There aren't many great cartoonists.

Schulz: Well, I am doing exactly what I want to do. There is no doubt about it. You know, I always thought if I could just do something as good as *Krazy Kat,* I would be happy. *Krazy Kat* was always my goal. It was done with a wonderful scratchy-pen effect. And it was quite literate.

Hall: What was your first job after correspondence school?
Schulz: The school sent me to a Catholic comic magazine in St. Paul. They just had stories about Catholic priests and nuns and other Catholics who did historic, heroic things. My drawing wasn't good enough for them, but they let me letter the entire magazine. Then they would give me translations in Spanish and French, which I didn't understand, and I'd letter again. I was very fast and a good letterer.

Hall: Do you still letter all of your own cartoons?
Schulz: I'm the fastest letterer in the West. And I still do all my own lettering. Not everyone does, but there are a number of purists around. Gus Arriola, who draws *Gordo,* is one. Not doing your own lettering is like Arnold Palmer having someone else hit his nine irons for him.

Hall: When did you graduate from lettering to cartooning?
Schulz: About that time the correspondence school hired me as an instructor, and I began selling some of my little kid cartoons to the *St. Paul Pioneer-Press.*

Hall: A friend of mine, Bill Greer, was city editor there in the '40s and he says you used to bring your cartoons into the city room when no one was there, because you were shy.
Schulz: But little by little, I was marching forward. And in 1947 I sold my first cartoon to *The Saturday Evening Post.* But I didn't really know it at first. I was so used to rejection slips. I got a little slip in the mail that said: "Check Tuesday for spot drawing of little boy on chaise lounge." I thought at first it meant I should check Tuesday's mail when I would get the cartoon back. I got $40.

Hall: Tell me about it.
Schulz: Well, the little boy looked somewhat like Schroeder. He was sitting way up on the edge of the chaise lounge, and his feet were out in front of him—resting on a footstool.

Hall: And then 17 years ago came my favorite strip, *Peanuts.*
Schulz: The strip was supposed to be called *Little Folks.* That's a much

better title, really. More comic strip-y. I don't like *Peanuts* for several reasons. Peanuts is an ugly word.

The only justification for the title would be a character named *Peanuts*. And there is none, you know. The man at United Features who named it hadn't even seen the strip.

Hall: Maybe he's one of those people who hate comics.
Schulz: People who don't read comics are in the same class as people who don't watch TV or listen to the radio. To be brutally frank, that's a form of ignorance or intellectual snobbishness. All comic strips and all TV and all radio aren't bad.

Hall: I'll bet I know who your favorite cartoonists are . . .
Schulz: Who?

Hall: All right. Gus Arriola and Walt Kelly and . . .
Schulz: You're right and you mustn't name any more. I know I'd feel bad if someone good made a list of favorites and didn't put me on it. I'm proud of the comic-strip business, and I think we do as well in our field as TV or the theater. Cartooning is not an art equivalent to painting or playwriting. But it is as good an art as writing for magazines or movies or as illustrating. And you can say things in cartoons. You can say things eloquently in many ways. Beethoven can tell you about loneliness, and so can Hank Williams. No one sang it better than he did, you know.

Hall: How much is memory in plotting *Peanuts,* and how much comes from your own children? This is a stupid question really, because it all comes from a wild, wonderful, whimsical mind, and I apologize for asking.
Schulz: That's a perfectly good question. The strip is based on memory, really, not on observation. But our first daughter, Meredith, was a fussbudget, and so is Lucy. And our first three children had blankets. This is where we got Linus and his blanket.

No comic strip is realistic. People talk about *Blondie* as a strip about people around the home, but that's not so. *Blondie* is exaggerated, and that is what makes it so wonderful. People wander through Dagwood's bathroom while he's taking a bath, and he has great battles with his boss. This is broad caricature and is necessary to a comic strip. Caricature separates the comic strip from the competing media, and this is the only way the comic can survive.

Hall: Is that because comic strips can't do what movie cameras can?

Schulz: And the camera can't do what the cartoonist does. If you stay in your own area, you're safe. Unfortunately, most people don't seem to realize this need for caricature, and their strips don't get off the ground.

Hall: There are quite a few soap opera strips around. What about *Mary Worth*?

Schulz: There's room for this kind of thing as long as the daily episodes remain interesting. But we need more *Gasoline Alleys*—and a revival of the old J. R. Williams and Clair Briggs type of humor—*When a Feller Needs a Friend,* and *Life's Most Embarrassing Moments* were panels with balloons in them. Now balloons have become relegated to gag lines. This was a bad trend and has damaged lots of strips.

Hall: We were talking about your own children. Please let's list them. There certainly are lots.

Schulz: Meredith is 17; Monty, 15; Craig, 14; Amy, 11; and Jill, 9. And through the years my children have given me a total of three lines for *Peanuts.* Nobody could give you all those lines I've used. They come from me. But one night Amy was talking so much at the dinner table that I said: "Couldn't you be quiet for just a little while?" And she was very quiet for a time. Then she buttered a piece of bread and said: "Am I buttering too loud for you?"

"SNOOPY IS A FIGURE SKATER, YOU KNOW. ISN'T HE A SILLY LITTLE DOG? BUT YOU WILL NOTE... WHEN HE IS PRACTICING A FORWARD OUTSIDE ROLL, HE IS DOING IT EXACTLY THE WAY SKATERS DO."

© by United Feature Syndicate, Inc.

And we were having a terrible time getting Craig to wash his hands. His fingernails were always dirty. One night he came downstairs with his nails so clean that we asked him how he did it. He said: "I used toothpaste."

Once when Monty was in kindergarten, I had read to him and was trying to get him to go to sleep. He said he didn't want to close his eyes because "It's dark in there."

Hall: If I were to describe this gorgeous estate you call the Coffee Grounds, I guess I would say it might be posh for Tuxedo Park. This part of California is redwood country and apple country, and it looks a lot like New England. This is a totally lovely country estate. And you have so many houses.

Schulz: Actually, there are four houses. Our house, which has six bedrooms; the former studio, which is actually two houses—it has two bedrooms, a kitchen and things, and my mother-in-law lives there. Then there is a renovated barn which is very nice, and our French exchange student lives there. And then there is my studio.

Hall: You know, it just suddenly occurred to me that your studio, which is one of the most peaceful modern buildings I've ever seen, looks a little like a church. I know you are very religious, and that you teach a Sunday-School class. Do your children like Sunday School?

Schulz: My children won't go to Sunday School. But my mother-in-law goes with me. The children say that it's boring, but I really can't believe that. I think they don't like to get up in the morning, and they hate to get dressed up. I think that once they attended a few classes, they would have to admit that they enjoyed it.

Hall: What grade of Sunday School do you teach in your church, which is the Church of God, isn't it?

Schulz: There is no church of that group here, so I go to the Methodist Church. And I teach adults. I couldn't possibly handle children. My class is all discussion and speculation and searching for truths that I want each individual to decide for himself. I couldn't stand before a class of little children and say: "This is what happened." I would have to qualify it and say: "Some theologians think. . . ." You can't teach little children that way.

Hall: But you've done religious books for children and teen-agers. One of them is the dearest and only thing of its kind I've ever seen. It's the one with one of my pet cartoons—a little boy standing in the huge doorway of a church and saying: "My name is Walter. I'm three years old, and I've come to get religion."

Schulz: That's in *Two-by-Fours*. Kenny Hall, who wrote the text, and I did that to help the Youth Fund of the Church of God. I did a teen-age book, *What Was Buggin' Ol' Pharoh?* Did you ever see that?

Hall: Certainly! And I loved it. You are talking to a typical American. Do you realize that if any newspaper had given *You're a Good Man, Charlie Brown!* a bad review when it opened off-Broadway, there probably would have been another newspaper strike—of subscribers.

Peanuts itself has been regarded as deeply Christian, and Robert Short dealt with this in his book, *The Gospel According to Peanuts.* It's an interesting book, and he is careful to say he writes what he *sees* in *Peanuts,* not what you may have put there.

Schulz: That's right, Mary, and you are the first interviewer who has understood this. Invariably, the first question people ask is: "Don't you think he has read too much into the strip?" That's not the point. His point is that this can be done with all works of art, and he would like to do this with all literature. Of course, the comic strip has appeal that other works of art do not have. What a press agent he has been for us on college campuses! He tells people all about the deep, hidden meaning in the strip. I couldn't ask for anything better. I don't appear at college lectures with him any more, though. Because it's not very good to have him tell about a Christian point, and then have someone ask me if that's what I actually meant and have me say, "Gee, I don't think so."

Hall: Short sees Snoopy at times as "a little Christ" and at other times as a typical Christian. By the latter, I think he means Snoopy has all our mortal defects. Snoopy is selfish, isn't he? It's funny how most of us go through life confusing selfishness with independence. Snoopy does that, too.

Schulz: Snoopy *is* typical. You're right. He is fairly selfish and thinks that this keeps him independent. But he is able to exist only because of the kindness of Charlie Brown.

Once he finished eating out of his dog dish and said: "So what is there to do the rest of the day?" That indicates the narrowness of his life. And Snoopy could be more appreciative. Not long ago Charlie Brown brought him a dish of dog food, and Snoopy stuck a little card in it—a rejection slip: "Thank you for submitting your material, but we regret it does not suit our needs." *Playboy* has asked for it, and several magazines want to use it as their rejection forms.

Hall: I'd love to use it. I don't think it would make authors feel any better, but it would be nice for the editor. Incidentally, Christian symbolism is easy to read into the Great Pumpkin. How did the Great Pumpkin come into Linus's life?

Schulz: I can't remember exactly. I know I was drawing some Hallowe'en strips about Linus, who is bright but very innocent, and he was confusing Hallowe'en with Christmas because he was one holiday ahead of himself. Now the whole thing has become a parody of Christmas, and Linus gives the Great Pumpkin those qualities Santa Claus is supposed to have.

Hall: Don't we give religious holidays characteristics that make them easier for us to understand?

Schulz: Sure, that's the reason religion takes on formality. Remember that Jesus said God desired Mercy, not Sacrifice. I think all God really requires of us is that we love one another. But this is hard to do. It is much easier to burn a sacrifice to God than to love someone. We take the easy way out by turning to formal religions and adding their customs to our theology. We find modern substitutes for sacrifices instead of just loving one another.

Hall: Substitution is a pretty childish approach to religion, but it's popular.

Schulz: My own private theological theory is that when Jesus said: "Be ye perfect, even as your Father in Heaven is perfect," He was talking about maturity. A psychiatrist was visiting me last month—just visiting, I wasn't his patient—and he was saying that no person can be truly religious until he has attained maturity. This is one of the big problems of the world. Lack of maturity.

Hall: I know a bigger problem—how to attain maturity. How does one become mature?

Schulz: I don't know. I am trying to find out. I suppose experience would be the obvious example, but you have to make an awful lot of mistakes to reach maturity that way.

Hall: What do you feel about the dropouts of thousands of young people from religion, from school and from society?

Schulz: Oh, Mary, you're beyond me, I think. But these kids who talk so much about love—well, I would just like to see them exhibit it. They have no more compassion than anyone else. Going off and being a free spirit and causing parents terrible anxiety is not exhibiting love. If they want to show love and their free spirit, they should try to make those two people who have devoted their lives to them feel happy.

I used to have more tolerance for these views, but I am losing patience with what I see. The test of anything is the fruit it bears. I see no good fruit being born. I think the church is having trouble recruiting people today, incidentally, simply because people now doubt everything in the world.

Hall: Are you pessimistic about mankind then, Charles?

Schulz: No, I am really optimistic about man achieving upward. Even though man continues to be evil and people continue to do unspeakable things. The greatest thing that has happened in our age is the conclusion we seem to be reaching that there is nothing glorious about war.

Hall: Only for the Red Baron and his fantasy world. Do you remember the William Faulkner short story, *The Mosquitoes,* about the torpedo boat and the beautiful, brave, frightened boy in World War I? But let's go back to *Peanuts.* I am glad you feel the way you do, though. A war-like Charles Schulz would be *tilt* somehow. I've noticed that your *Peanuts* children don't play much with toys—except of course with baseball equipment. How come?

Schulz: My ideas just don't come along those lines. And toys can be a terrible thing to draw, too, you know. Did you ever try to draw a tricycle? And with a four-panel cartoon, you have to draw it four times. Charlie Brown can't ride a tricycle anyhow. His arms and legs are too short. There are a lot of things Charlie Brown can't do. He can't get his arms up over his head.

Hall: The cover of our magazine this month shows a boy with Snoopy goggles playing in a cardboard box.

Schulz: We never had intricate playthings as children. We force our kids to live in a ready-made Disneyland. Disneyland is a wonderful place, but we try to move it into our homes. I think children still are happiest when they are creating something. We used to think of every toy ourselves and make it out of paper or cardboard. Most of the fun was in the construction. Now toymakers do all the making, and we wonder why children don't play with their expensive toys.

Hall: Your own children have just about everything here, Charles, including a four-hole golf course.

Schulz: Golf courses are not toys. They are wonderful things, and everyone should have one.

"LINUS IS BRIGHT BUT VERY INNOCENT. HE HAS A WAY OF SAYING POMPOUS THINGS AND THEN BEING . . BROUGHT DOWN QUICKLY."

© by United Feature Syndicate, Inc.

Hall: Do you find it more productive working here in the country, miles and miles away from the newspapers who use *Peanuts*? Did you move here from the Twin Cities to get peace and quiet?

Schulz: No, we just like California. Actually, I've always thought it would be fun to have a private office in a newspaper building. Then I could have coffee breaks with the columnists and pick up inspiration from being with people. It would be exciting.

Hall: Why haven't you done that?

Schulz: No newspaper office has ever invited me.

Hall: Every profile I have ever read about you clearly says that you think of yourself as Charlie Brown, that you *are* Charlie Brown. And yet when we talked before, you said that this was just journalistic license.

Schulz: I think of myself as Charles Schulz. But if someone wants to believe I'm really Charlie Brown, well, it makes a good story. I used to read about George McManus, that he really *was* Jiggs. So, why argue. You can't win. But *I* think I'm Charles Schulz.

Hall: Except for one thing. You are Charlie Brown—a little bit. And I am Charlie Brown—a little bit. Isn't that the whole point? He is everyone.

Schulz: Good grief, what a nice thing to say. I don't think you are one bit like Lucy, Mary. You wouldn't take away anybody's football.

Penthouse Interview: Charles M. Schulz

JIM PHELAN / 1971

From *Penthouse*, 1971,
pp. 36, 38, 40, 42, 104.

The comic strip *Peanuts,* the creation of Charles Monroe Schulz, is the
most popular newspaper cartoon of all time. More than 1100 newspapers in the United States and other countries (including Britain's high-
brow Sunday, *The Observer*) serve up the serial aspirations and frustrations of little round-headed Charlie Brown, his wildly imaginative dog
Snoopy, his severest critic Lucy van Pelt, and their friends Linus,
Schroeder, Peppermint Patty et al. The daily readership amounts to
more than 100,000,000, a peak no other comic artist has ever
approached. And the figure might easily be doubled but for syndication
restrictions by United Features, which limit the strip to only one paper
in a competitive circulation area. An editor of a *Peanuts*-less newspaper
in California, the Long Beach independent *Press-Telegram*, recently
suggested that *Peanuts* be declared a national resource and made

63

accessible to all, like the right to vote. Meantime dilemmas persist like that of a woman resident in Wichita, Kansas, when it was still a two-newspaper town, who kept complaining that she hated the *Wichita Eagle,* its news coverage, its editorial policy, even its typography. So why, asked a friend, didn't she switch to the *Wichita Beacon*? "I can't," she grumbled, "The *Beacon* doesn't carry Charlie Brown!" The creator of this comic-page phenomenon is a mild-mannered, faintly harassed but unflaggingly pleasant 48-year-old artist. A transplanted Midwesterner, Schulz resides, with his wife and five children, on a 28-acre spread in Sebastapol north of San Francisco in the wine country of Northern California. Charles Schulz is that fortunate man who knew early in life what he wanted to do, went ahead and did it, succeeded magnificently at it, and still enjoys doing it. Those who believe in Kharma will say that he was destined to become a cartoonist. When he was only a week old, his parents nicknamed him "Sparky" for the cartoon character "Sparkplug" in the comic strip *Barney Google.* He began doodling cartoons when just a boy, and other than a stint as a sergeant in World War II he has never worked at anything else. Despite a reported income of more than $1,000 a day, Sparky Schulz shuns the production-line techniques employed by many other top comic-strip artists. As he did when he started out 21 years ago with only eight newspapers. Schulz still draws every line of every cartoon and refuses to delegate even the lettering of the balloons. Though constantly besieged with gratuitous ideas for the strip, he finds himself unable to make use of them—even when he recognizes that they are excellent. "It has to come directly from my head," he says. One of the few strip ideas that didn't, came from his own family. One evening at dinner he complained that his daughter Amy was talking too much and too loudly. She lapsed into silence, picked up a piece of bread and began buttering it. Then she asked him, in a line so exquisitely pure *Peanuts* that it found its way into a Charlie Brown balloon: "Am I buttering too loud for you?" The fantastic success of Charlie Brown has spun off a whole conglomerate of related products until Schulz has become the core of a little big business. There are *Peanuts*-inspired greeting cards, stationery, bridge pads, posters, pillow dolls, sweatshirts, wastebaskets, sleeping wear, tee shirts, bedspreads, draperies, rugs, lunch kits, lamps, baseballs, music boxes, and paperback books that sell far up in the millions. There has also been a highly successful musical comedy. *You're a Good Man, Charlie Brown,* a series of animated cartoons for television, and coming soon is a full-length movie. Amid all this action, Schulz scorns the celebrity role, remains riveted to his drawingboard and the work that he likes. He did not even attend the opening of his musical comedy. The authenticity of Charlie Brown comes naturally because most of it derives from Sparky Schulz's childhood. An avid sports fan, he recently built a magnificent ice arena at nearby Santa Rosa, where he maintains a modest workroom on the second floor. In his youth he tried to play hockey on little bumpy rinks home-made by flooding the backyard in winter. Now he has his own rink and has largely abandoned golf (five-handicap) in favor of hockey. In this exclusive *Penthouse* interview, conducted by writer **Jim Phelan,** he reveals the personality behind the favorite cast of thousands.

© by United Feature Syndicate, Inc.

Penthouse: Does *Peanuts* reflect life in the U.S. today, or an escape from it?
Schulz: I feel that *Peanuts* reflects certain attitudes of life in our country today and perhaps some basic fears. However, I like to think that these things are part of the entire human condition and not simply something involving one generation of people in one country.

Penthouse: Can you account for the enormous appeal of the strip?
Schulz: I suppose the strip is reasonably consistent in its content from day to day, and it is also quotable, which is very important in cartooning. The drawings are pleasant to look at and the characters themselves are quite real.

Penthouse: There seems to be a broad age spectrum to your fans, from the teens all the way up to quite elderly people.
Schulz: We get a strong group of letters each day from little kids, but we also go right on up through teenagers to grandparents. We get letters from quite a broad spectrum of professions, too—doctors, priests,

lawyers, nuns, rabbis, athletes, pilots, servicemen, musicians. I hope it is
because I comment on their interests in a reasonably intelligent way.
That doesn't mean that I'm an authority on them but the things I draw
I research to a certain extent. If you're going to do humor at all, you
have to know something about the subject you're dealing with. We frequently get 100 letters a day—sometimes more.

Penthouse: Is there any personal antecedent to Charlie Brown in your
own boyhood?
Schulz: Anyone who creates a comic strip and is involved in doing it
day after day works in the same manner as a novelist does. I've been
doing this now for 21 years and if you're going to survive on a daily
schedule you survive only by being able to draw on every experience
and thought that you've ever had. That is, if you are going to do anything with any meaning. Of course, you can grind out daily gags but
I'm not interested in simply doing gags. I'm interested in doing a strip
that says something and makes some comment on the important things
of life. I'm probably a little bit of Charlie Brown and a little of Lucy and
Linus and all the characters. It would be impossible in this kind of strip
to create any character and not be part of it yourself.

Penthouse: Somehow *Peanuts* seems to span the generation gap. As
both the father of Charlie Brown and a member of the middle-aged
generation, how do you view the present chasm between the young
and their parents?
Schulz: I find the gap with children unpredictable—sometimes frighten-
ingly so. As your children grow up, you're convinced that you're a
good father and that you're doing everything right. Then all of a sudden things just run off the track and you have no idea what went
wrong. I don't think it's anyone's fault. I think that suddenly this personality that has been growing up in your home is released from some
of the bonds of parental pressure and the real personality comes shin-
ing through. This is just the way the children were born to be, and has
nothing to do with what you have taught them or not taught them.
They're now in a new age. Television always gets brought up as a factor in what is happening to children, and we just can't deny that TV
brings them the whole world in such an easy manner it just has to have
something to do with it. Also economic freedom—the young have
more money than any other generation ever had. Today you just can't
know what is going to happen with children. You can talk about

parental guidance but I don't think you can teach children any more than what you have lived yourself. They see you for what you are and they *know* what you are, and they either admire you or they don't admire you and that's all there is to it. As far as your influence is concerned, if you think you can tell them something and you have not really lived it yourself, you're just fooling yourself. Perhaps it's about time to start going by some new rules; I think some of the old rules were not very good. I have a feeling if we can just survive for the next few years—I hate to say five or 10 or 25—we'll come out of our present problems the better for it. I think we've made tremendous strides in just the past five years. We've accomplished things that no one could have predicted. I think the whole business of race relations, for example, has made tremendous progress.

Penthouse: Talking about that, you introduced a little black boy into the strip.

Schulz: Yes, and that brought the strongest criticism I remember. There weren't many letters, but they were quite vehement. Of the critical letters we receive—only a total I would say of maybe 25 in 21 years—some are quite fascinating and show how the human mind works. I've had letters recently complaining that Woodstock and Snoopy appear too much—that Snoopy seems to be taking over the strip. I have the feeling that these are readers of the Sunday page only. It is true that I use Snoopy and Woodstock more on Sunday because they provide more action, and the Sunday strip is supposed to be slanted more toward children. But the fact is that Snoopy is simply the most popular figure in the strip. I listen to such criticism, if it's valid, I do something about it. This has resulted in my doing several stories recently without Snoopy at all. I also have been criticized now and then for quoting scripture in the comics by people who say that scripture should never be used in such a lowly art form. I think this is terribly insulting, not only to me as a creator, and one who loves the scriptures, but also an insult to what the scriptures were originally intended for.

Penthouse: Wasn't there a book written on the religious ideas of the strip?

Schulz: Yes, *The Gospel According to Peanuts* by Robert Short. I had not known him at the time, but he wrote for permission to do it and since then we've become very close friends. His book took the approach that any art form—even such a lowly art form as the comic

strip or literature such as Kafka's—could inspire one to spiritual thinking. It was reviewed in *Christian Century* and sold millions of copies.

© by United Feature Syndicate, Inc.

Penthouse: How was Charlie Brown born?

Schulz: It is all the result of a life-long ambition to draw a comic strip,
simply from a fascination with the "funnies." As a kid I read all of the
comics and was a great fan of such strips as *Popeye* and *Buck Rogers,
Mickey Mouse, Terry and the Pirates, Captain Easy, Li'l Abner, Prince
Valiant, Krazy Kat, S'matter Pop*. I drew all the way through grade
school and high school. I never drew anything of any importance and
never sold anything. I didn't even work for my high-school newspaper.
In fact, the cartoons I drew for our high-school annual never got printed, which was a bitter disappointment to me. After World War II, I was
living in St. Paul with my father, who was a barber, and I began seriously to try to get my cartoon career going. I got a job with a correspondence school in Minneapolis called Art Instruction Schools, and I
ended up working for them for five years. While I was there, I developed my drawing and creative ability. Suddenly one day, just by mailing
it in blindly to the *Saturday Evening Post,* I sold my first cartoon. It was
a one-column cartoon for which they paid $40. During the same period
I began drawing cartoons that involved little kids, and the St. Paul
newspaper agreed to publish them on a once-a-week basis. I drew
either three or four of them. They were panel cartoons grouped together in one feature. They printed them two columns wide each Sunday,
hiding them in the women's section. This went on for two years. It was
a wonderful way to start because I had to think of only three or four
ideas each week and yet there was a schedule to which I had to hold,
so I learned to think of ideas on schedule. It gave me a chance to
develop my drawing and my creativity. At the end of this period I
began to sell some more cartoons to the *Saturday Evening Post* and
finally I decided I ought to try to improve my standing with the St. Paul
paper. I asked the editor if he wouldn't run them on a daily basis,

rather than just on Sunday and he said No, he didn't have room for a
daily feature and, besides, he had a lot of syndicated material. They
were paying me $10 a week at the time, which was normally what
they might pay for a top quality syndicated feature. I was always
appreciative of his just giving me the start so there was no bitterness. I
asked him if he could run it along with the Sunday comics, but he said
this as absolutely out of the question. So I said: "Maybe you could give
me a little more money for doing the feature?" He said No, the budget
wouldn't allow it. Having a little more confidence, having sold those
cartoons to the *Post,* I said, "Well, perhaps I should just quit drawing
it," and he said "All right." I'll never forget that. He just said, "All
right," and that was the end of my two-year career with the *St. Paul
Pioneer Press.*

Penthouse: How did you get started again?
Schulz: I wasn't too disturbed, because I knew I was getting better all
the time. I used to bundle my efforts together and take the train down
to Chicago and visit two or three syndicates there and get rejected and
get on the train and come home. In the spring of 1950, I took all the
best cartoons I'd done for the *Pioneer Press* and redrew them and submitted them to United Feature Syndicate. They liked them enough to
ask me if I'd care to come to New York and talk about it, and I did. I
took along six daily comic strips which had a new approach to humor
in strips. If you were to see them now they wouldn't look like much,
but at the time it was new. There was a very light touch to them and in
a way they were subtle and it was a unique approach. They decided
they would rather have a strip than the panel cartoons. So when we
signed the contract it was with the agreement that I was to create definite characters and draw a daily comic strip. I took some of the little kid
characters I had been drawing, which were anonymous, and named
one Charlie Brown and one Patty. I'd always been drawing little dogs in
the strip, so I named one Snoopy, the one I would be using the most.
Actually he was named Sniffy at first. But I was walking past a newsstand one day and saw a stack of comic magazines and one was called
Sniffy, and it was about a little dog, so I had to go back and change the
name to Snoopy. The real dog who was the forerunner of Snoopy was
named Spike. He was bigger than the beagle that Snoopy has turned
out to be, but he was kind of a wild dog marked in a way similar to
Snoopy. I had another boy character named Shermy, who was named

after a friend of mine. Those were the four characters in the strip the first week. Later on I added Violet who was supposed to be the pretty girl in the strip, and then Lucy came along and her brother Linus. It was about that time, close to a year later, that the strip began to take shape. It has grown in many different directions down through the years.

Penthouse: Do you have a favorite character in the strip?
Schulz: I suppose my favorite is Charlie Brown, simply because I like him so much. However, I have a fondness for all of the characters and feel that Snoopy is the one with which I work best.

Penthouse: How long does it take you to draw the daily strip?
Schulz: I can draw it in an hour. Some strips I could probably draw in ten minutes, if it's Snoopy and Woodstock doing something simple.

Penthouse: So you stay on top of the strip pretty well, in terms of time?
Schulz: Oh no, I'm always fighting the schedule, simply because I have so many other things to do—people like you coming for interviews, for instance. Yesterday someone was here at noon, and Thursday I have to spend the entire afternoon in San Francisco helping to record voices for our new movie. I suppose that if I had nothing to do but the strip, it would be the same thing. I'd just think about the ideas longer and worry about them and still let things interfere. I've never been one who can shut himself off and say I absolutely refuse to see anyone—no phone calls. I'd feel guilty about it, because I feel an obligation to see people. If anyone is kind enough to call, I feel I should answer the phone and talk to them. I'm also not one who can work steadily at the drawingboard. I simply can't sit there and grind out cartoons all day long. I get jumpy and I want to get up and move around and do something else.

Penthouse: But you also say that you *like* to draw cartoons. You sound like most writers, who talk about the agony of writing but refuse to do anything else.
Schulz: Oh yes, I'm at my happiest when I have a good idea and I'm drawing it well, and it comes out well and somebody laughs at it. This is what I enjoy doing more than anything else. If there is such a thing as being born to do something I think I was born to draw comic strips because my ability seems to fall in this line. I'm able to draw just well enough, and I'm able to write just well enough. I've said before, if I

could draw better I'd be a painter, and if I could write better I'd be writing novels, but as it is I'm just right for this medium.

Penthouse: Do you know the exact syndication?
Schulz: I'm not quite sure. The size and quality of the papers are more important than the mere numbers. We were fortunate with this strip that we got off to a pretty good start as far as big newspapers were concerned. A lot of times you start with a lot of papers but they aren't very big. We were fortunate in that we had the Minneapolis paper, the Chicago *Tribune*, the New York *World*, the Seattle *Times*, the San Francisco *Chronicle*, all within the first month, and this was a big help.

Penthouse: You have been quoted as terming *Peanuts* a "chronicle of defeat." What is it about defeat that intrigues such a cheerful and optimistic artist?
Schulz: If *Peanuts* chronicles defeat it is probably because defeat is a lot funnier than victory. Most of us know what it is like to lose some kind of contest, and we can identify with the loser.

Penthouse: Your strip also has a great sense of the hero. Charlie Brown is a great hero-worshipper, and there's Schroeder and Beethoven. How about you personally—do you have any heroes in the age when everyone complains that there are none anymore?
Schulz: I'm not so sure that it isn't a good idea for us to find out that heroes are really human—particularly the military ones. The heroes I have are mainly athletes. I was a great admirer of Sam Snead. I once watched him play a round in the St. Paul tournament when he hit every green in regulation figures—and all the par-fives in two—for a truly flawless round. I think the great athletes supply us with something that we need—an example of excellence.

Penthouse: Sport is clearly a major enthusiasm of yours. What ever gave you the idea of building this magnificent arena?
Schulz: Well, there was one in town, smaller than this, which had to close because of structural difficulties. We had taken a new interest in skating, and my kids all enjoyed it so much that we hated the idea that we'd have to quit. When I heard that the rink had to close, I said I wished there was something we could do about it. My wife said: "I was hoping you would say that, because there is something we can do." She already had plans in her mind for building a new one. She's great at building things and gathering together people who can put

things up. So she got the people together and built this under her own supervision and it is literally the world's most beautiful ice arena. Joyce did it all. I had nothing to do with it. I'm just the chairman of the board and the star hockey-player.

Penthouse: When did you take up hockey?
Schulz: I just played around the neighborhood when I was 14 or 15. In St. Paul we used to play on backyard rinks my dad used to make for us, or we'd sneak onto private-school rinks at night and play under the light of the moon. But I was never specially good, never good enough to play high-school hockey. But since the arena is open here and we can play on good ice and with plenty of room, I think I'm a better player than I was in those days.

Penthouse: How does a man who played golf so well switch to another sport in middle age?
Schulz: It's better exercise. And besides, the hole is bigger. I took up golf when I was 15 and became a real fanatic. I had seen Bobby Jones in a series of shorts he had made years ago, and I had always admired good golfers. But I had no one to show me the game. A friend of mine and I took an old borrowed set of clubs with wooden shafts and went up to a public course in St. Paul one morning at 5:30 and played our first game of golf. I remember I shot 156 and I thought the next time we go out, I'll do better. The next time I shot 165, but four months later I broke 80—I had my first 79. The next year I made the high-school golf team. From then on that was all I thought about—drawing cartoons and playing golf. I had this dream that some day I'd become a great cartoonist and win the National Open. But I never qualified for the Open, though I tried a couple of times. That was what was great about playing in the Bing Crosby tournament—it was the next best thing to getting in the Open. I was very dedicated to golf until a few years ago, when some of the friends I'd played with regularly just drifted apart. Our weekly foursomes broke up, and since opening the arena here, I've discovered that hockey is better for you physically. Walking around a golf course is a deception. It isn't really good for you—it fools you into thinking you're exercising.

Penthouse: But you've never used golf in the strip, have you?
Schulz: Well, once Snoopy started to go down and play in the Masters at Augusta, but then he found out that no beagle had ever been invit-

ed to play in that tournament. Baseball is the ideal sport for the kind of humor I've used in the strip. There is the contemplative quality of the baseball player—of the pitcher standing still there on the mound, rubbing the ball, and there are two out and men on second and third and it's the last half of the ninth. Then someone walks up to the mound and what does he say? You have the suspense right before you. It works perfectly for Charlie Brown.

Penthouse: Were you as good at baseball as you were at golf?
Schulz: Not really. I was pre-Little League. We played on vacant lots, with baseballs that had the covers knocked off and had been taped up with black electrical tape. And we used old cracked bats. We played from the early cold days of spring until football season in the fall. I remember I was always disappointed when the kids brought the footballs out, because I liked baseball much better than football.

Penthouse: A few people felt that in your last television show, *Play It Again, Charlie Brown* the humor was a bit more abrasive than in the earlier TV animations. Were you out of sorts, or was it just a reflection of the general deterioration of gentleness in our world today?
Schulz: This is very difficult for me to respond to because—this may surprise you—I never saw the show. I saw only some pencil tests of the show without the music. We did receive more bad comments on that show, but at the same time, a lot of good comments. My problem with these things is not being able to work close enough with the animators down in Hollywood. This is my own fault; I just don't go there often enough and work carefully enough with them. I'm going to try to make up for it in the next movie.

Penthouse: What is the next one?
Schulz: It's called *Snoopy Come Home.* The story is completed and I have written the entire show and blocked out every scene myself. I've created all the funny business for the entire thing and if it doesn't work it will be only my fault—my inability to translate what I want to the animators, so that they can turn it out. This is where it gets lost, as I discuss what I want with the director, and he takes my wishes and has to impose them on the animators. The animators are then at the mercy of the inkers and painters, and along the line lots of things can go wrong. It's our obligation to look at these things and say "That's not quite right" and "We'll have to correct this or that." This doesn't hap-

pen because of time and money. It's not an art form that you can polish and re-polish until you get it just the way you want it. There is
always a schedule to be met and a budget to which you have to hold,
and this is unfortunate. But I think this will be a better movie than the
first one. It has a better story and it flows better. It involves Snoopy in a
decision whether he will go off and live with another girl instead of
staying with Charlie Brown, and it involves a little journey that he and
Woodstock take and some of the problems they have.

Penthouse: Where did Woodstock come from?
Schulz: I've been drawing birds in the strip for some time—at least 10
years. Like a lot of things in this medium, suddenly your drawing starts
to work. At one point I began to draw the bird a little better. I needed
a name for him, and with the Woodstock festival being so prominent in
the news, I said "Why not?" I've run into a little trouble with Woodstock because he is frequently a secretary for Snoopy and it would be
better if his secretary were a girl. This has spoiled some of the ideas in
my mind, but you can't have everything.

Penthouse: Two of your critics . . .
Schulz: My *critics?* . . .

Penthouse: Yes, William Zinsser in *Look* and Richard Schickel in *Life*,
both complained about the same thing: the use of Charlie in commercial advertising—in the Falcon car ads and those for Weber bread.
Schulz: I have a lot of answers for that. My number one answer is:
"Can anyone prove to me that the feature is not as good today as it
was two years or five years ago?" Someone else did an article for
another magazine and claimed to have definite proof that the strip had
deteriorated in quality as a result of my having put in too much time on
other things. That was five years ago. *Peanuts* is now listed in the
Guinness Book of Records as the most widely read comic strip in the
world. I think the strip this last year has had things in it as good as anything anyone has ever done in comic strip history. Therefore, I don't see
why there should be any complaint about what we do outside the
comic strip, if it doesn't affect the strip. These critics don't have to buy
the greeting cards, or the Charlie Brown books, or look at the TV
shows. The comic strip is there in the daily paper and it is as good as it
ever has been. If I'm just kidding myself and it is not as good, then
there is nothing I can do about it—to go back to the quality they think
it once had. No one can go back. Maybe the quality of discovery for

some people is gone. They like to discover unique new things in enter-tainment, and once an author becomes popular they no longer like to enjoy it. They like to hold a new writer to themselves. Once he becomes part of the public, he no longer is unique for them. I *don't* put in that much time on other projects so that work really suffers.

Penthouse: It wasn't so much that they thought Charlie had deteriorated as that they thought Charlie was too pure for commercial exploitation.
Schulz: I would answer that in another way. No one has ever given us credit for taking part in a pure art form. *Time* magazine, when it would write about the strip, would not list us as part of the Art section; it was always in the Press section. Comic artists are never given the Pulitzer Prize. We are never given the Nobel Prize. No one ever gives us any awards except our own organization. So how can they criticize a com-mercial enterprise for being commercial? We would like to be regarded as art, and I think it would be nice if they said, "Gee, what you are doing is pure art," but no one has ever said that. It is just a plain old comic strip, which helps to sell newspapers. If athletes can use their names to sell sweat shirts, why can't comic-strip artists? If movie stars

© by United Feature Syndicate, Inc.

can use their faces to sell cosmetics and other things, why can't a car-toon character?

Penthouse: At least there is the consolation that Picasso made ceramics.
Schulz: That's a *very* good consolation. As for what William Zinsser said, he was far off the track too, in talking about my little books such as *Happiness Is a Warm Puppy*. He complained that the world is more complicated than that. This is an outrageous accusation. I never said that it wasn't more complicated. But I will defend to my dying day the statement that Happiness is a Warm Puppy. I defy him to give me a bet-ter definition of what happiness is. It may take him a 12-volume set of books to do it, but in one sentence let him try to tell me better what is more happy than a little kid putting his arms around a warm puppy. If that isn't happiness. I don't know what is. And I'd rest my case on that.

Penthouse: Mr. Schulz, thank you.

You're a Good Sport, Charlie Schulz

CHARLES MAHER / 1973

From Los Angeles *Times,* August 28, 1973,
Sports Section, pp. 1, 7. Copyright © 1973
Los Angeles Times. Reprinted by
permission.

Rats! The way things stand, we won't get to see Lucy hold the football
for Charlie Brown this fall and then snatch it away just as he's about to
kick it. So there won't be any final panel showing Charlie Brown tumbling through the air with that wry, wounded look of his, muttering
something about this latest triumph of treachery.

It's become a tradition, a rite of autumn, for Lucy to pull the ball
away from Charlie Brown. Knowing Lucy (and to know her is to loathe
her), one suspects she'd be doing it again this year. But her idea man,
Charles M. Schulz, couldn't come up with a punch line.

"I was trying to think of one the other day," he said. "Instead I
came up with another idea: Peppermint Patty running through Charlie
Brown four times, crashing right over him. That led to another idea,
involving Snoopy. So I drew two football pages (for Sunday papers)

76

and I'm just tempted to let it go at that and not do one with Lucy pulling the ball away."

"How many years has she been doing that?"

"Oh, I'd say 16 or 17."

"And this will be the first year she hasn't?"

"Unless I can think of an idea at the last minute. In the one I thought of, where Peppermint Patty blasts right over poor Charlie Brown, she fumbles on the fourth time. She says, 'I fumbled the ball, Chuck. Why didn't you jump on it?' Charlie's sitting there all dazed and he says, 'I thought it was my head.'"

Over the years Schulz has used sports themes in hundreds of *Peanuts* strips. In baseball, for instance, Charlie Brown has piloted his team to uncounted reverses. ("How can we lose," Charlie once asked, "when we're so sincere?")

There's a lot of little Charlie Schulz in little Charlie Brown. Things that happen to Charlie Brown in the comics once happened to Charlie Schulz in St. Paul. And a lot of them happened in sports. Schulz was talking about it the other day at his studio, a modern, one-story building situated at No. 1 Snoopy Place in Santa Rosa.

"You'll notice," Schulz said, "that a lot of my sports ideas don't deal directly with sports."

"You mean you just use sports as a vehicle to express a philosophical point?"

"That's right. But you'll notice when I deal in some of these areas I deal authentically with them. I put in little touches of authenticity so the reader will know it's being done right."

"Were you once on a baseball team that lost 40-0?" he was asked.

"Yeah. We had a game after school and this other team was a shade bigger than us and we couldn't see the ball and it was a disaster. We had a terrible team anyway."

"You had a 40-0 game in your strip once."

"Oh, yes. A lot of things in the strip are autobiographical."

Schulz sat at an easel in what might be called his drawing room. It's a paneled, split-level room about 40-feet long, 18-feet wide. He works in a corner on the upper level. "It was designed so I would work on the lower part," he said, "but I discovered I was too far away from the ceiling light and I really like this corner business—being backed into this corner. I like the coziness."

Schulz, 50, is a slender man, just under 6 feet, with wispy, grayish-brown hair, high forehead, kindly countenance. He speaks precisely with a gentle voice, often using soft chuckles for punctuation marks. He wears metal-rim glasses and a tired expression. If he worked out of Central Casting, he'd probably get calls when they needed a professor or a judge.

"I liked baseball best when I was a kid," he said. "The trouble was we never had any good places to play. The playground in my neighborhood in St. Paul was terrible, so we played a lot of our sports out in the street. Later, after I moved, we had to play on a crushed-rock playground and a good hot grounder through short was a home run because it just kept rolling. In the winter my dad made me a little ice rink in the backyard and we'd play hockey when the weather was right. I was never a very good skater."

"How good were you at baseball?"

"I was a good player but I was never big and strong enough to play high school baseball. There was no Little League or anything so our baseball was just our neighborhood team against another one."

"How old were you then?"

"I would have been around 12 or 13. And when I was 14 I experienced one of the outstanding summers of my life. There was a playground manager named Harry. He organized a four-team league and worked out a schedule and we played all summer long, every Tuesday and Thursday. I could hardly wait for Tuesdays and Thursdays to come. The first game was at 9 but I'd always be down there, the first one, at 7:30 in the morning with all my equipment."

"What was your position?"

"Well, I was either pitcher or catcher. We alternated. I was also the team manager. I pitched a no-hit, no-run game that year. Our team won the championship."

A most unCharlie-Brownish development.

"Things kind of fell apart the next year," Schulz said. "Harry left the playground. You know, I have no idea what his last name was. But somewhere in this country is a fellow named Harry, probably close to 60 years old, and I wish there was some way I could say, 'Harry, thank you for a great summer.'"

"What other sports did you play?"

"Well, all those years I had wanted to play golf. I had seen a Bobby Jones movie short when I was 9. I was fascinated by that. But my dad (a barber) didn't play golf. He loved fishing. I never really cared much for it. Didn't like sitting out on the lake in the cold. I guess I was kind of a disappointment to him. When I was 15 I finally got to play golf. A friend and I went to a public course and I shot a 156 with a miserable set of three or four clubs."

"Yeah. Never got the ball off the ground. But I thought the next time I'd do better. So two days later I shot a 165."

"You must be up over 200 by now."

"Well, I really became totally immersed in the game. The next spring I started playing again and within a month or so I had a 79. I improved very fast. And I played on the Central High School team when I was 17."

Schulz played touch football in the street, and a little hockey on his backyard rink, but golf was the only sport in which he made the school team.

"I kind of resented the whole public school system of that time," he said. "It didn't cater to the many kids who weren't big and strong. The gym teachers paid attention only to the school athletes. The rest of us were shunted aside. I really resented that."

Schulz followed hockey as a kid and still does. He drives 11/2 hours to Oakland to watch the Seals, who have lately played like one of Charlie Brown's teams.

"I have season tickets," he said, "but I'm pretty much limited to going Friday nights now because of my own hockey playing and refereeing."

Schulz plays in a $2-million rink he built for himself and the kids of Santa Rosa. It's a handsome Swiss-style building two blocks from his studio.

"We've tried to correct some of the things I thought were wrong with sports programs when I was a kid," he said. "I don't know if I've been successful but in our hockey program I declared that every boy who signed up was going to get a uniform and play on some kind of team regardless of ability. He wasn't going to sit on the bench."

"What teams use the arena?"

"We belong to the Northern California Amateur Hockey Assn. and our boys play teams from other towns. We have kids from about 5 or 6 up to 19."

"And you're a referee?"

"I'm the referee-in-chief. I've been refereeing about four years now."

"Are you a strict enforcer of the rules?"

"I like to think I'm very fair but there are people in other communities who think I'm prejudiced and deliberately make calls in favor of our teams, which is astonishing."

"You take a lot of flak?"

"From the coaches and players, I think, you should take only something like, 'Hey, ref, that was a bad call.' They should never get away with swearing at you. (Schulz abstains from profanity, as well as smoking and drinking.) From the crowd, I think, you have to take a little more, until they become directly personal. Last year I kicked a father out of the stands because several times I heard him say, 'Schulz, you're a creep!' I don't think any sane person should say that and I don't think anybody should be allowed to say it, especially in this kind of game, where youngsters are playing and it's supposed to be for fun."

"How often do you referee?"

"Every Sunday night. We work as many as three or four games a night, which is very exhausting. I know tempers can run high. When I'm playing I get mad at the referees. But I think you should draw a line when they become personally insulting. I've had boys deliberately kick me, deliberately hit me with their sticks on the faceoff, just for revenge. I've had boys spit on my back. Here I have built a $2-

million arena for their enjoyment, not to make money for myself. I'm refereeing the games for my own enjoyment, I must admit, but also for their benefit. And yet they'll do these things, with no comprehension of what they're doing. But I suppose this is the way people are."

Schulz plays right wing on a local men's team. "Playing hockey is one of the few things that takes my mind completely off everything else in my life," he said. "You don't have time to think of anything else. That's when I think sports have their greatest value . . . I think one of the biggest thrills I ever got in sports was when I scored our only goal in a game here two years ago against a team from Korea. They beat us, 3-1. I certainly wasn't the best player on our team but I can still remember the goal. I had about a six-inch opening between the goalie's foot and the pole and I slid it in just like a perfect putt. I can still see it sliding in there and hitting the back of the net. That was really exciting."

Schulz would join those who criticize the American obsession with winning. "No sooner does the season start," he said, "than we begin to record how far a team is out of first place. A game between two teams in 7th and 10th place can be just as exciting as any game. But all we're worrying about is who wins. It should be the plays, great goals being scored, great baskets being made, great overhand shots hit. These are the things that count in sports."

Worse yet. Schulz said, adults pass their obsession along to their children.

"I think the Little League setup is deplorable," he said. "First, the players are judged by age. Age has almost nothing to do with evaluating or placing players. If there's a 12-year-old kid who stands 6 feet and can throw the ball so fast the other kids can't see it, he shouldn't be allowed to dominate the game. He should be pushed up to a higher league, where he fits in."

"Your boys went through this?

"Oh, yeah. I saw the whole thing first hand. It's deplorable."

"Have you commented on it in your strip?"

"I did once, just a little bit. Last spring Charlie Brown's team won a game. First game they'd ever won. But they got a call to report to league headquarters. They had discovered that one of the players had a nickel bet on the outcome of the game. So a group of the parents got together and took away Charlie Browns' only victory.

© by United Feature Syndicate, Inc.

And Linus said something like, 'In all the world, Charlie Brown, there's nothing more frightening than when a group of parents gets together.' And that's what happens all the time. A group of kids are out playing together and a group of parents gets together and decides something and mainly the decision is according to their own interests."

Schulz used to live on a 28-acre estate in nearby Sebastopol. The address was 2162 Coffee Lane and the place was called Coffee Grounds. A magazine story said Schulz had a wife, 5 kids, 11 ducks, 5 cats, 4 dogs, 3 horses and 2 ponies.

"Lots of changes since then," he said. "Now I'm divorced. We sold the Coffee Lane property and Joyce lives out on a ranch with three of the children. Meredith, our oldest daughter, is married now and Monte, my hockey-playing son, is leaving for Concordia College in Minnesota."

"Where do you live now?"

"I don't have any place to live. I'm trying to get re-established."

"Where do you sleep?"

"Right here on the couch. I've been living here about six months.

Joyce has remarried and I have to start my life all over. Strangely, I've drawn better cartoons in the last six months—or as good as I've every drawn. I don't know how the human mind works."

"What's your work schedule?"

"I usually start around 9:30 and work to about 5. I don't work real hard. I'm not one who can sit at the drawing board all day. I work generally five days a week. I used to work four. I played golf every Thursday. But I've given that up."

"What was your handicap when you played regularly?"

"Oh, I suppose about 3 or 4. Something like that. I've played in the Crosby tournament. But last year I didn't. I was so upset with everything that was happening to me. I don't know if I'll play in the next one because I'm going to be grand marshal of the Rose Parade. That's on the first and the Crosby starts on the third. I don't know if I can stay away from home that long."

"What percentage of your strips would you say have sports themes?"

"It goes in streaks. I've done a lot of baseball things this year. Last year I almost ignored baseball. This year I've done 15 or 20 tennis strips. I play tennis now most every day." (He has a court next to his studio.)

"What are some of your favorites among the sports things you've done? "I noticed a couple of framed ones on baseball out in the main office."

"Yeah. There's one out there I like a lot. It's where Schroeder gets nicked on the finger with a foul ball."

That, of course, would be Beethoven Schroeder, the miniature pianist with the minia-

ture piano. When he gets nicked Charlie Brown asks, "Is it all right? Are you going to be able to play?" Whereupon Beethoven runs home, bangs on his piano a while and returns, announcing, "It's OK. I can play." And Charlie Brown, looking out from the last panel with mild exasperation, says, "It isn't exactly what I meant."

"Do you reproduce genuine Beethoven scores for Schroeder?"

"Oh, yeah. I've got a book of some of Beethoven's things and I just copy out of that. It's hard work, drawing all those notes."

"Are you a musician?"

"Not at all. I can't read music."

"Who's the premier athlete in your aggregation—Snoopy?"

"I suppose he would be."

"Why give the role to a dog?"

"It's funnier. Apparently Linus is a good player and Schroeder is a good catcher. I think Charlie Brown's outfield is no good. He has the three girls out there. Lucy is obviously a bad player. But we've never found out, really, why they lose all these games. Charlie Brown looks as though he's pitching pretty well."

"You talk as if you're puzzled yourself."

"Yeah. I really don't know why it is."

"Well, if you don't know, we're in trouble."

"Yes, I suppose. You know, we don't even know who they're playing."

"Do you watch sports events on TV?"

"To a certain extent. I like to catch the major ones. I suppose I like football but I'm not a fanatic about it. Basketball I've never watched. Never played it. Never cared much for track because I was never into that, either. And I was a lousy swimmer so I don't watch that. I like some of the big tennis matches."

Schulz offered to show his guest the ice arena. A public skating session was in progress when they entered. "I'll be lucky to get out of here without having to draw a Snoopy," Schulz said.

Sure enough, as he was showing his guest the arena gift shop, a little girl came up, said she was from Oklahoma and handed Schulz a piece of paper to draw something on. He drew a Snoopy and wrote "SCHULZ" underneath.

"How often do you have to do that?" he was asked.

"Oh, I wouldn't ordinarily come over here on a day like this," he said. "I could be here doing this all afternoon."

"The townspeople haven't gotten used to you?"

"No. Sometime it's almost maddening."

Schulz and his companion slipped out of the arena and parted. Schulz had given up more than two hours for the interview. Time to get back to the drawing board.

Charles Schulz:
"Comic Strips Aren't Art"

STAN ISAACS / 1977

From *Newsday*, August 28, 1977, pp.
15–17, 36, 38.
Reprinted by permission.

Charles M. Schulz once said, "I worry about almost all there is in life
to worry about, and because I worry Charlie Brown has to worry." If it
seems that Charlie Brown doesn't worry in the strip *Peanuts* as much as
he used to, it may be because Schulz for a long time has had less reason to worry.

Peanuts is probably the most widely read comic strip in the world—
90,000,000 readers is one broad assessment—and it has been estimated as a $150-billion industry where artifacts include books, greeting
cards, records, T-shirts, pillows and just about every *shmata* that can
stock a novelty store shelf, along with regular TV productions based on
the strip and *You're a Good Man, Charlie Brown*, the most performed
musical comedy in history.

Schulz employs five people in his studio on Snoopy Lane in Santa

Rosa, about an hour's drive north of San Francisco—an area he has lived in since he moved to Sebastopol from Minneapolis in 1958.

Schulz has five children by his first wife. He married his second wife, Jean Clyde, in 1973. His 12-room house on four acres adjoins his studio. A new indoor tennis court he built on the grounds was christened with a game the day of this interview. Schulz then invited his guest to hit some balls with him, showing a form that was practiced and graceful, though not as furious as the action of his strip alter ego, Snoopy.

Schulz is known by local townspeople as Sparky—a nickname derived from the horse "Sparkplug" in the comic strip *Barney Google*. Schulz, a youthful 54, who uses soft chuckles for punctuation, once said, "When I was small I believed my face was so bland that people would not recognize me if they saw me some place other than where they normally would."

Q: What were you doing on Oct. 2, 1950, the day that your first *Peanuts* strip appeared in newspapers?
Schulz: I can't recall if the paper in Minneapolis was one of the initial subscribers. About half-a-mile uptown in Minneapolis there was a large newsstand which sold out-of-town newspapers, and I had a very close friend named Jim Sassaoill who was very interested in my getting started, and we might have gone up to that newsstand that day and bought any papers that had the strip. I remember a few days later poor Jim going up there and asking if they had any papers with *Peanuts* in them, and the newsdealer said, "No, and we don't have any with popcorn either." That was doubly and triply obnoxious because I hated the name, and I knew that things like this were going to happen. It made me more and more angry . . . I despise the name.

Q: What would you have called it?
Schulz: I don't know. Originally, it was supposed to be called *Little Folks,* but we couldn't use that name. I think I would have settled for just *Charlie Brown* because most comic strips are named after the lead character.

Q: How did you become a comic strip creator?
Schulz: I was working at Art Instruction School, which is a correspondence school in Minneapolis. I was an instructor after having taken their course when I was a senior in high school. It was called "Federal

School" then, and it's the same correspondence school which advertises the "draw me and try for free art course." I answered an ad in a newspaper when I was in high school. My mother showed it to me, and it said, "Do you like to draw? Send for free talent test." And a salesman came out to the house, and I was sold on the textbook simply because they had things about cartooning in them. I really was afraid of art school because I didn't think I was good enough. But I wanted to be a cartoonist, so I signed up for that art course and eventually, after the war, I began to take my drawings over to the instructors and show them to them, and they hired me as an instructor for five years. And that's where I was the day my first strip appeared.

Q: You have said, "I do not regard what I am doing as great art." Why?
Schulz: I said that in the opening remarks to *Peanuts Jubilee,* one of my books, which the publishers subtitled "My Life and Art with Charlie Brown." I wanted to make it clear that I didn't want anybody to get the impression that I regarded this as art even in its broadest sense. Comic strips aren't art, they never will be art. They are too transient. Art is something which is so good it speaks to succeeding generations, not only as it speaks to the first generation but better, and I doubt that my strip will hold up for several generations to come. I don't know any that have. *Krazy Kat* is good, but I notice that even now I am bored with reading *Krazy Kat.* Comic strips are not made to last; they are made to be funny today in the paper, thrown away. And that is its purpose, to sell that edition of the newspaper. Just because something has drawing in it doesn't make it art, just because something has words in it doesn't make it literature. In an age where we label things like pop art, I didn't want to be accused of thinking I was better than I really was.

Q: I think many people might argue that 50 years from now a lot of Charlie Brown will have meaning to people.
Schulz: Well, you have convinced me. As long as *you* say it; *I* don't want to say it.

Q: What inspired you to conceive some of the themes of the strip? First, Schroeder playing Beethoven?
Schulz: That came from a music book I was looking at the very first year the strip began. I was looking through this book on music, and it

showed a portion of Beethoven's Ninth in it, so I drew a cartoon of Charlie Brown singing this. Now this was a long time ago, and the humor was much different from what it is now. I thought it looked kind of neat, showing these complicated notes coming out of the mouth of this comic strip character, and I thought about it some more, and then I thought, why not have one of the little kids play a toy piano. We had just bought a tiny piano then for our youngest daughter, Meredith; she was then only 2 years old. And then I thought, why not have Schroeder, who had just come into the strip as a baby, play the toy piano. And that's how it all started. If I had known that it would work as well, I would have planned it more carefully. Actually, I drew three or four strips and then I ended it. But then I kept thinking of new ideas and I brought it back. This is what happens in a comic strip all the time. You are never sure when something is going to work, so you don't plan things out as carefully as a novelist might because you don't have the time. The schedule is always right there on top of you. And you have to get something in. When you discover that something has worked, you wish then that you had really plotted it out more carefully. But it really doesn't matter. You just go back and work it around. The only thing that matters in the strip is what is in today's paper.

Q: I see your secretary has a sign on her desk that says, "Advice, Five Cents."
Schulz: I wonder where she got it.

Q: Lucy as psychiatrist: What is the inspiration for that?
Schulz: I haven't the slightest idea. I think it had something to do initially with a parody of children and lemonade stands, which you always used to see in comic strips. I think that is how it started out and again it worked. So I simply kept it going and gradually polished and refined it. It doesn't appear so much. We seem to be out of that phase. Things which seem funny one day don't seem so funny the next.

Q: Lucy taking the football away from Charlie Brown as he tries to kick it?
Schulz: That was a recollection of when I was a little kid. It was impossible for one boy holding a football for another to let him kick it without pulling it away. It would happen every time you went out to play football. The kid would pull it away; actually he would roll it away, but you can't draw that. I was thinking about that today because it is

almost time to start drawing the one for next year. It just works. It's kind of neat to establish something that is unique. This is the only running gag in comic strip history which appears annually that way, outside of Sadie Hawkins Day in *Li'l Abner,* and I don't know if Al Capp is doing that any more.

Q: I read a couple of years ago that you were thinking of cutting out the football sequence because it was too hard. But now it is permanent, I take it?

Schulz: Yes, and it varies. Sometimes I think of it right away in September, sometimes I haven't done it until late in November because I couldn't think of one. We had lunch with Governor [Ronald] Reagan once, and he told me that was his favorite series sequences. If the governor liked it, I guess I ought to keep it up.

Q: Now that you have this football monkey on your back, can you give us any insight of how you are thinking of working out the next one?

Schulz: Yes, I was thinking about it just today. I will start with the conversation in my mind of Lucy saying, "Come on Charlie Brown, I'll hold the ball and you'll kick it." And of course his initial reaction is one of outrage. He'll say, "Boy, you really must think I'm stupid don't you." From there I'll think of what the response will be. I almost got one this morning of what this year's will be. I'll have to think about it a bit longer to see if it is funny enough. I think my favorite is the one where he is lying on his back and he quotes from Isaiah and he says, "How long, oh Lord, how long?" and she says, "All your life, Charlie Brown, all your life." Another good one was where they shook hands on it and she said, "A woman's handshake is not legally binding."

Q: The security blanket?
Schulz: That came, of course, from our first three children. Three out of five of our children dragged blankets around, and that was one of those observation things which I started. And again it wasn't plotted very carefully at first because I think even Charlie Brown had a blanket in one or two sequences. And then I used to do sequences where Snoopy would try to get the blanket from Linus, but he doesn't run on four feet any more, which sort of kills that form of humor. But it worked out well, and that is probably the single best thing that I ever thought of. "Security blanket" is now in the dictionary.

Q: You say Snoopy hasn't been on all fours for a long time. What brought this about?
Schulz: Oh, you just progress from one gag to another and finally as he became more literate, and as he began to do more and more things which were more and more fantastic, it just seemed funnier at times to get him up. Some things demanded that he walk on his two hind legs. In a lot of instances, once you commit yourself that way you can't back up. It would be too late to put him back on four feet now. It would just destroy him.

Q: Snoopy writing at the typewriter. How did that start?
Schulz: It probably began with the dark and stormy night sequence. It might have been that I thought of that first and simply applied it to the dog writing at the typewriter. But since then I have done a lot of things with it and I have enjoyed it. Again, each theme that you think of seems to serve its purpose by giving you an outlet for all the ideas that come to you. Now some of the ideas for puns that Snoopy writes could never be used in this strip itself; they are simply too corny. But when Snoopy writes them, and writes them with all sincerity, then they are funny. You don't think that Snoopy is being stupid or anything like that.

You like him for his naivete because he innocently thinks he has done something great, and that makes it acceptable.

Q: What was the inspiration for terms like "good grief," "rats," and "you blockhead"?
Schulz: These are just things that I normally say myself.

Q: You don't look like the kind of person who would say, "You blockhead."
Schulz: What else can you say?

Q: "Good grief," or rats." I guess I think of stockier people saying, "You blockhead." I've seen reports that you might buy a professional hockey team or the San Francisco Giants baseball team.
Schulz: A person would be insane to do that. That's a whole different kind of wealth too. I make my money sitting here at the drawing board. I am not a Rockefeller or a Hunt. I don't play with money. I'd be insane to get involved where you lose money to make money. I don't understand that. It doesn't interest me at all. I have to sit here and draw comic strips. That's what I am alive for.

Q: How many papers are you in now?
Schulz: I think the last count that I read was 1,665. I can't estimate the number of readers. All I know is that King Features continues to say *Blondie* has more readers than I do, but I'd be glad to make a little side bet.

Q: I have seen the figure $150 million to describe the volume of business by Peanuts commercial enterprises.
Schulz: Somebody made up that figure once, and it was printed in a business magazine, and again I wouldn't have the slightest idea.

Q: What is the danger of over-commercialization for Charlie Brown when people see it that much away from the strip itself? How concerned are you?
Schulz: I am not the least concerned, because we have passed that point of concern now. The only danger that I can see is one that I've spoken of quite often—and that would be if I became so involved in all the commercial activity that I turned the strip over to somebody else, or if I began to go on a daily television show telling everybody how to run the world and all these other things. Then the strip would start to go downhill, then I think the whole thing would begin to crumble. But I

maintain we have not robbed our primary client, who is the newspaper editor. He still gets what he pays for, and I turn out, I think, a better strip today than I ever turned out, so the newspaper editor today is still getting what we agreed to give him 25 years ago. Nobody is forcing anybody to buy the T-shirts or anything; the strip is there to be read in the paper. I still draw it, I still think of all the ideas, I do all the lettering, I do the whole thing. So what's the complaint?

Q: What was your reaction to Robert Short's *The Gospel According to Charlie Brown* , which pointed up the religious themes inherent in the strip?

Schulz: My reaction was fair amount of delight because I was flattered that he should have treated the strip in this way. It is a book which is quite often misunderstood. I think Bob's theory is that even such a lowly thing as a comic strip can prompt some kind of spiritual thought, which is why he quotes everybody from me clear up to Kierkegaard. Obviously Kierkegaard prompts spiritual thought. There are country-western songs, and there are all sorts of things which can make us think about life in different ways, and this is what he was talking about. I liked the book. It's difficult to talk about what my beliefs are and what his beliefs are. I don't know about him, and I think the last thing we ever discussed is my belief that the only theology there is that there is no theology. The only true theology is that there is no theology. Obviously this could be argued, but that's my belief. It could make a very short book.

Q: After Short's book people began to think of your strip more in terms of theology, that and the fact you taught Sunday school with the Church of God. And now I understand you have stopped teaching Sunday school.

Schulz: There were a whole flock of misunderstandings along the way, misquotations. I even have been given the credit of being a lay minister, of actually being a minister. I taught adult Sunday school classed in a Methodist school here. I enjoyed it, but after doing it for almost 10 years I simply ran out of things to say, and I figured when one runs out of things to say then it's time to stop, and so I simply did. I enjoyed the studying of the Bible and reading all sorts of things to find out what different people think about difficult passages, but I no longer have any desire at all to try to influence anyone in my own beliefs or thoughts. The minute one propagates some kind of theological thought I think he is drifting away from what true theology is.

Q: You have said you worry constantly about the strip being the No. 1 strip in the paper each day, that you are no loser when it comes to drawing a comic strip. What is your reaction to Gary Trudeau, who draws *Doonesbury,* winning the Pulitzer Prize?

Schulz: That's an inaccuracy. He won the Pulitzer Prize for political cartooning; he did not win it for a comic strip. And I think he deserved it. Some cartoonists have been trying for years to persuade the Pulitzer Prize committee to award a prize for the best comic strip, but they have not been successful.

Q: It could be argued that in the broadest sense your strip is more than a comic strip, and if they were going to give the prize to anybody the first Pulitzer Prize should have gone to *Peanuts.*

Schulz: They just don't want to give it to comic strips for some reason. We're low down on the scale. I keep insisting that we are right next to vaudeville or burlesque as the lowest form of entertainment there is.

Q: But you don't believe that?

Schulz: It puts you in an untenable spot. You never quite knew where to stand. One moment you are praised and the next moment you are pushed aside. You don't know whether to think you are good or not. You can't take yourself too seriously, because if you do you'll get shot down right away. You are not in a dignified profession.

Q: And yet a religious writer has written that you are a preacher with a wider audience than Billy Graham, Norman Vincent Peale and others.

Schulz: But you are still a comic strip, and you still get letters from people saying, "Don't quote Scriptures in such a lowly thing as a comic strip." They are offended by it. Scriptures on streetcars is fine, but put them in a comic strip and they say you are sacrilegious. So you are stuck.

Q: When somebody is No. 1, people are always comparing you to yourself and with others. And you get something like a recent *Time* magazine profile on Trudeau, in which it said that Trudeau seemed to be relevant, and commenting on things that were happening in the world, whereas: "*Peanuts* kids are still too wrapped up in security blankets and warm puppies to say much about the pressure of events."

Schulz: Unfortunately when they write articles like that they seem to think that if you do an article on one man and praise him they have to knock somebody else. This criticism is not valid at all, in my opinion. I think I make comments which are much more important than what

Doonesbury does every day, much more lasting. And this again does not take away from *Doonesbury*. I think what Trudeau does is very funny. I couldn't do what he does. He's bright along those lines. I do what I do. But I really think that in the long run the things that I talk about are more important.

Q: Is it true that you once took a course at the local junior college on the novel?

Schulz: Oh yes. Greatest experience of my life.

Q: Why did you do it, and what was it like?

Schulz: I am very interested in writing, in the novel as an art form. I am reading a book by Margaret Drabble these days. I am only a high school graduate, and I really want to know more about great writers and writing. So I took this class and I was a good student. I got an "A" on my term paper, a great paper. On *Pale Horse, Pale Rider* by Katherine Anne Porter. Getting the "A" on that paper was as exciting to me that evening as when I won my first Reuben from the National Cartoonists Society. Because I knew what I wanted to do, how I wanted to write it, and the professor came up to me afterwards and told me, "I want you to know that your paper is a perfect example of what a term paper should be like." That's great. I had never written a term paper before. I wrote it as if I were writing for *The New Yorker,* starting off in one direction as the *New Yorker* does and then coming around to the point.

Q: Have you ever created a character who became more popular than you thought it would be?

Schulz: Pigpen is kind of a nuisance. Everybody kind of likes Pigpen. I don't like to draw him. He's only useful if you have him involved in dust and being dirty. I don't have many ideas on that; I ran out of these. And I don't even enjoy them. Now and then I think I ought to draw him, but my mind doesn't work in that vein, but people are always saying, "Why don't you draw Pigpen?"

Q: If you were to put only one of your strips on the wall, which would it be?

Schulz: Not one, I don't think. But the strip that seems to get the most attention is the one where the kids are looking at the clouds. That seems to be the one guaranteed for a laugh. It's a long strip. They are trying to imagine what they are seeing in the clouds. Linus says all sorts of pompous things which he sees and which just overwhelms Charlie Brown. Then Lucy says, "What do you see, Charlie Brown?" He says, "Well, I was going to say I see a ducky and a horsie, but I changed my mind."

Q: Does the strip speak at all to the disadvantaged?

Schulz: I suppose it doesn't. I think about that every now and then that there must be certain kinds of people who can't appreciate it because the strip, I suppose, is about middle-class kids and the things that they have. But I can't do anything about that.

Q: It's nice that you put Franklin in the strip, but he could be a white kid; there's nothing particularly black about him.

Schulz: I think it would be wrong for me to attempt to do racial humor because what do I know about what it is like to be black?

Q: You recently mentioned for the first time that you may not always be doing this, that you might stop.

Schulz: The burden of drawing this becomes oppressive at times. And I begin to think, do I really want to sit here for the rest of my life and fight this schedule? I see other people taking a vacation. The only way I can do that is by grinding out a whole batch of strips; it takes me months to get a few weeks ahead. I am beginning to wonder, beginning to have second thoughts. I think drawing a comic strip is the world's easiest job, but if you want to draw a good comic strip then it's one of the world's hardest jobs.

Q: If Charlie Brown were drawing an epitaph for Charles Schulz someday, what might you like to see him write?

Schulz: Just, "He made us happy"—which I think is what it's all about.

Cartoonist Profiles: Charles Schulz

Jud Hurd / 1979

From *Cartoonist Profiles,* No. 44
(December 1979): 46–55.
Reprinted by permission.

Hurd: I think readers would like to hear something from you about your Redwood Empire Ice Arena which is near your studio building. I know it has been called "The World's most beautiful Ice Arena."
Schulz: Joyce, my first wife, was really the driving force behind the designing and building of the arena. She had a real knack for being able to accumulate talent in the building of such constructions and she wanted to make sure that it was done really well. She was very much inspired, of course, by the marvelous way that Disneyland was run, and also by the Madonna Inn down in San Luis Obispo. The Inn is a pretty fancy place and she was fascinated by the attention to detail in the building of each room, and she was also intrigued by the well-run operation of Disneyland. So when our arena opened, she had all of the employees dress properly, and they were instructed in how the whole

place was to be run. And this is why it has earned the reputation as being "The World's most beautiful Ice Arena." She's not around anymore of course—she lives out on the ranch now—and I've remarried. I inherited the Ice Arena and I think we've done well in keeping it up since then. I've made several improvements myself in the place.

Hurd: I know you lived in Minnesota before you moved to California some years ago, and I'm wondering whether you missed some of the benefits of living in cold country when you came out here.
Schulz: The only thing we missed in moving from Minnesota was ice skating. We weren't fanatics about it, we weren't even especially good at skating but we did like to do it. We found that there had been an arena in Santa Rosa, but just as our family began to get into skating, and all the kids were learning how, that arena was forced to close down. And I can still remember the day that Joyce came home and said, "The Ice Arena is closed and I don't think they're going to be able to open again." At that point I said, "Gee, I wish there was something we could do about it." We liked the two Baxter brothers who had been running it—one of them had been on the U.S. Olympic Team. Joyce said, "I was hoping you'd say that because I've been thinking about it on the way home." That's the way she operated—she had great ideas for things—so we investigated the possibilities of buying some property and building an arena, thinking perhaps that we could build it for an estimated $170,000. By the time the building was finally constructed two years later, it cost $2,000,000. That was in May 1969 and we're celebrating our 10th anniversary in May 1979, and we hope to have Peggy Fleming back, as well as a few of the people who were there for our grand opening. We had a $25-a-seat charity opening and Joe Garagiola flew all the way out from New York one day just to be the master-of-ceremonies, and then I remember him getting on a plane and flying all the way back that same evening. I don't think I'm going to ask him to come out this time because he's such a good guy I think he'd go to all the trouble of doing it, and I'd be embarrassed to ask him. So that's the story of the Ice Arena—we've installed a ballet room recently because ballet is very important in figure skating, as are jazz dance classes. These days, in its highly competitive form, you have to know how to be a good dancer, as well as a good skater. We have a flawless sound system—one of the finest available—and we can convert the Arena overnight into an auditorium by covering up the ice, and

covering the boards with carpeting. This gives us a warm, comfortable theater and we've had men such as Bill Cosby, Bob Newhart, and almost any entertainer you can name, come in and do performances. We don't do this as much as we would like because most of the entertainers are forced to charge too much and we can't get that many people in for one-night stands.

© by United Feature Syndicate, Inc.

Hurd: Let me go back for just a minute and ask about those beautiful murals on the walls of the Arena.

Schulz: We sent a photographer to Switzerland and he took some beautiful photographs of the Swiss countryside. Back here we had them blown up so that they are approximately 5 to 6 feet in height. A woman from Carmel came up and painted the black-and-white photos with oils and the result helped to give the whole place more warmth. The photographer also took many pictures of Swiss homes and chalets in order that the carpenters would have something to use as models for the facades which are around the building. You sort of get the feeling that you are skating in a little park when you're in the Arena. Warmth was the thing Joyce was after in the Arena—she didn't want a cold place. The coffee shop has been a very great success—there are people who come to the coffee shop every day for lunch, and there are people who literally come to the Arena every day just because it's a nice place to be. There are a lot of lonely people in the world—they don't want to hang out in bars, they can't sit home and watch TV every night, they have no place to be, and the Ice Arena is a perfect place to go where they know they're going to see people who are their friends. They can just sit in the coffee shop, they don't have to buy anything if they don't want to, and if they want to nurse one cup of coffee the entire evening, they can do it. It's just a comfortable, friendly place to be, and this is one of the reasons I keep it open. This operation costs me a lot of money but I do it because I like it myself, and I realize there are people that need it, and of course I'm grateful that my own children have gotten so much enjoyment out of it. Two of my three girls now have become excellent figure skaters. Amy, who is now 22, did her first solo performance on our last television show "Snoopy's Musical on Ice" which starred Peggy Fleming. Amy did a number near the end of the show where she skated to a medley of hymns—something which has never been done before and which was challenged as not being appropriate or even very entertaining, but it came off marvelously because it fitted her style of skating. Her younger sister, Jill, who will be 21 very soon, just passed her 8th figure-skating test which is the ultimate test in skating—the Gold Test—and I think both the girls are capable of being in ice shows whenever they're ready to make that jump so this has been very gratifying. Jill will probably take it up professionally but I doubt if Amy would be willing to go on the road with a show. Outside in the front of the Arena I have copied the Grauman's Chinese Theater idea. Circling a little planted area I have cement blocks and when a famous skater comes to the Arena for one reason or another, we always ask him or her to sign their name in cement, and it makes a nice record of the people who've been here. And it's entertaining for visitors to wander around and be surprised at the many famous people who've been here, including a few nonskaters like Phyllis George, who's hosting our next television show. We always have something around to keep the people intrigued.

Hurd: I gathered from something you said earlier that the Arena isn't exactly a profit-making venture.

Schulz: No, it isn't. The tax situation is very difficult, the property taxes on it are enormous, and the monthly electric bills are also enormous. Last year the PG & E bills were up around $9000 a month, and you have to have a lot of skaters in there just to pay the electric bill. And we run a pretty quality operation—we have many more employees than your average ice arena, which is probably run by 2 or 3 people. We employ probably 40 or 50 people and we have no vending machines or anything cheap like that on the premises. It's something to be proud of and I like to do it and we're also the host of the Senior Olympics, which is a hockey tournament at the end of July each year. This year 28 senior hockey teams came in from various parts of Canada and the United States—the minimum age being 40—and in my bracket you have to be at least 55 to play. This was a tremendous success—we had about 800 people and we hosted a banquet for them on Saturday night of the tournament and everybody had a good time.

Hurd: Just what are the Senior Olympics?

Schulz: They involve all sports but they are hosted in various parts of the country by different people who are willing to take them on. It has nothing to do with the Olympics that you're familiar with. The head-quarters is in Los Angeles and it is run by a Mr. Warren Blaney and his son. The hockey segment of the Senior Olympics started in Burbank, California and we took our team down there for two or three years. I could see that they would have difficulty building up the sport, not owning their own plant, having to rent the ice, and having compara-tively few people to be involved. So I volunteered to take over the pro-gram, figuring that we could expand it into something that we hoped would be meaningful for the men. And I think it has been a tremen-dous success, and we really do it for the sake of these men who give so much of their own time to youth in the sport of hockey. It's just our way of returning to these fellows some of the work that they do. Although I do get tired of losing—I play right wing for our team—I'm on the first line and we did win our bracket one year but we've lost now for the last three years in a row. This last year we came in second and we're quite content just to do that.

Hurd: As we were walking over here to the Arena from your studio building, you mentioned that you like to concentrate *first of all* on the *Peanuts* strip, even though you have become involved in so many other related activities.

Schulz: Quite often people come up to me, tell me how much they like what I do, and say, "You are a second Walt Disney." Well I'm not a second Walt Disney by any means—it's just a bad comparison. I could never do the things that Walt Disney did, and I doubt seriously that Walt Disney could have drawn the comic strip that I am drawing. So it's a foolish comparison, but nevertheless the comparisons are made by well-meaning people, because I suppose we do overlap in some ways, both having covered so many different mediums. But my main objec-tive has always been to try to draw a good comic strip every day, and this is the foundation of everything that we do. When I say "we," I mean the syndicate, myself and our licensees. I regard the comic strip as the center of the wheel, and all the spokes that go out are the various projects that take place. Connie Boucher, of Determined Productions, has undoubtedly been our No. 1 licensee, and she set the standard for licensees by the quality of the work that she did back in the early days, when she got the idea for producing the Peanuts Date Books. And then it was her idea to publish *Happiness Is a Warm Puppy*. I never thought I'd be able to think of the ideas for that, but I did very easily, and that was the No. 1 selling book in 1963, so that set Connie Boucher going. Since then, of course, we've accumulated such licensees as The Ford Motor Company and Hallmark Cards, and of course Lee Mendelson Productions, with Bill Melendez the animator, have been doing all of our television shows, and this has been a wonderful association. But all of these things grow out of the comic strip, and I think what makes our licensing different from many others is the fact that our program is built upon characters who are figuratively alive—they are continually growing and doing new things—we're not simply stamping these characters on the sides of products just to sell the products. Every new thing that Snoopy does, or Charlie Brown does, becomes somehow an idea for a licensed product and it just seems to work. Snoopy is so versatile he just seems to be able to fit into any role and it just works. It's not that we're out to clutter the market with products. In fact anyone that says we're overdoing it is way off base because actually we are *underdoing* it. We could be turning out much more material than we do and there's no comparison between the amount of products that, say, Walt Disney Productions turns out, and what we do.

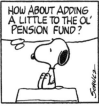

I think our license program is watched more carefully than any other license program, if for no other reason than the fact that I see every product that is done. The foundation is still the strip—I still think of every idea and I still draw every comic strip. I think it would be a big mistake if I would become overly involved in these other things and turn the strip over to other people. This does not mean—and I want to stress this too—that I have any criticism of those who employ assistants or gag writers. It's just that I, at the present time, have no need for this. I wouldn't know what to have an assistant do, although it would be kind of fun, kind of a relief maybe, to have somebody do the lettering, but I'm never quite sure what the character is going to say, sometimes, until the very last minute, while I'm actually in the process of doing the lettering. So I think I'd be a little bit nervous having somebody else around in the studio.

Hurd: Do you get the same fun drawing the strip as you did years ago?
Schulz: Yes—it depends on the idea. If it is what I think is a good idea, I enjoy drawing it as much as I ever did. I have a slight difficulty these days—my hand is not as steady as it was at one time. I used to pride myself upon being able to whip out a perfect pen line, and I still can on my better days. This makes the drawing a little more of a chore than it used to be, and it is a handicap having to draw to the confining sizes that we have to work in these days. But I have no sympathy for most of the other people who complain about this because, if others will recall, when *Peanuts* first started in 1950, it was the smallest comic that had ever been in existence. It was sold as a space-saving strip and it had 4 panels which were not much larger than 4 airmail stamps. Yet, in spite of this, with what I regard as being sheer quality, I have been able to move on, day by day, week by week, year after year, and have passed up all these men that had, in many cases, three times the size that I had to work with. So that I now have more newspapers than any other comic strip in the history of the business.

Hurd: I know that Jim Freeman, the longtime Managing Editor of the United Feature Syndicate, was the man who bought *Peanuts.* Would you say a word about that?
Schulz: Everything in life seems to hinge upon certain bits of good for-tune—odd coincidences and things like that—although I suppose quality eventually rises to the surface in sports, in entertainment, in writing, and in everything else, but I'm sure that the fact that Jim Freeman was the gentle man that he is had a lot to do with it, as did his love for children. Also Jim Freeman had a daughter whose name was Patty, and in my original submissions one of the girl's name was Patty. He liked kids, he noticed the little girl character and I think he just liked the gentle humor

that was there. Jim and I always got along very well as I did with all of the people at United Features. There was an attempt to make a few changes when we were first starting. My original submission was a panel feature and somebody had the idea of having little kids in the top panel and then having teenagers in the lower panel. But this was abandoned almost immediately as an idea that wasn't practical, and then they discovered that I would rather draw a strip than a panel.

Hurd: Would you say something about the hour television special called *Happy Birthday, Charlie Brown* which our readers will have seen by the time they read this conversation.

Schulz: Several years ago we had an hour special celebrating my 25th anniversary, and the January 1979 special is really in anticipation of Charlie Brown's 30th anniversary but it is also celebrating his 15th year on television. I think we are right behind Bob Hope now in having had the longest run of specials on television—especially in prime time. Lee Mendelson once again is the producer and Bill Melendez has always done my animation. Bill and I have now been associated for about 17 or 18 years, and we became acquainted back when we were doing Ford commercials. We did Falcon commercials and openings for The Tennessee Ernie Ford TV shows and we got along so well I always said that if we ever did any other television work, I would never do it with anyone other than Bill Melendez. So our association has been long and good. This show will be a combination of things that have happened during the past 5 years, some new animation, some scenes from the next movie that we are working on which will be called *Bon Voyage Charlie Brown, and Don't Come Back.* In this movie the kids go overseas to England and France as exchange students and Charlie Brown ends up in "The Chateau of the Bad Neighbor," which is the same chateau that I was stationed in for 6 weeks during World War II. Last year Bill Melendez and our wives and I visited that chateau, and I have tried to put down on film some of my feelings about visiting a place that I had not seen for 32 years. We may get something out of this, so we went over again this past August and took along a cameraman and his wife to film my feelings as we walked around this chateau and up a nearby road to a cafe we used to visit. As I said, we hope to get something out of that in the way of a documentary on what it is like to revisit old places.

Hurd: What happens when the time comes for you to do a new television show?

Schulz: The first thing that happens is that Lee Mendelson calls me up and says that we have a time period now in a certain portion of the year to do a new half-hour show. So the first thing that governs our thinking is when the show will appear—whether it is to be summer, winter or something like that. A lot of this is governed by shows that we already have—we've covered practically every season and holiday so we actually got down to something like "Arbor Day" for one of our shows and it won the National Arbor Day Award. Next, Bill and Lee and I meet here in my studio and we just start talking about what might be a good basic theme for the show. Now there are unique exceptions to this, such as the time a couple of years ago when I was reading a *Sports Illustrated* article about Alaskan sled dogs. Immediately it hit me—wouldn't it be funny if Snoopy were hijacked and forced to become part of an Alaskan sled dog team. His being overly civilized would cause him terrible problems, so I called up both Lee and Bill immediately and said, "I've got a great idea for a new show!" This was just a different way of doing it but most of the shows depend upon the holiday season at the time we're talking about. So we start talking about a show. I never do any actual writing at a typewriter and I do not do the storyboards. I just sit here in the room with Bill Melendez, we talk out the stories and we make suggestions back and forth. Then he goes back to Hollywood and he will make his preliminary story-boards. After that he will return here, we'll go over them, sometimes making drastic changes, always polishing the dialogue, and trying to think of new "funny business." When he's back in Hollywood, some-times I will think of something and just call him on the phone and he'll say, "Yeah, that's good, we'll add that" and he makes a note of it. So, after several trips back and forth, we finally get the whole storyboard down exactly where we want it. I go over the dialogue one last time, making sure that it all is authentic *Peanuts* dialogue. Lately, in the last few shows, I've gone down to a little studio just south of San Francisco with Lee, and have worked with the recording of the voices because it is very important that these kids read the lies the way I have written them. It's a tedious job, and at times an exasperating one, but it seems to produce necessary results. This job was expanded in our *Bon Voyage* movie because we're using a couple of French children. Naturally, when Charlie Brown goes to France, he attends school and he stays at the home of a little French girl, while Peppermint Patty and Marcie stay at the home of a French boy. It was fun doing that because we had some

French dialogue and then we also had a lot of English dialogue which needed a broad French accent, so we hired several students from a local French-English school in San Francisco. It was really neat getting these cute voices, because there's nothing more fascinating and beautiful to our ear than to hear someone speak English with a French accent. It just gives it a charm which is unparalleled. And for the first time we're using adult voices in the movie—adults do not appear however. Adult voices will be heard as the kids arrive in England, go

through customs, and then ride with the cab driver. Snoopy plays tennis at Wimbledon. They rent a car at Calais, of course they have a terrible time renting the car from this Frenchman, Snoopy drives through French traffic and gets into arguments with French drivers. So the potential there of some delightful scenes is really good.

Hurd: This will be a full-length movie for theaters, won't it?
Schulz: Yes—we've made three of them so far and they are all eventually sold to television so it will go on TV later.

Hurd: When will this be completed?
Schulz: It will take Bill at least a year to draw this movie. Bill hires the people he needs to complete one—I don't know what the staff would be, but Bill is normally satisfied if he can have 6 months from beginning to end. The very first and most successful show we ever did was

A Charlie Brown Christmas which was done in 4 months but that is *not* enough time. Budgeting is always a problem—we always wish we had more money to do our shows with.

Hurd: Your studio is really impressive—I'd like to include a photo of it with this conversation.

Schulz: We could have built a much more fancy place than we did, and it would have been fun to build a studio which was really unique, not only on the outside but on the inside. But, for one thing, I didn't want to attract a lot of attention. As it is, we have become too much of a tourist attraction here and have problems with busloads of tourists pulling up in front of the studio, all wanting to come in and get drawings and autographs and things like that. I think the building really resembles a dentist's office, or a realtor's office, and if someday I quit, I can just sell the whole place to some brand new dentist or an opthalmologist. I have two very nice, large rooms to work in, but I don't think this is important. In fact I think a cartoonist should work in a small, bare room where he'd probably do better work. I can close the door, this is a very quiet neighborhood, and the phones are fixed so that I do not hear them ring and I'm buzzed by my secretary only when I need to answer a call. I'm amazed at the amount of things that you have to accumulate that I never had when I first started. Right after Joyce and I got married, we lived for two weeks with my father and stepmother, and I drew the *Peanuts* comic strip down in the basement of my stepmother's house, on a card table. And when I sent the drawings in, I would get cardboard boxes, cut off the ends, get some old butcher paper, wrap the strips up, and mail them in. Now I have a 7-room studio here, we have a Xerox machine, a postage meter, a huge safe for storing drawings overnight, we photograph everything that is sent out, we have negatives on file of every drawing that is made, I have my own accountant who handles all of my financial affairs for me and for the arena, we have a storage room where we keep all of the licensed products, we have a conference room with a beautiful table that seats 8 people, we have a movie screen with a 16mm projector, we have a television set on which we can play our shows, with tape if need be, so I've simply graduated from a card table to a very comfortable place to be. But, as I say, I think it could be much more fancy and ostentatious, but I don't want to attract attention. I've always had the fear of being ostentatious—of people thinking that these things have gone to my head. A lot of things have been written about me which are not true. I'm still intrigued by the business of cartooning, I still like drawing comic strips, I still like reading them, although I don't search them out like I did 30 years ago, and I'm not anxious to meet every cartoonist in the business like I was the first year I attended the National Cartoonists Society Award Dinner. I remember that night—I went around and was anxious to meet Harold Foster, Roy Crane, Al Capp and Hank Ketcham, and everybody else. I still enjoy seeing whomever happens to pass by in the business and I'm always willing to welcome anybody who comes by to talk about cartooning. I have become also slightly bitter about the business—I'm not quite sure that I approve the way syndicates handle cartoonists. I think they take advantage of young cartoonists by forcing them to sign contracts which should never be signed. In fact I'm very much against this and I don't know what can be done about it but I think something should be done. But I suppose this is the same thing that happens to young actors and young athletes. There's always the conflict between the team owner and the guy who plays second base—the conflict between the man who produces the play and the actor who acts in it—and there's always the conflict between the syndicate and the cartoonist—between the business man and the artist. They never do understand each other and I doubt if this can every really be solved.

Hurd: I think you've mentioned that there's a lot of imitation in the comics field these days.

Schulz: I think there's a terrible trend these days in strips being so much alike. I think the worst trend is this business of setting strips in various historical backgrounds but having the humor then all relate to modern day dialogue, which can be funny, but why should they all be alike? This is wrong. I think there's a great need for comic strips about real people done in cartoon style but with real problems. We've really drifted away from that—I think there's a need for it—and I don't think space limitations would prohibit something like this.

I still try to cooperate with the National Cartoonists Society and the Newspaper Comics Council in whatever projects they have, although my views on the way the Reuben and the other awards are given out are pretty radical. I've won my share and I don't want to sound like a poor loser—that has nothing to do with it—but I just think so many good men are being deprived of our greatest awards, and some that *are* made shameful.

I didn't cooperate with that recent project in which various cartoon-ists did original collector's-item-type lithographs for sale, for the simple reason that if someone wants something of mine to hang on their wall, I don't want it to be something which is aside from what I regularly do. I do not like drawing group pictures of my characters. For one thing, their heads are so big I can't group them all together and I'm no good at it. The second reason I didn't participate is that the comic strip I draw is what I do best, and if somebody wants something of mine to hang on their wall, I want it to be one of my comic strips and not something else which I think is a contrived bit of art work. So I just want it known that this is the *only* reason why I backed away from that lithograph project.

© by United Feature Syndicate, Inc.

Atlanta Weekly Interview: Charles Schulz

EUGENE GRIESSMAN / 1981

From *Atlanta Weekly,*
November 15, 1981.

Charles M. Schulz, despite the fact he dislikes the name *Peanuts,* is the creator of the most successful cartoon strip of all time. Although he is the most publicized and honored cartoonist in history, no less than legendary in his profession, he considers himself more of a thoughtful craftsman than a pure artist, one who looks upon cartooning as a job to be done between 10:00 and 5:00 on weekdays.

Schulz's characters, Charlie Brown, Lucy, Linus, Snoopy, Woodstock, Schroeder, Peppermint Patty, Frieda, have come to symbolize the largely unfulfilled hopes and dreams of America's Inferiority Majority. What he draws and the stories he tells are, more often than not, autobiographical. The characters, including the perfectly crafted Snoopy, are based on animals and plain folks he met while growing up.

A kindergarten teacher once prophesied, "Someday, Charles, you're going to be an artist." His grades in high school indicate that such a career may have been made possible by the process of elimination, for by his own admission, he was an awful student. When he was in high school, his mother showed him an ad from the Art Instruction Schools. His parents paid for the course—170 middle-of-the-Depression dollars. Although the school was located in the Minneapolis-St. Paul area where he grew up, young Schulz mailed in his lessons because he was too embarrassed to show them personally. He still maintains that he can't really draw, although he would probably be very unhappy if someone else said the same thing.

The studio of America's most famous cartoonist is located at One Snoopy Place in Santa Rosa, California. The area where Schulz draws is more like an elevated den than an airy loft. A visitor is astounded by the lack of clutter and the absence of nameless assistants slaving away at rows of desks. Schulz's work for the week, five panels of half-finished cartoons, rests on the left side of an elegantly simple desk.

"I like things neat," he responds to my surprised look.

Unlike many other cartoonists, Schulz insists on doing all the work on the strip himself.

"When I sit behind the drawing board," he says, "I feel I am in command. It's one of the few situations in my life where I feel totally secure."

Wanting to be in command is perhaps what one should expect from the creator of Charlie Brown, the quintessential loser. Dignity may be what the world of Schulz is all about. Dignity lost—his characters constantly do stupid things and abuse one another. Dignity sought—they do anything to look important and get respect. Dignity found—rarely and briefly. One gets the impression that Schulz himself tries to balance two wishes: to be dignified, on the one hand, and to give free rein to ideas that might seem outrageous to the people who are his constituency.

Who needs a security blanket in such a world? Everyman.

Q: Has humor changed, insofar as you are aware of it, during the past few years?

Schulz: I don't know about humor as a whole. I think that's too difficult to answer. Comic strips have changed.

Q: Let's talk about comic strips. Have you had to change your approach noticeably or consciously?

Schulz: I've changed it considerably since I first began. I think the humor that I introduced to the strip back in 1950 was a very concise sort of humor. It grew out of magazine cartooning where the humor was simply one panel. I drew very brief incidents in the very first *Peanuts* strip. Then as the strip began to grow and the characters developed, more conversation entered into it, and the characters themselves developed more intricate personalities, and the humor began to flow from those personalities. Then I began to develop a sort of humor where the same thing was happening day after day. It all started, I think, with Charlie Brown standing under a tree, and he stood there for five days as people—the other characters—came by and said different things to him, and he reacted to it. And that was a new sort of humor that I developed. As the years went on, as Snoopy became more human, the strip became more abstract and became more of a fantasy. I grew away from drawing upon the actions of real little kids playing in sandboxes and riding tricycles. I just don't draw those anymore. So now the strip has become much more of a fantasy. They say that my strip is always being described as being about children who talk like adults, but I don't think it's necessarily true. I think that children do talk the very way these kids talk. I don't think the exaggeration is that great. But then as the strip went on, I began to do little stories, and I enjoyed drawing those very much, because I think a strip should have a change of pace. I think a three-, four-, or five-week story is good to have every now and then, and when that is through, then you just have a lot of brief, daily gags that stand on their own for a while until you can come up with another kind of story.

Q: But you do try to make every day's episode funny, don't you?

Schulz: I think the most important part is that each episode stands more or less by itself. I don't think, however, that it's necessary for every reader to understand every strip that you draw. I think that you can demand attention from your readers that follow the strip every day. I think an editor who worries that someone who comes in the middle of a story won't know what's going on, is worried about the wrong thing. I think that it's not unreasonable to demand loyalty from your readers; but then I think that you should reward your loyal readers with the sort of humor that they can appreciate for having been loyal. There should be little "in" jokes and remarks in the strip that will reward the reader for his or her loyalty.

Q: You say that humor is very important. Insofar as you view cartooning, is that the most important thing for you, or are you trying to say something more important?

Schulz: The only important thing is that you be funny each day, because your client is the newspaper editor, and he's paying out good money in his comics' budget to buy a strip that will help sell his newspaper. And I don't think you have any business promoting your own personal views at the expense of the humor in your strip. So the main thing is to give the editor what he has purchased. If out of your ability to create something funny, you are also able to say something meaningful that is not offensive or is not a personal vendetta of some kind, that's fine. If you can say something that will speak to people who are lonely or frustrated or fearful of something, that's fine. But the main thing, of course, is to be entertaining each day so that you can help the editor sell the newspaper.

Q: You're an entertainer then?

Schulz: Yeah. Surely. The same way as an author's an entertainer—someone who writes mystery stories or things of that kind.

Q: You are not then primarily a commentator on the social scene?

Schulz: No. I would never think of myself as being that. I don't mind being described that way by someone else, but I would never be presumptuous enough to describe myself in that manner. I don't mind just being a comic strip artist.

Q: Can you think of a time when you have been, on the one hand, entertaining, and on the other, really tried to say something important.

Schulz: Last summer I did a series where the kids went to summer camp, and they didn't know what kind of a camp they had gone to. They discovered, unknowingly, that they were in what apparently was some kind of a religious camp, because when they were asked to go to the meetings in the evening, they heard somebody who was preaching to them that the world was coming to an end—that we were in the last days. I think this is irresponsible preaching and very dangerous, and especially when it is slanted toward children, I think it's totally irresponsible, because I see nothing biblical that points up to our being in the last days, and I just think it's an outrageous thing to do, and a lot of people are making a living—they've been making a living for 2,000 years—preaching that we're in the last days. And so that's why I did that series. But it was kind of funny and I enjoyed doing it.

Q: Are you religious?
Schulz: I don't know. I . . . that's not for me to decide.

Q: You've been called religious.
Schulz: I know, yeah, but I don't know what that means. I don't know what religious means.

Q: You taught a Sunday school class for a while.
Schulz: Uh huh.

Q: And you no longer do?
Schulz: No. I ran out of things to say. And I think when you run out of things to say, it's time to close the book and let somebody else take over the class. We went through the Old and New Testa-

© by United Feature Syndicate, Inc.

ments word for word twice in a class that I was conducting. And the situation just got to a point where I no longer felt that I had anything new to contribute. [I felt] perhaps it would be better if somebody else took over the class who could give it a fresh approach. I enjoyed it very much.

Q: Do you still attend church?
Schulz: No. No.

Q: Why did you stop attending?
Schulz: I don't know where to go. Besides I don't think God wants to be worshiped. I think the only pure worship of God is by loving one another, and I think all other forms of worship become a substitute for the love that we should show one another.

Q: Did you arrive at this conclusion gradually?

Schulz: It took me a long time to figure that out. But I was always bothered by the inconsistency in church worship and a lot of the Scriptures, which I've studied very carefully, and the words of the Old Testament prophets, and Jesus himself. And these are the conclusions that I've reached. It's always dangerous to talk about these things, because then the letters come criticizing me . . . as they did once. In an interview I said that I no longer taught Sunday school. Well, I immediately got critical letters from people saying that I was setting a bad example by doing that. That I should go back in order to set a good example. But I think we place the wrong emphasis upon examples, that we're treading on very weak ground when we set ourselves up as examples for others to become religious. If people are going to look to me for religious guidance, then I think they're looking in the wrong place. But I love talking about the Scriptures and I love discussing religious things because I *think* that I'm completely open for whatever truth there is that exists. I have no ax to grind. But I defy anybody to prove to me that their denomination has all the truth. I don't pretend to be able to discuss profound theological problems, but I do think that the only true theology is no theology at all. I think the only theology that exists is that God exists as a spirit, and that we live in His world, and the minute we begin to form some sort of theology, we begin to drift away from the truth. I don't know the meaning of life. I don't know why we are here. I think life is full of anxieties and fears and tears. It has a lot of grief in it, and it can be very grim. And I do not want to be the one who tries to tell somebody else what life is all about. To me it's a complete mystery. But this doesn't mean that I don't enjoy studying biblical things.

Q: Your life has been—from your report and from others—a good life. Has it had its share of tears and grimness?

Schulz: Oh, I guess it's all relative, so I find it difficult to talk about that. No matter what you say, there's somebody else who's had it harder. There's always somebody else who had it better, too.

Q: You say you are not very sophisticated at all. Why do you say that? Is it because you're modest or because it's true?

Schulz: I really think it's true. In the first place, I don't really think I'm especially smart. I'm lacking in formal education which I now wish I could make up for. Not that it's necessary in drawing a comic strip, but I think I could do even a little bit better. I think formal education goes together with sophistication. I don't regret not being highly sophisticated, but who even knows what it is. I don't even think about it.

Q: Do you feel a little inferior in some areas?
Schulz: Oh, I feel inferior in a lot of areas. I feel inferior that I can't draw better than I can, that I don't have a wider, broader knowledge, which I would love to have. I feel I don't have the extensive vocabulary I think it would be nice to have. I suppose this is why I'm able to function so well with Charlie Brown, because I know what it's like to be inferior, and with Charlie Brown I can caricature all of these faults, realizing as I've grown older that these are common feelings and you'll meet almost no one who deep down really does not have feelings of inferiority. That is why, I guess, the readers can identify so completely with Charlie Brown.

Q: But you also know that you are good at some things, don't you?
Schulz: I don't know how *good* I am at drawing a comic strip, but I think I know as much about drawing comic strips, if not more, than anybody there is. I think I'm really an expert on the comic strip as a medium. This does not mean that I think I'm the best that there is, but I do think that I've contributed a lot to the profession. I think I've contributed a lot to the art of the comic strip, and I'm very proud of what I've done, and I think I've created some of the best comic-strip characters that have every existed. But this does not mean that I'm the best. Nobody is best at anything. That's a foolish, modern thought that there has to be a number one in everything. Art—if you can call a comic strip art—shouldn't have to be that competitive. But I think I really understand the comic-strip medium. I seriously doubt that cartooning is a pure form of art for many reasons. For one reason, you have to please an editor, and no art form can exist when it has to please an immediate audience. Also the true test of art—my own definition, right or wrong—is how well it speaks to other, future generations. If a cartoon lasts generation after generation, is reprinted over and over, and speaks just as well to the fifth generation as to the generation when it was drawn, I suppose it could be labeled as art just as much as a painting could. If it gives joy 100 years from now, then it's just as much a work of art as a painting. But in the long run, again, what does it matter what we call it. Is it serving it's purpose for the person who's doing it? Is the person who's reading it getting something out of it? What somebody else labels it . . . what the critics call it usually doesn't mean much anyway.

Q: I have the impression that you feel that cartooning is not taken as seriously as it ought to be taken.

Schulz: Well, this is a continual argument. I suppose some cartoonists complain about this, but it's just a product of what we are, and I think a lot of us are taken seriously and receive all the attention that we deserve.

Q: Do you think you have?

Schulz: Oh, I've probably received more attention than any other cartoonist that's ever been around. I've been on more magazine covers, and been interviewed more, been on more TV programs than any other cartoonist.

Q: And your characters have been on the moon.

Schulz: Right. Snoopy's the only one who actually went to the moon. The others have always *thought* they went to the moon, but Snoopy's the only one that did go there.

Q: Inferiority is just one of the themes that your characters have explored rather fully. What are some other themes?

Schulz: One of the very first themes that I tackled in the strip was this struggle that takes place out on the front sidewalk or on the playground or in the schoolroom among children. It's not an easy life to be a child, especially when you're out there on your own, unprotected by supervising adults. Adults forget this, and adults forget the problems of being a child, because as they get older they learn to protect themselves, and they learn to avoid uncomfortable situations, and they learn not to go places where they either might be in danger or might be uncomfortable. And they have a tendency to forget that they leave their children in these situations, and I suppose this is all part of growing up. The embarrassment of standing at the blackboard, not having the slightest idea what you're supposed to be doing or how to solve the problem with everybody kind of looking at you and giggling and the teacher being mad because you haven't been able to learn what you're supposed to have learned. And the hassle of having to write continual reports about books that you don't understand.

Q: Were you ever the object of ridicule when you were a kid or later on where people actually laughed at you?

Schulz: Oh yeah, yeah. I don't think I was ever regarded as being a very strong kid. I don't know if I was ever regarded as being a sissy, because I don't think I was that; but I was certainly not a tough little kid, and that always bothered me. But I felt . . . is the term *exonerated?* by World War II by becoming the squad leader of a light machine-gun squad. And I felt that was as tough a job as anybody can have— although I didn't see a lot of combat—but at least I was a squad leader of a light machine-gun squad, and you couldn't be a sissy and be that.

And I was always a good athlete. I was always a good baseball player and an excellent golfer and all of that. So I think it was an unfair criticism. Also, I was never very smart in high school. I was made fun of for one brief period of time in school, when I failed everything. Those are kind of sad days. I failed everything there was to fail one year in high school.

Q: You really failed?
Schulz: Oh, everything.

Q: Why?
Schulz: I just didn't know what was going on. It sneaked up on me along about the seventh grade. I got my first E, which was the lowest thing you could get, in arithmetic.

Q: Earlier we were talking about the fact that *Peanuts* is you. You said to me earlier, it would be fatal if you had someone to do the lettering or to suggest the ideas. Why?
Schulz: I just have a feeling that the quality of the strip would probably suffer. This doesn't mean that I can't find somebody who can draw even better than I can. Maybe somebody else could think of better ideas, but if he could, then he really should be drawing his own strip and not working for me. So I think this strip should live or die on what I do to it. Plus the fact of whether I want somebody else drawing it. This is my life. This is what I do, and why should I hire somebody else to help me do it when I can do it all by myself?

An Interview with Charles M. Schulz

LEONARD MALTIN / 1984

From *Charlie Brown: A Boy for All Seasons*
(New York: Museum of Broadcasting,
1984), pp. 19–23. Reprinted by permission
of Leonard Maltin.

Maltin: Let's talk about animation. It's rare that a comic strip has translated so effectively and so durably to another medium. And I don't think there has ever been an example where the creator has been so intensely involved. How did you get started in animation?

Schulz: We were approached by several different people but it started with doing the Ford commercials. I was introduced by the people at J. Walter Thompson to Bill Melendez, which was a very fortunate thing because Bill and I became very close friends.

Bill has so many great qualities. What helps us work together is that we each appreciate what the other does. I've heard Bill say many times, "I could never draw a comic strip," and I like to have somebody admit that he could not draw a comic strip because a lot of animators probably think they could—there's nothing to it.

121

I'm not sure I could be an animator, but I'm not quite as humble as Bill and I won't say that I don't think I could be an animator. I think I could be an animator but I wouldn't want to be. I like to create part of it. I like to be able to think of the funny things, and then I know I don't have to draw it! Some poor animator is going to have to sit down with the terrible task of transferring some monstrous idea that I've had into little tiny bits of action. I think I have been able to make the transition from comic strips to animation because working with Bill I can see things in my mind and see how they're going to work on the screen. I don't think all comic strip artists have been able to do that. It was fortunate that Bill and I got together. We appreciate what each other does.

© by United Feature Syndicate, Inc.

What has made our animation efforts different from the others is the fact that our characters really talk to each other. Our characters do not feed each other gag lines and they do not speak in tiny flashy expressions—they actually converse. Off hand, I can't think of any other animated series where the characters converse in a natural way using real, live sentences. It makes the characters become very real. Of course, they're still cartoon characters. They're still drawn in the same style as in the comic strips with a little expansion which is nice, because this is a different medium. With animation, they're able to do some things with backgrounds and other things I can't do in the strip and there are also sound effects and all of that. But it is still basically the same group of *Peanuts* characters made almost real—because they talk to each other.

Maltin: What is the biggest hurdle in taking a two-dimensional comic strip and turning it into an animated, color television special?

Schulz: One thing was learning how to write an episode, which is very important. Each separate episode must contribute to the story as a whole. If you think of a story first, you're likely to end up with weak episodes. So, I try to think of episodes first and then put them all together and fashion a story out of them.

From the drawing point of view, the most difficult part was the fact that these are comic strip characters and they were not designed for animation which means that they don't have the rubber-like quality that animated characters need. On the other hand, I can't really think of a good animated character that also has become a good comic strip character because the rubber quality that goes into animation does not transfer into comic strips very well.

For example, Bill Melendez has had a terrible time drawing Charlie Brown's head and making it revolve because I only draw it from the sideview and from two three-quarter views the same way Popeye used to be drawn. Popeye is always drawn from the three-quarters view. Suddenly Charlie Brown had to revolve, so things had to change and this has been difficult. Fortunately, we are now working with limited animation, and I've told Bill that our characters don't have to show the perfection of the old Walt Disney animations.

We're not working with human characters. If they were we wouldn't need cartoons. We could use live actors and they could do it better. Also, we must remember that they have to remain cartoon characters, so there's nothing wrong with a character turning from one position to another. You don't have to have it flow that smoothly. It's a cartoon and it looks fine.

Maltin: After successfully doing half-hour television specials, was it an even bigger hurdle to tackle a feature length film?

Schulz: Yes. The biggest hurdle, of course, is that you have to please so many different people. You not only have to please the people with the networks but also those who are going to distribute the film. They also give you a time limit saying this film must run 75 minutes. Well, that's absurd to set a time limit on something. You either have to stretch it out to make the 75 minutes or you have to reduce it to some time limit and that's always bad.

We've learned how to handle it but we suffered because of it and I think our films have been better when we've gone back and trimmed them for running on television.

Maltin: When the first Peanuts special came along I remember one of the things that was most exciting and most curious to me was listening to the voices. I'd been reading *Peanuts* for so many years and like every other reader I had been speaking the lines silently to myself without ever having a clear picture of what those voices would sound like. What was it like when you had to face the actual problem of casting voices for those characters?

Schulz: One of the qualities that makes comic strips good is that each reader hears a different voice and that's all right. When we started doing the Ford commercials, the biggest problem was what we were going to do with Snoopy. Snoopy couldn't think out loud any more, and some of the advertising people wanted to give Snoopy a voice which would have been a terrible mistake. They actually brought in some Hollywood character actors who tried to use funny voices for Snoopy's thinking but I just didn't like that and said, "Well, we'll lose a little something but in animation and action we're doing something else".

The animators can do something with Snoopy with their drawing that I can't do in the strip. Since that beginning, we've learned how to handle that but we also tried adult voices with the kids and discovered that really didn't work either. So we began using little kids' voices and we happened to get some real gems. I think in *A Charlie Brown Christmas* the Linus voice was a marvel.

As the years have gone by, we've learned that we have to keep down the Lucy voice, otherwise she shrieks too much. We have trouble now and then with the very young characters like Sally because the children get so young that they can't pronounce the words. Frequently, Bill Melendez has to take a long word and chop it up on tape and paste if back together to make it work.

Some of the little kids can't read so they have to take their cues from someone reading their lines to them. All sorts of problems come up. Sometimes they can't emote as well as we would like. When we did *The Big Stuffed Dog* it was a pleasure working with adult professional actors who took some of the lines I had written and really brought them to life. I'm afraid that many of the child actors don't bring the lines up to the level you would really like.

Maltin: Was it tough for you the first time you heard children's voices doing the voices you had heard in your head all the time?

Schulz: Oh yes, but I was also pleased that some of the voices were really good. For instance, we discovered that there were a lot of Linus's voices around. Charlie Brown is the hardest voice to get. We want a voice that is bland and dull and without character and we've always had the most trouble finding voices for him.

I wasn't there for the initial recording sessions. I don't think I attended a recording session until we had done several shows and then I discovered how difficult they are. It's just a lot of plain hard work.

Maltin: Was the Tennessee Ernie Ford show the first Peanuts animation?

Schulz: That's right. And we kept on getting better and better. By the time the show was finished, we really knew what we were doing in animation. The drawing was improving and we did some funny things that served as a wonderful background for our eventual stepping up to do *A Charlie Brown Christmas*. Bill Melendez was ready when he had the opportunity to do the first special.

Maltin: The first television special had one of the great credits in animation history. It was called "graphic blandishment." I had never seen a credit like that . . .

Schulz: That was a Bill Melendez bit.

Maltin: Would you describe how your collaboration with Bill Melendez works?

Schulz: One of the first things that happens is that our producer, Lee Mendelson, has to find out when the network is ready to accept another show. For instance, we'll take the fall. We'll go back to Halloween and Lee Mendelson will say that the network wants a Halloween show, and, okay, how do we write a Halloween show.

Bill Melendez comes up here to my studio, and we sit down and start talking about different things and out of the first conversation comes a rough story. Bill goes back down to Hollywood and roughs out a storyboard and then brings it back up here again, and I go through it and we try to think of some more funny things. After about the third session we're ready to polish the dialogue and get it just the way we want it. Now that's one way of doing it.

Another way is that suddenly I'm reading a magazine, or I'm lying in my hospital bed three years ago, and I get an idea and call up Bill

Melendez and say, "Bill, I've got a great idea. I'm going to make you rich and famous." And out of this one little idea a whole show came about.

I'm thinking of two shows—the one where Snoopy was hijacked onto a dog sled team—I got that idea from reading a *Sports Illustrated* magazine article about Alaskan sled-dog teams, and it occurred to me that Snoopy would have a terrible time if somehow he was forced to become a sled dog. He runs on his hind feet and he's just not in shape for that sort of thing. Bill has always said that it became his favorite show because it had a little lesson in it, too.

And then the other one I'm thinking about is *What Have We Learned, Charlie Brown?*, the one where the kids visit Normandy. I wrote that in my head lying in bed in the hospital at 3:00 a.m. in the morning. I was searching for a certain key phrase and when that came to me, the whole sequence of *What Have We Learned, Charlie Brown?* fell into place. Three or four days later when I got home, I called up Bill and he, in his usual enthusiastic manner said, that's a great idea, and we did it and won a Peabody Award for it a few months ago.

So those are the different ways of doing it. There's no one way. I think the spontaneous way is the best. I think being told you must have a show done six months from now for a certain date—and because it's a certain time of year and it should be about this or that—that's the worst way to do it. It's too mechanical and it will usually show up as being on the forced side.

Maltin: What about some of the nuts and bolts of your collaboration? How involved were you, and are you, in the actual process of turning script into film?

Schulz: When we first began I think I made a couple of rough drawings to show them the way I thought the characters should be drawn, but since then I just trust it to Bill Melendez. I really should go down to Hollywood more often to see what's going on, but drawing the daily comic strip is still the basis and foundation for the whole thing and I feel this studio is where I belong.

And, of all the things we do—books, licensed products, television, etc.—I think the most important thing is drawing a good comic strip for a newspaper editor every day. A newspaper editor is still our number one client and he's the person who got us where we are and he's the person that I think we have an obligation to please. So, if I have time to go to Hollywood during the animation work, that's fine. But drawing a comic strip every day is my first priority.

Maltin: How would you sum up what you do?
Schulz: When you're talking about people who make their living at this, I think you are simply discussing someone who just likes to draw funny pictures and that's what I like to do. I would be doing this even if I had to do something else to make a living. I just enjoy drawing funny pictures. That doesn't mean that I'm having the time of my life every day. Sometimes it's plain hard work.

I think cartooning has a certain quality and a certain charm unlike any other medium, whether it's somebody drawing for over 2,000 newspapers or if it's somebody drawing a little cartoon on the outside of an envelope in a letter to a friend. There's a communication there, a bringing of joy, a bringing of happiness without being too pompous about it. I simply like to draw something that is fun.

Good Grief! Charlie Brown Is 35

LEONARD MALTIN / 1985

From *International Herald Tribune*, October 2, 1985. Reprinted by permission of Leonard Maltin.

He doesn't look a day over 10, but Charlie Brown and the rest of the Peanuts gang are celebrating their 35th birthday today.

Peanuts, which sprang from the fertile mind of Charles M. Schulz when he was 27 years old, has generated 30 television specials, four movies, two Broadway plays and countless merchandise. The collected strips have sold more than 300 million copies in book form. In a recent interview with Leonard Maltin of *Entertainment Tonight*, Schulz, 62, reflected on the evolution and longevity of his *Peanuts* comic strip. Excerpts:

Maltin: Do you feel that your whole life has been pretty much tied to this medium?

Schulz: Yes, I sometimes say that I'm not sure that it was a very great ambition, but my dad and I enjoyed the funny papers. My mother used to say, "How could you sit there and laugh at something out loud? I don't understand that!"

Maltin: Did you ever have any wavering of thought about what you were going to do with your life?

Schulz: I had a few doubts that I wasn't able to do it. Right after high school I sent an application to Walt Disney and got turned down flatly, but that didn't discourage me. I used to see how good some of the cartoonists were and I used to sit at home in my bedroom and draw comic strip after comic strip.

But I think I've always been obsessed by the medium. It's a strange medium because it isn't given much glory in our society. It's still regarded one notch below burlesque, I'm afraid. And so, you have to be very careful to judge the compliments that you get when people say how good something is that you're doing.

Maltin: Are you the kind of person who believes that if you want to get a job done right, you've got to do it yourself?

Schulz: No, and I'm not sure that I'm the person that probably can even draw this strip the best. There are other people who can draw much better than I can but I think I have a certain feel for this. I think I may not be the best comic strip artist that has ever lived, but I bet I know more about drawing comic strips than anybody who has ever been in this business. I have a feel for this rather insignificant business.

Maltin: There was a time when everything was very detailed in a comic strip, particularly the serious ones, but even some of the funny ones. When you came along with *Peanuts,* you simplified all that.

Schulz: Well, for one thing I wanted to get the reader right down on the level of the characters. We never use camera angles so that we're looking down on the kids. There has to be a consistency here and I think there is a consistency in the style of the caricature all the way through. The ears are caricatured to the same extent that the nose and eyes and fingers and everything is. Now, I think warmth is very, very important. Cartoon characters should have warmth.

Maltin: What about the actual style or format? Has any of that changed over the years?

Schulz: It's difficult to tell until I look at some of the reprint books and then I see that, gee, I could have drawn that better. You don't notice it when you're drawing day after day after day. The characters do change. They get smaller, they get taller and they shrink, and then you find a reprint book coming out a year or two later and then you think, Charlie Brown is getting a little too tall, or Snoopy's stomach isn't quite drawn the way it should.

Now, what is interesting is that as you become better at something you no longer can draw it. I think of Snoopy lying on the doghouse and the way I did the drawing at that time. Now that I've learned how to draw it better I find it doesn't work anymore.

Maltin: What character has changed the most in your eye?

Schulz: Snoopy! Snoopy started off as simply a cute little dog, a cute little puppy and then he grew to a very grossly caricatured dog with a long neck and I can't believe I drew him that way in those days. If the syndicate had any sense, they would have called me up and said, "You're fired, we hate the way you're drawing." But I have to keep going back to warmth. There was harshness to some of the things that I was drawing at a certain time.

Maltin: How do you keep your enthusiasm working on a strip day to day?

Schulz: Yeah, sometimes it's not that fascinating. Some Sunday pages, when you think of the idea you know it's just going to be plain hard work. And others you can hardly wait to draw it because it's going to be so much fun—especially if there's a lot of action and a lot of wild expression and things like that. Then it's fun to do. But if it's going to be Schroeder playing the piano with Lucy leaning on if for 12 panels, that's just plain hard work.

Maltin: I know you get a ton of mail.

Schulz: I received a letter from a young girl last year who said she thought it was time for Lucy to stop pulling away the football from Charlie Brown and that it was kind of cruel. Now, she may be right. As the years go on, you look at things a little bit differently. I mellowed considerably, I'm not as sarcastic as I used to be and the characters in the strip aren't as sarcastic.

Maltin: Do you feel that you are consciously trying to do a moralistic comic strip?

Schulz: It is pretty decent humor. Everything that we have done has been pretty decent. Maybe it sounds prudish but I don't think there is anything wrong with being prudish and I don't see anything wrong with being nice.

Maltin: Have you ever caught yourself consciously changing something about the characters?
Schulz: I suppose the most conscious thing would be trying to tone Lucy down so she is not as mean as she might have been. I've eliminated characters because they just didn't work. I eliminated Frieda's cat because I discovered that I really didn't draw just a very good cat. Also, the introduction of certain characters spoil the other characters. I introduced another brother for Snoopy a couple of years ago simply because I thought the name Marbles was a great name for a dog who would be spotted, but I discovered having another dog in the strip took the uniqueness away from Snoopy. It destroyed the little relationship between him and the kids.

Maltin: In 35 years time have you ever thought about really shaking up some of the conventions that you yourself have developed? Have you

© by United Feature Syndicate, Inc.

ever thought about not having Charlie Brown be a loser at a certain point?

Schulz: That would be the worst mistake you could make. It would be like Li'l Abner getting married, which was the worst mistake Al Capp ever made. And once Charlie Brown begins to win, and you give into these little temptations, your whole structure will collapse.

Maltin: How would you sum up what you do?

Schulz: I think cartooning has a certain quality and a certain charm unlike any other medium, whether it is somebody drawing for 2,000 newspapers, or if it's somebody drawing a little cartoon on the outside of an envelope to a friend. There is a communication there. There is a bringing of joy, a bringing of happiness—without being too pompous—but it is worth something and people like to draw funny pictures. Even if you don't draw, it is still fun to do it and I guess that's why I do it. I like to draw something that is fun.

The
Peanuts Progenitor

CYNTHIA GORNEY / 1985

From *The Washington Post,*
October 2, 1985, pp. D1-D2.
© 1985, The Washington Post.
Reprinted by permission.

All he had ever wanted to do, from the first Minnesota Saturdays when he waited with his father for the earliest Sunday comics, was draw cartoons. He was quick. He was funny. Ideas leapt into his head and crowded up one behind another until he could scarcely sit still; when an art teacher suggested one day that the students try drawing anything they could think of in sets of three, he snatched a pencil and drew, as fast as he could: three sabers, three springs, three hockey sticks, three parachutes, three light bulbs, three smokestacks, three tombstones, three ink pots, three golf clubs, three ears, three fishhooks, three Wheaties boxes, three fountain pens, three megaphones, three bugles, three ghosts. The hand was sure, the drawings simple and precise, and as the other students were still gazing at their papers and wondering what to draw, he had filled two whole pages and was lettering triplets of a signature so practiced that even the name looked confident beyond his years: CHARLES SCHULZ. CHARLES SCHULZ. CHARLES SCHULZ.

"She held it up in front of the whole class, and said, 'Look at Charles—what an imagination he has,'" Schulz says. His voice is so gentle and almost uncertain that he might still be triumphantly recalling the day to his father over the evening dinner table: See, Pop, I *told* you I was good. When he was 18 he found a local cartooning class and champed for Tuesday nights, when he could bring in his pens and pencils, and sit in a studio with a real comic artist, and draw.

"The first night, he put up big drawings of different cartoon characters from the papers that we had to copy," Schulz says. "There was a Blondie, a Dagwood, different ones like that. And I was done *way* ahead of everybody else, you know, and I could draw them just as well as he could. Now, that made me feel good. Because I knew then that I really had something special."

Thirty-five years ago today, under the copyright name *Peanuts* and a signature that read simply *Schulz,* seven North American newspapers carried the first syndicated comic strip by Charles M. Schulz. In the strip two simply drawn children sit at the edge of a sidewalk, watching a third child trot toward them. "Well! Here comes ol' Charlie Brown!" says the sitting boy. "Good ol' Charlie Brown . . . Yes, sir! Good ol' Charlie Brown . . ." And then, scowling, as Charlie Brown disappears from sight: "How I hate him!"

It was an acerbic, almost nasty bit of work, and to this day Schulz cannot remember just why he wrote it that way. "I think there was more of that kind of bitterness and sarcasm in comic strips for a while there," he says. "Maybe it was a little harsh in those days. Of course, I was a lot younger, and as you get older, you learn not to be so sarcastic, and to temper yourself. But I would never have drawn that now. The odd thing was, that was the first strip that appeared, and a few days later, in the Minneapolis paper, there was a letter from a Lutheran minister, saying, 'Don't we have enough hatred on the front page without having it in the comic section?'"

Schulz smiles. "I thought, 'Here I am. I've worked for 27 years to finally sell a strip. And the very first one, I get a complaint on.'"

There is not a single cartoonist alive whose work has matched the extraordinary celebrity of the young and large-headed persons in Charles Schulz's *Peanuts.* He is read in Welsh, Arabic, Serbo-Croatian,

Malay, Basque, Chinese, Catalan, and the Alaskan language Tlingit. His cartoon books, many of which now bear titles like "Het Grote Snoopy Winterspelletjes-Boek" or "Du bist Sub, Charlie Braun!" have sold 300 million copies. Fierce philosophical debates erupted over the accurate Italian translation of "Good Grief!" ("Misericordia!" was the final compromise), and when *Peanuts* was translated into Latin last year as part of a language revival effort, the famous beagle made his appearance as Snoopius.

The five *Peanuts* television specials have earned Emmy Awards, Peabody Awards, and astonishing audience ratings. *You're a Good Man Charlie Brown*, the off-Broadway musical based on the strip, had grossed more than $6 million by 1969. When the 1970 feature film *A Boy Named Charlie Brown* premiered in New York, it opened to the largest advance sale of any picture Radio City Music Hall had ever booked. Oscar de la Renta and Willi Smith have designed evening wear for Snoopy. A minister had considerable success with lectures and books discussing his interpretation of the *Peanuts* theological references, and when the Oakland Museum organized a Charles Schulz retrospective this summer, the exhibit's glossy catalogue included lengthy essays analyzing *Peanuts'* humor, its role in American popular culture, and the philosophical messages implicit in Schroeder's piano and Linus's blanket.

"You could never grasp the power of his *póesie interrompue* by reading only one, two, or ten episodes," wrote the Italian novelist Umberto Eco in a catalogue essay that had originally appeared as the introduction to the first *Peanuts* volume in Italian. "You must thoroughly understand the characters and the situations, for the grace, tenderness, and laughter are born only from the infinitely shifting repetition of the patterns . . . the poetry of these children is born from the fact that we find in them all the problems, all the sufferings of the adults, who remain offstage. In this sense Schulz is a Herriman [George Herriman, creator of the surrealistic early 1900s comic strip *Krazy Kat*] already approaching the critical and social tendency of a Feiffer. These children affect us because in a certain sense they are monsters: they are the monstrous infantile reductions of all the neuroses of a modern citizen of the industrial civilization."

Charles Schulz, leaning back in the padded brown chair that angles between the desk and drafting table in his split-level studio, smiles broadly when this passage is read to him. Then he looks embarrassed.

Then he chuckles. "I think that's wonderful, that he should be able to say that," he says. "But it scares me, because I'm afraid somebody's going to say, 'That's all nonsense.' I think anybody who can write that well and thinks that much of my strip—that's really frightening."

Eco calls upon Freud in his essay, Schulz is advised, and Adler, and Beckett, and Thomas Mann and Rollo May. "Rollo May," Schulz murmurs, and then looks embarrassed again. "I don't pretend to know anything about those things. I'm not a psychology student. I'm not a philosopher. I really don't think I fit in anyplace. I've always felt like kind of an outsider, even though I have a lot of friends, and I think I have some good friends. I still feel like an outsider—that people would really rather be around somebody else—that I'm not that interesting."

Such a Charlie Brown sort of voice, which of course Schulz knows. He is a spare, sharp-nosed, gray-haired man, gentle and upright and exceedingly cordial, and he likes to tell stories of small, awful wounds suffered casually in the business of daily life: the girl he loved but never won, the leather school patrol belt he never got to wear, the day the St. Paul movie theater promised free Butterfingers to the first hundred matinee customers and Charles Schulz turned up one hundred and first. When he pulls his high school yearbook from a shelf, it is to tell the story of his overwhelming excitement the year a teacher asked him to draw cartoons as yearbook illustrations.

"And June 1940 came," Schulz says, slowly flipping the pages of the blue bound volume. "And I thumbed through it—and I thumbed through it—and no cartoon. For a year I wondered why."

He says he never found out. "Look at all the activities of some of the other kids," Schulz says mildly, running a finger down the annotated columns of high school head shots. Next to "Schulz," the page reads only, "Cehisean." The name of the yearbook. "For the drawings that didn't get printed," Schulz says.

He grins down at the pleasant-looking blond kid, the ears a little big but the smile nice and shy, gazing up from the yearbook page. "This is what I looked like," he says.

Handsome he is told, and he snorts. "No!" Schulz cries. "*Innocuous.*"

He was born in Minneapolis, grew up in St. Paul, went by the nickname Sparky, and spent one odd childhood year in the California desert town of Needles before his father gave up visions of the Western life and moved the family back to the apartment and barbershop in St. Paul. (Yes, that *is* why Snoopy's brother Spike lives in Needles; Spike, for that matter, was Schulz's first dog and once made a dubious appearance in *Ripley's Believe It or Not* as A HUNTING DOG THAT EATS PINS, TACKS, AND RAZOR BLADES.)

He cannot remember not wanting to draw, and always, it seems to him, the goal was cartoons. "I used to buy every comic strip that came out, literally, until I became overwhelmed by them," he says. *Famous Funnies* reprints cost a dime, and there were the fat Big Little Books, and the Sunday papers, which exhilarated him simply by rolling off the St. Paul presses with their colored comics fresh inside.

At school the teachers forced Sir Walter Scott on them, page after page of numbing description, but this was so different. "You hated the things you had to read, because there wasn't enough dialogue," Schulz says. "But comics—there's the characters, right in front of you. And they're funny-looking people, and they talk to each other. And that's what people like to read."

He copied the drawings in the comics. He would go down to the dime store and buy big blank books of paper and fill the pages with grandly illustrated Sherlock Holmes stories, inventing the mysteries to go along with the drawings. His mother watched him work, and when he was in his teens she took him one day to a St. Paul library exhibit of cartoonists' original drawings.

"I had never seen an original, professional strip," Schulz says. "And I looked at them, and went home, and took all my strips and tore them up and threw then away and started all over again. I knew I had a long way to go."

He was a kid of considerable determination, and he says it never occurred to him to pack it in. When he came back from the front in World War II he found work teaching art through the mail at a correspondence school, and kept drawing cartoons; it was a Catholic magazine, *Timeless Topix*, that finally offered him work, first lettering cartoons and then drawing some of his own. "This was the first page I ever had," Schulz says with some pride, opening a bound scrapbook to a yellowed newspaper clipping of four cartoons under the heading "Just Keep Laughing." They are sweet, single-gag cartoons: a small boy presents a vase to his mother and says, "Happy Birthday, Mom, and if you don't like it, the man said I could exchange it for a hockey puck!"

After *Timeless* there were some cartoons in the Minneapolis paper, and then the St. Paul paper, and the *Saturday Evening Post,* and finally the packet that the syndicate United Features liked well enough to ask if Schulz would turn it into a strip. He was drawing principally children by then, and although they had no names in the cartoons, the suggestions of character were already there: the impertinent beagle, the sharp-tongued girl with the bow in her hair, the entirely adult-sounding language issuing from what looked to be 5-year-olds.

Why children? "They sold." Schulz seems incapable of a wicked grin, but he is coming close. "It's the only reason. Literally. People are always saying, 'I'd like to tell you about this school project because we know of your interest in children.' And I'd say, 'I have no interest in children.' Just because I draw kids doesn't mean I have interest in children."

The personalities of the principals came without much difficulty, Schulz says. "I knew I wanted a little dog, and I asked my friend Charlie Brown if I could have his name. And that's how it was started . . . Charlie Brown was supposed to be a round-faced, bland character, without much personality or anything. And the others were the ones that had personality. That's why he had the round head with kind of a blank face. Now he still has the round head, but somehow . . ."

Schulz cocks his head, studying a large, freshly drawn cartoon panel on his desk. "That's kind of a nice round head," he says. "I like the way he looks."

He follows a schedule of some precision, driving his little yellow Mercedes every morning from his hilltop spread down to the wood-and-stone studio where he does his drawing. It is an unpretentious place, modestly landscaped and looking, as Schulz says, rather like a suburban dentist's office. He works much as he has for the last 35 years. "We're pretending it's Monday morning," Schulz says, since it is, "and I have no ideas, and I haven't thought of anything . . . So now, here I am with the blank pad."

Schulz brandishes a yellow legal pad. "And I'm thinking of Snoopy dancing. And Lucy says, 'How do you know that you're just not happy on the outside and crying on the inside?' Well—what does he say? I don't know. I can't think of anything. So I'll go in another direction, and that's the way I go, until I think of something."

What he has thought of, finally, courtesy of a newspaper article, is "fixed income." I had been thinking about Peppermint Patty getting nothing but D-minuses. So when I came back, I wrote out this strip here, which is—see—" Schulz reaches over and pulls out a large panel of empty cartoon squares with scarcely legible letters penciled at the top. "She says, 'I got another D-minus. That's what I got yesterday, the day before, and every day before that. All I ever get are D-minuses.' And Marcie leans forward and says, 'That's like living on a fixed income, sir.' And she says, 'Thanks, Marcie.' And that's it. That's the business. That's how I make a living."

That is not entirely how Schulz makes a living, of course, which raises a slightly sensitive subject, referred to in this conversation as The

1950

1951

© by United Feature Syndicate, Inc.

Things. There are, as is known to anyone who has ventured inside a variety store over the last couple of decades, a multitude of Things. There are Charlie Brown music boxes, Lucy picture frames, Woodstock bedroom slippers, Snoopy straws, Snoopy clocks, Snoopy doghouse lights, Snoopy coasters, Snoopy gumball machines, Snoopy toy car garages, Snoopy cookies, Snoopy ice cream, Snoopy calculators, and Snoopy address books with the labeling written in Portuguese.

"Does it bother you?" Schulz asks, sounding genuinely interested.

"You know, it starts so slowly . . . Eastman Kodak called the syndicate one day, and wanted to know if they could use the characters to make an instruction book on how to use the little Brownie camera. Now, should I have said no? Would that have been the time to say, 'No, I'm a purist'?"

Schulz is quite intent about this. "But I'm *not* a purist, see? I'm a commercial cartoonist. Nobody cared when Picasso drew pictures on plates and sold them." And the little rubber characters came some years later, and then the datebooks, and then the sweatshirts, and then—Schulz waves his hands, looking momentarily and unconvincingly helpless. "But I still had five kids to support and put through college. And I have United Features Syndicate that takes half the money, and they're pushing for things—and it keeps getting bigger and bigger."

Comics in general are not what they were when Schulz began, and he wonders about that, about the brash young cartoonists who lunge into a hundred newspapers at once with their smothering cuteness or the undisguised politics that seem to him terribly critical and self-righteous. "We could make a little 50-cent wager that they will not be around 35 years from now," he says. "I think they burn out faster, and I don't think the appeal is that broad."

And he knows, because so many still write to him—Schulz has received mail addressed to "The Great Pumpkin, c/o The Pumpkin Patch"—that his own comic still breaks a lot of hearts, that there are readers out there desperate to see Charlie Brown win a baseball game, or kick the football before Lucy can snatch it away, or dance away with the little red-haired girl.

"But I can't do that," Schulz says. "Because then your basic premise disappears. The foundation collapses. And at the risk of repeating myself, this was the biggest mistake that Al Capp ever made, was when Li'l Abner got married. The bottom dropped out of the strip, because that was the basic premise. We all wish we were big handsome guys pursued by blonds."

Schulz *likes* writing sad things, he says.

"May I read this?" he asks.

He picks up a copy of *But You Don't Look 35, Charlie Brown,*" the volume just published to celebrate the anniversary. The passage, which Schulz wrote, is about Lucy and the dismal predictable-as-spring-floods betrayal as she jerks the football away from Charlie Brown at the start of each fall season.

"'She really can't help herself,'" Schulz reads. "'Perhaps she is annoyed that it is all too easy. Charlie Brown isn't that much of a challenge. To be consistent, however, we have to let her triumph, for all the loves in the strip are unrequited; all the baseball games are lost; all the test scores are D-minuses; the Great Pumpkin never comes; and the football is always pulled away.'"

A Conversation with Charles Schulz

FRANK PAUER / 1987

From *Dayton Daily News and Journal Herald Magazine,* May 3, 1987, pp. 1–4, 13. Reprinted by permission.

Charles Schultz's unique insight into the frailties of human nature has kept *Peanuts,* at once, both apart from other comic strips and the best of them all. More than in any other comic strip, readers have come to identify with characters from *Peanuts.* Readers have also made *Peanuts* the most popular comic strip in history—begun in 1950 in seven newspapers, it now appears in more than 2,000 newspapers in almost 70 countries.

Any look back at the strip's modest debut is tempered with Schultz's look forward, work that will certainly not approach another 36 years. A 1981 quadruple bypass operation has left Schultz more reflective about his work, but with few regrets, as he approaches four decades at the drawing board.

Q: Did you think it would last?

A: Oh yeah, I had no intention of doing something that was not going to last, especially since I had worked all my life and dreamed about doing it. I never had any anticipation that it was going to achieve the amount of newspapers that we now have. But as far as lasting, I always thought, "Well, this is it—I'll draw this thing now for the rest of my life." Now I'm not so sure.

Q: Is it easier?

A: It doesn't matter, it's not any easier, it's not any harder. I'm more particular about what I draw now. I think I have discarded more ideas the last two or three years than I ever used to—I used to almost never discard an idea. I probably am more fussy now and work harder now than I ever have.

Q: The drawing must be easier.

A: Except for my hand shaking. I have a problem and I don't know if it has been since the heart surgery, but I have to draw much more slowly. I'm not as facile as I used to be.

Q: What led up to the surgery?

A: I just woke up one morning with a tight feeling in my chest and I didn't know what it was. It wouldn't go away so I thought I'd better call my doctor. He took an EKG, called a cardiologist and the next thing I knew I was lying in the emergency ward. Never had any indications of any problems. The next morning they took an angiogram and discovered that I had one artery totally closed and about three others that were anywhere from 50 to 80-90 percent closed, so the probabilities of another, or more severe, heart attack were very high. We thought about it for several weeks, and finally decided to go ahead with the surgery.

I stopped all autographing and answering the phones and just worked hard at getting three months ahead in my work because I had no idea how long I'd be out. As it was, I only lost a month of my lead time. I had a little trouble lettering when I first came back. In fact, I didn't do the lettering, just did the drawing and let the lettering set aside for several days until my hand steadied down. I'm not sure if the way my hands shake now has anything to do with the surgery or not. Some days drawing is extremely difficult, and I almost despair of being able to keep it up.

Q: You've thought of dropping the strip?

A: Sure. I mean, why not? Most people don't work in jobs for 35 years. Sometimes I wonder do I really want to do this for the rest of my life? People ask me all the time, and all I can honestly say is, "I simply don't know."

Q: You knew you were going to be a cartoonist at an early age.
A: I'd hoped to be one. I always liked the funny papers—my dad and I always read all four papers published in the twin cities. I followed *Buck Rogers* and *Popeye* and *Skippy* and all of those great strips. We didn't get the encouragement in school that I think we should have. Cartooning was looked down upon as not a dignified or worthwhile occupation.

Q: What encouragement from your parents?
A: My dad was a barber, and he and my mother only went to the third grade with their education, so they had no idea of how a person should go about fulfilling this ambition. They were always encouraging and never, never discouraging. My mother saw an ad in the paper one night that said, "Do you like to draw? Send for free talent test." A salesman, from what is now Art Instruction Schools, came out and my dad signed me up for this correspondence course because it had a lot of cartooning in it. I think it cost him $170, and even at that he got behind in the payments.

After WWII when I returned to St. Paul, I got a job as one of their instructors. I worked there for five years, which is where I met my friend, Charlie Brown. I asked him when I sold my strip if I could use his name as the lead character. I remember him coming over to my desk and looking down at Charlie Brown's face and saying, "Is that going to be Charlie Brown? I was always hoping I would look more like Steve Canyon."

Q: How did the strip evolve? You were drawing a panel cartoon, *Lil' Folks*, for a newspaper.
A: I had been drawing different types of strips. I drew some adventure strips, some war pages for comic magazines and I did a lot of lettering. Then I started drawing little kids, and somehow my type of humor seemed to fit these little kids. My first major sale was to the *Saturday Evening Post.* I got $40 for a little one-panel cartoon, and so I kept drawing the little kids—I think I sold 15 over a period of two years.

It was when I started to develop these panels that I really began to find my direction. The *St. Paul Pioneer Press* ran these *Li'l Folks* cartoons for two years. I only had to draw three or four panels per week that they ran back in the women's section each Sunday in black and white. It taught me how to hold to a schedule, to create on demand and develop my drawing style and lettering.

Q: How did it evolve from a panel to a strip?
A: Once I took all my best ideas and thought I've got to come up with an angle, something that nobody else has done. My style was getting more and more simple, so I thought why not draw a panel that has two cartoons to it instead of just one? This way the editor will be getting twice as much as he would normally get. So, I measured out the size that a panel would appear in a newspaper and then I drew one kid cartoon above the other. I drew them up really beautifully, and I sent them to United Features.

The syndicate looked at them and they said, "We really like it, but maybe it would have more appeal if one of the ideas was about teenagers." Typical of a syndicate trying to fiddle around with what you're doing. So I tried a few and sent them back, but they didn't like that. So they said, "Well we still want to go ahead with this, come to New York."

I then had this package of strips that I had been working on that were quite unique. They were three panels wide and they were little kids, but they were involved in extremely brief incidents. In those days characters in comic strips talked a lot, the ideas were overly involved. My strips were very simple and the action was really brief. I was quite proud of those and I took them along to show them what else I could do. After officers of the syndicate saw that I had drawn a strip, they decided right then and there that they would rather have a strip than a panel and that's how *Peanuts* was born.

Peanuts was originally sold under the title of *Li'l Folks*, but that had been used before, so they said we have to think of another title. I couldn't think of one and somebody at United Features came up with the miserable title *Peanuts,* which I hate and have always hated. It has no dignity and it's not descriptive. So the strip started in 1950 with seven newspapers.

Q: But what about the name?
A: What could I do? Here I was, an unknown kid from St. Paul. I couldn't think of anything else. I said, why don't we just call it *Charlie Brown* and the president said, "Well, we can't copyright a name like that." I didn't ask them about *Nancy* or *Steve Canyon.* I was in no position to argue.

© by United Feature Syndicate, Inc.

Q: How long did it take for *Peanuts* to really take off?

A: Probably not for five or six years. Just a whole series of fortunate circumstances: Snoopy finally getting up, walking around on his hind legs. Using the thought balloons also pushed it forward a little bit. Robert Short wrote *The Gospel According to Peanuts.* The musical, *You're a Good Man Charlie Brown* came along. Lee Mendelson came to me with the idea of television shows, and we won an Emmy with our very first show, the Christmas show. Hallmark came along with their greeting cards. One by one we kept adding things—some things worked, some things didn't work.

Q: The strip has changed over the years, is this a conscious decision, or does it just evolve?

A: The evolution of the drawing in comic strips is something that you're not even aware of. I'm not aware that Charlie Brown gets a little fatter, he gets a little thinner. Snoopy's nose gets longer, narrower, fatter or shorter. I'm not aware of it until I see the reprint books a year or two later.

Q: Do you bounce ideas off people?

A: No, never. I never take anybody else's ideas. If somebody tells me something that they think is funny I always say, "Well why don't you draw it up?"

Q: What about the decision not to portray adults in the strip?

A: I don't think I even thought about it. As the strip progressed, it just seemed something that made the strip unique. Now, as I look back upon it, I think it was a wise decision. The strip became abstract, like a fantasy. The minute that Snoopy became what he did drove any adult out of the strip. I don't think adult characters could fit in with a little dog writing novels on his doghouse or thinking he's a WWI flying ace. Kids accept him for what he is. It just wouldn't work.

Q: Any big mistakes over the years?

A: Snoopy had a sister, Belle, whom I discovered I really didn't like. I brought in Spike and I like Spike a lot. But when I brought another brother in—I thought Marbles would make a great name for a dog—I discovered almost immediately that bringing in other animals took the uniqueness away from Snoopy. So the only other animal character who works now is Spike, as long as Spike stays out in the desert. You have to be very careful that you don't destroy the personality of a character. You can do it without knowing it.

Q: What about public reaction?

A: I don't pay any attention to that. I like getting the good letters. Years ago people used to write and tell me I was using the dog too much in the strip, bring back the kids. Now I get letters saying I use the kids too much.

Q: Are you your own toughest critic?

A: I'm a fanatic about comic strips. I don't think I'm the greatest comic strip cartoonist who ever lived, but I really think I know as much, if not more, about drawing comic strips than anybody in the business. That isn't saying very much—knowing a lot about comic strips is not great in world affairs. But for what I do I really think I understand the medium. I think I understand it as much as anybody who has worked in the medium.

Q: Is there much of a routine to your week?
A: If I come in here on a Monday morning with having nothing started, none of the other million and one things that get in the way, the first thing I would do is take out my blank pad. I would probably look at the calendar to see when these strips are to come out because I don't want to skip Mother's Day, or Thanksgiving or Veterans Day, where Snoopy goes over and quaffs a few root beers with Bill Mauldin. Then I just start doodling around, showing kids yelling at each other, or Woodstock sailing into Snoopy lying on the doghouse, and all of a sudden there's an idea. I just sit there until I think of something. I'll rough it out in pencil, maybe put in the lettering and then set it aside and try to think of another one. I'll do that until I can think of three or four ideas and then I'll go ahead and start to finish them.

I can draw a strip completely in an hour. I don't like to draw six strips in one day, although it's possible and I've done it many times—it's too tedious. I like to finish six daily strips in two days, and then it will be time for a Sunday page.

I like to think the Sunday pages should have a little more action than the daily strips. I don't like to draw a Sunday page that is too simple or doesn't have a funny picture in it. I think it's a mistake to forget that cartooning is still drawing funny pictures. We are in a medium that can do things with which no other medium can compete. Just to use verbal ideas over and over is a big mistake, because other people can do this better than we can.

Q: Are you happier now with your art than you've ever been?
A: Oh, sure, no doubt about it, but I'm never totally happy with it. Cartooning is solving little problems while you're drawing—each panel becomes like a painting, you're trying to break up the area into pleasing shapes.

Q: But you're not entirely happy with your style?
A: I think I've trapped myself in a drawing style which I've had to use

to fit the amount of space that was given to me. Fortunately, it fits very well with the kind of humor that I'm using.

I've often thought that I would like to draw a strip about real children, where the cartooning was just slightly exaggerated. I think it would be a mistake to draw it realistically, because that doesn't do you any good. By trapping myself in this real extreme style, it has inhibited some of the things that I do. I've never completely resolved the drawing of interiors to my satisfaction. I don't really cartoon them funny. Now, if I show Sally sitting at the table trying to write, I could draw several different camera angles and show her sitting at a real table, but I don't think it would help. What she says is consistent with the drawing.

Q: How does the licensing of the characters work? Do you have final approval of drawing, style, colors?
A: I have final approval of everything. I can do anything I want as long as it doesn't destroy the feature, and no one can do anything that I don't want them to do.

Q: Were there concerns about overexposure?
A: They've been talking about that for 25 years. No one ever talks about Walt Disney having overexposure, yet they do infinitely more than we do. We never sought out licensing products like they do today. Everything that we have ever done was usually the idea of somebody else who came to us. Little by little we did these things.

It is also far more subtle than people realize, too. In the first place, it hasn't harmed the feature. As long as I continue to draw this strip every day and think of every idea and make every drawing, how am I hurting anybody? The people don't have to buy the books, they don't have to do any of the other things but they do.

Q: Is there a tendency today for syndicates to consider licensing too soon?
A: Yeah, but they deny it. But if they deny it, why is it as soon as a new strip starts, they go to the greeting card companies, and then try to put it on television—it's just going about it all wrong. You have to give a strip a chance to develop, find out what direction it's going to go, which characters are going to work. There's no way of telling when a strip starts what characters the person is going to be drawing 10 years from then. Popeye didn't come into the strip *Thimble Theater* until it ran for a long while.

Q: Do you give a considerable amount of thought to introducing new characters?

A: I never try to create a character just because I think that it's about time. That's a fatal thing to do. I think a new character should be produced out of something that you happen to be doing.

Years ago, I developed the character Peppermint Patty because I happened to be walking through our living room. I saw a dish of Peppermint Patties and I thought that would make a good name for a character, so I drew the face to match the name. One day I sent her to camp, and a little girl came into her tent one night and said, "Sir, my stomach hurts." That was Marcie. Now I think Marcie and Peppermint Patty are as much of the strip as any of the other characters.

I think all the characters in the strip are really very fond of each other, but they are also very hard on each other. Some are kind of innocent, some are brighter than others, but they all work. If a character works, and if the personality that you give the character provides you with ideas, then that character will stay. If the character just doesn't work, then out he or she goes.

Q: Is there something about your fame that you do not like?

A: Autographing. I despise autographing. My readers are nice people and I really appreciate that they like what I draw. I never try to draw anything that is offensive, because it would be ungracious of somebody who's been allowed to make such a good living doing this. I don't mind so much if somebody has bought a book and they want it signed, but to give me a gum wrapper to sign, or to draw a picture on a napkin really bothers me.

Q: Are you at all uncomfortable with all the analyzing of the strip?

A: In the days when I used to give speeches, somebody would ask, "What do you think of Robert Short's book *The Gospel According to Peanuts?*" I'd have to say well, it was his book. Robert Short wasn't trying so much to show what I was saying in the strip—what he was trying to show was that even such an insignificant thing as a comic strip could promote certain spiritual thoughts.

This doesn't mean, however, that in some of the strips that I haven't said some theological things. I like biblical study and I've done a lot of it with my meager education. I think I'm the first one who's really done some fairly deep things in this medium with biblical quotations. Of course somebody always hates it, too. I get letters from people saying that it's a monsterous thing to do and that the strip should be thrown out of the paper—you should never quote the Bible in a comic strip. Some people just think comic strips are awful and next to burlesque probably one of the worst things ever.

Q: Any philosophy?
A: My philosophy is just one of kindness, I think. There's not a lot of cruelty in the strip, although they do insult each other. You notice that Snoopy never throws his supper dish at Charlie Brown's face. They're always getting hit in the head with fly balls and it goes "bonk," but this is typical comic strip stuff and it's typical of the medium.

Q: How much of you is Charlie Brown?
A: I don't know what percentage of me would be Charlie Brown—certainly some. I'm a little bit of all the characters because that's what I draw. I used to be more Lucy than I am now, but I'm not much anymore—I've learned to temper my sarcastic remarks. The strip is very personal and all the things in the strip are things that I think about.

Q: Every other person must wonder where you get your ideas.
A: Yeah.

Q: What do you tell them?
A: I tell them I'm very clever.

Q: You've written that you don't believe that *Peanuts* can be considered art.
A: No, no, I don't think it is. I think maybe a hundred years from now, if some of these strips survive, maybe one of them could be called art in some way. In the first place, it doesn't matter what you call it. I think this comic strip is better than a lot of things around that they *call* art, but I don't think it's as good as anything Picasso ever did. I also don't think Picasso could have drawn a comic strip. This is a very demanding profession, but I'm not sure it is art, and I'm not sure it really even matters. The same way as is tap dancing as good as ballet dancing—who cares? Those discussions baffle me.

Q: How would you like to be remembered?
A: As just somebody who drew a real good comic strip. I think I'll be lucky if I get remembered that way.

A Chat with
Charles Schulz

MARTY JONES / 1994

From *The Aspiring Cartoonist,*
No. 2 (1994): 2–5. Reprinted
by permission.

Q: Think back to when you were a young, aspiring cartoonist. What was some of the advice and direction you got from professionals?
A: When I was very small, I really got no advice at all. My mother and dad both knew what my ambitions were, and when I was a teenager, they used to ask different friends or people what I could do to get started, or was there anybody I could talk to, because they had no knowledge of the business. And there was just no one around to talk to. It wasn't until I took the correspondence course and went over to Minneapolis from St. Paul and visited Mr. Frank Wing, an elderly cartoonist, and got some tips on drawing and rendering and things like that. But when I was very young, I had no advice. Just a few things I'd read here and there, but nothing of any real importance.

Q: Many young cartoonist send you their strips and come to you for advice. What are some of the common mistakes you see?

A: I suppose the common mistake is to follow the trends too closely. To imitate those who seem to be reasonably successful at that period, rather than just following their own leanings. I think also it's a big mistake not to read up and study the work of the really old timers, like *Krazy Kat* and *Skippy,* and what have now become old timers, I suppose, such as Al Capp's *Li'l Abner,* and J. R. Williams *Our Our Way.* [Young cartoonists] seem totally ignorant of those sorts of people, and many of them, almost all of them, have never heard of people like Roy Crane. They seem to follow only the very modern ones, and in many cases follow the wrong ones.

Q: When you started, then, how were you able to avoid being drawn into making that same mistake of copying something you really admired, such as *Krazy Kat,* and find your own voice?

A: I consider that nothing I did before World War II, which would have been up until I was 20 years old, was worth anything at all. Roy Crane was my hero, and I tried to draw comic adventure strips the same way he did with *Wash Tubbs* and *Captain Easy.* I remember trying to do a Foreign Legion Sunday page once, patterning it after *Prince Valiant* designs—a huge page. Things like that. And then I tried gag cartooning, of course, which I still think is one of the best places to get started if all you're trying to do is market your work. I sent gag cartoons out to the *Saturday Evening Post* and *Collier's,* and got them all rejected. I felt that I was somewhat on the right track, but none of this really meant anything until I came back 3 years later from the war and got a job at the correspondence school in Minneapolis, Art Instruction. They hired me as a temporary replacement for someone going on vacation that summer, and I ended up staying there for 5 years. That's when I seriously went to work trying to develop what I wanted to do.

Q: What well-meaning bad advice have you heard professional cartoonists give?

A: I think the worse advice I read is someone who's been telling cartoonists they should look around and see what the market seems to need. Are there any comic strips about firemen these days, or any comic strips about a different kind of animal, or something like that. To see what the market seems to need, and then do that—that's the worse thing you could possibly do. I think what you have to do is draw from your own personality and your own experience. Each one of us is, obviously, unique, and you should draw only about the things you really know well or reasonably well, and draw from your own personality.

Q: Little direction is given on how to make a cartoonist a writer. Do you become a good cartoon writer by looking around and writing about what you know well?

A: I don't know how you become a good cartoon writer. I think you either have it or you don't have it. But I do think that it is necessary to be reasonably well educated. I think you should read a lot, that you should be well informed about all forms of literature. I think a good knowledge of history is important, and knowledge of the whole world around us. I think knowledge is very important, and to maintain an interest in people, and try to grow as a person yourself.

Q: Do you have any thoughts on how to take that observation of life and turn it specifically into humor, and conform that to the confines of a four-panel daily strip?

A: I'm not sure if this can be learned. I think a person can maybe learn it himself or herself, but I'm not sure it can be taught. There was a time when I was working on my book, *Peanuts Jubilee,* and I thought maybe I could explain the thought process of how some of these ideas occur. But I found you can only carry them so far, and then I don't know what happens. I don't know how you twist that little phrase to make it funny, or how you apply something. I'm not sure that it can be explained, and I'm not sure I have the energy to put it all down on paper and try to explain it.

Q: You're considered one of the great cartooning minimalists, to the extent you'll exclude a mouth from a character if the character isn't speaking. Is this a conscious application of a style, or is there a significance in the things you leave out of a drawing in order to convey humor?

A: I think that it is very important not to include a lot of extraneous details in the characters themselves, in the drawing of them, or in the background, or all of that. Anything that would interfere with the flow of the dialogue or the idea itself. I would advise someone to go back and read Percy Crosby's *Skippy* to see what I'm talking about, rather than my own work. Now, I resent the fact I was forced to draw the worlds' smallest comic strip at the time, simply because I'm sure the people at United didn't have much faith in it, so my work was reduced almost to the size of 4 air mail stamps. A lot of my style was developed so that I could accommodate it to those small panels. I'm also a strong believer in not overly cartooning your figures. I think people should be able to recognize right away where the nose is, where the mouth is, where the eyes are, and what the expression is. I think that this is very important. So I'm a great believer in *mild* cartooning. I can't think of a single superstar in the comic strip business that employed an exaggerated style of cartooning.

© by United Feature Syndicate, Inc.

Q: Exaggerated in what way?
A: Extreme caricature. Now, I'm only talking about comic strips, of course. I know nothing about the comic magazine business these days and a lot of other things. I'm just totally unacquainted with that. I'm talking about just newspaper comic strips.

Q: How important is authenticity in drawing? For example, your use of the musical staff above Schroeder's piano when he's performing classical music. The notes look real, as if you've researched and copied down exactly what they should be.
A: I think that has been one of the secrets to whatever success I've had. Everything that I cartoon or write about is done with authenticity. The notes are actually notes from different piano works, and I copy them out very carefully. And this was one of the reasons I got my very first *Peanuts* book published, because one of the editors for Rinehart in New York noticed that Schroeder was playing a Beethoven sonata. It

struck his eye, and that's how he started reading the strip, and decided to publish it as a book. So when I do things about medicine, or historical things from World War I, where Snoopy is over in France, it's all very authentic. I think it's important to try to break beneath the surface in everything you are doing, rather than just drawing surface cartoons.

Q: To keep a daily strip going for 43 years, you've developed a consistent routine in order to produce the strip. How do you cope with the common disruptions in your life that upset the routine, such as prolonged illness, family crises, or vacations?

A: Actually, it drives you crazy, because I never have a total 5-day work week with no interruptions. I'm interrupted continually. I was just thinking about that this morning driving to the studio. You get up in the morning, and you think this is going to be good; I've got all day now, and maybe if I can think of three or four ideas, I can get this week's batch done. And then, either on the way to work, or after you get someplace, or the first couple of phone calls come in, or maybe somehow you have a stomach ache, or something happens to you, and—BANG—the whole day, rather than being tremendously productive, just goes down the drain and nothing really good happens. But this is just one of the things you have to put up with, and you learn to live with it. The actual drawing and the mechanical part of it is not difficult, it's that it interrupts your thinking, and your quiet time of just sitting here and staring into space and trying out all sorts of ideas that either work or don't work.

Q: Overall, how do you assess the state of the comic industry today?
A: I'm afraid that we are slowly being driven out of business.

Q: How so?
A: Well, in the first place, we don't have the room in which to work. This is the obvious complaint. Beyond that, there seems to be no room for a lot of experimentation. We seem all to be channeled down the same path, and I don't know what the solution is. I think that if some editor had the great notion to run a comic strip large all the way across the bottom of the paper, or something like that, it would be revolutionary. It just might start everything all over again. But I'm afraid it's just not going to happen.

Q: Is there room for editorializing on the comic's page?
A: Oh, there's always room for it, I guess, if a person wants to do that

kind of thing, sure. But it's just a personal response. It's something that some people like to do. It just doesn't interest me.

Q: We ask that question because of the notorious "to remember" strip you did on the anniversary of D-Day. It was different for you to do something that was devoid of humor, and get away from what you usually do.

A: It takes a long time to develop, to be able to branch out, and go off into directions of this kind. I think it takes a lot of maturity, it takes growing, and it's a product of a lot of memories, and, of course, for my generation, World War II was one of the most important times of our lives. And you live with those memories all of the time. Actually, that whole thing happened because I

JUNE 6, 1944, "TO REMEMBER"

© by United Feature Syndicate, Inc.

was looking at my calendar to see when my next Sunday page was going to be printed. It said June 6th, and all of a sudden—BANG—it hit me, because I remembered that day so distinctly. I did that Sunday page at home, and I remember going through book after book after book trying to find some photographs that would really work for Snoopy. There were almost none that would, so I had an awful time drawing it. The impact of the strip had to be that one large picture. But for Sunday papers that print the half page, you still need the title panel and throw-away panel in the right-hand corner. And I had to draw something that wouldn't disturb the impact of that one, solid picture. So it took me all day Saturday and Sunday to make it finally come out the way I wanted it. Then, of course, it really needed the color to bring out the impact of it all. Now my big problem—I didn't realize at the time I was doing it—that that was the 49th anniversary of D-Day. Now I've got the big 50th anniversary coming up this year, and D-Day does not fall on Sunday, so I've already begun trying to think of what I'm going to do this coming year.

Charlie Blue:
The Fragile Child
Lurking Inside the Cartoonist

SHARON WAXMAN / 1996

From *The Washington Post,* October 22, 1996, pp. D1–D2.
© 1996, The Washington Post.
Reprinted by permission.

Charles M. Schulz surveys the bustling ice rink he had built a few steps from his art studio in Northern California. "My whole life has been one of rejection," America's most successful cartoonist says. "Women. Dogs. Comic strips." A moment of silence while this curious information sinks in.

Dogs?

"I've been reading F. Scott Fitzgerald's short stories lately," he goes on. "I like them because everyone gets rejected. Ever read 'The Rich Boy'? He frequently puts his head in his hands and cries."

The fact is, Schulz—creator of Charlie Brown, Snoopy, Linus and other indelible icons of baby boomers' carefree youth—never forgets a slight. Like the high school yearbook that rejected his drawings. Like the red-haired girl who turned down his proposal of marriage, or the wire-haired fox terrier, Andy, who died on him a few years back. Like

159

the post office clerk in 1950 who asked Schulz what was in the package he sent out to United Feature Syndicate every week. Schulz explained: That comic strip about little kids. The clerk shrugged and said he didn't think much of it.

"I still get things rejected," he says, munching on a platter of fish and chips at his habitual window table at the ice rink. His expression is even and friendly, as if by now he has come to expect rebuffs. "Three years ago I had a whole TV series rejected. CBS decided it would like a Saturday morning series of Snoopy and his brothers and sisters as puppies. I wrote eight of them—the more I wrote the better they got—I sent them to an animator who sent them to CBS. A couple of weeks went by, I didn't hear anything. Finally they said, no, they didn't want it, because the dogs didn't talk. I said, 'Well, dogs *don't* talk.' But they never even called me to discuss it."

He sighs. "That's the way it is with most people. Most of us are acquainted with losing. Very few of us ever win. And I've never been especially good at laughing at myself."

Well, good grief.

Perhaps a bit of perspective is in order. *Peanuts,* which debuted in 1950, now appears in some 2,600 newspapers around the world, reaching an estimated 355 million readers in 75 countries. It has inspired 40 animated television specials, four feature films and a long-running Broadway play *(You're a Good Man, Charlie Brown),* sold some 300 million books and spawned an industry of retail products from greeting cards to bed linens to "Chuckwear" clothing. The success has not only been commercial; an exhibit of Schulz's work was displayed at the Louvre in 1990, and a *Peanuts* concerto, believe it or not, by contemporary composer Ellen Taaffe Zwilich will premiere at Carnegie Hall next spring.

As if this weren't enough, HarperCollins is unleashing a new line of 30 *Peanuts* books this month, a million copies altogether, marketed for children and the adults who grew up with the strip ("Love Isn't Easy" and "Me, Stressed Out?" are some of the titles).

In truth, the 73-year-old Schulz appears to live an almost impossibly idyllic existence. His plush, roomy studio is nestled in a wooded glen near the community ice rink he had built 27 years ago, and both are but a short drive through the Santa Rosa Hills to the house he shares with his lively, loving wife of 23 years, Jeannie. He begins every day with breakfast at the ice rink, which he built when the one his kids used closed. Then he heads to the studio to answer mail and draw the strip. He strolls back to the rink for lunch, where he banters with the regulars and checks on the progress of the annual Christmas show, an original production in which he has a hand. He's back in the studio until 4 and then he usually has dinner with Jeannie at a local restaurant.

Schulz is fit, a tall, handsome man with a head of silver hair. Thrice weekly he does an aerobic workout; he also plays golf and ice hockey. He is rich—he has an eight-seater jet for short trips and more money than he could ever hope to spend. He is famous and beloved by the American public.

But with all his success, Schulz remains a fragile and melancholy soul; he cannot help but see the world through the prism of a painful and frustrating childhood. Schulz's father was a barber in St. Paul, Minn., keeping the family afloat on a sea of endless 35-cent haircuts. Both parents had only third-grade educations. "Sparky," as everyone called (and still calls) Schulz, did all right socially as a kid and skipped ahead two half-grades, but by junior high school, "the roof fell in," as he puts it. He couldn't keep up. His grades were miserable. He had pimples. No one paid him any attention.

"In high school I was a nonentity. I failed everything," he says. "I was a decent little kid. A son of a barber—at least my father had a job. I didn't belong to anything. I was never given credit for knowing how to draw. Why didn't someone ask me to work on the high school paper? They didn't even come close."

That, of course, is not the whole truth. In fact Sparky and another girl in elementary school won diplomas as the smartest kids in class the year his family moved to Needles, Calif. (they moved back to St. Paul after a year). He made the golf team as a senior in high school; he shot up to nearly 6 feet and wasn't a runt anymore. And he once got the highest mark in an illustration class. But to a sensitive boy with secret ambitions, every cut was a lasting scar.

Schulz reserves a special derision for his teachers. There was one in elementary school who assigned the class to use the encyclopedia to write an essay. Schulz wrote his using a small set he bought from the corner five-and-dime with money he had painstakingly saved. "I handed it in and she said, 'Not much material here.' I told her it came from my own encyclopedias. She said, 'Then I think you need a new set of encyclopedias.'" He smiles, a wry wrinkle across his face. "Here was a chance for a teacher to talk to someone who wasn't stupid, who was

shy and sensitive. She blew the whole opportunity." He pauses. "She was an idiot."

School as a whole was a painful experience for Schulz, whose trials can be recognized in those of Charlie Brown. "Once a teacher asked what I had learned in class," he says. "I wanted to say something wonderful. But I couldn't think of anything to say. I remember a girl turning and whispering to me, 'Say *something.*' And the teacher said, 'Well, Charles, apparently you didn't learn anything. I'll have to give you a failing grade.'" He pauses, the 60-year-old humiliation as vivid as yesterday. "I felt so awful. I wanted to say something decent. But I couldn't think of anything. Now I can. But now it's too late."

These experiences indelibly marked the young Schulz and became a bottomless fount of creative irony and bittersweet humor for the artist. In a strip completed in recent years, Peppermint Patty tells Marcie that being subdued is the key to success at school—"Subdued, Marcie, that's the secret," she says. Then she gets her report card with a D-minus and the teacher's remark: "Student fails to speak up in class."

In the sharp-edged reality of today, Schulz's pen-and-ink world is an island of comfort, familiarity, and warmth. Happiness is a warm puppy. "Rats!" is as profane as it gets. *Peanuts* does not have the forced gaiety and one-dimensional heroism of Disney. Instead, it has pathos and pain; it is funny because the protagonists are vulnerable. They yearn and strive and they fail. Charlie Brown never gets to kick the football; Peppermint Patty has yet to pass a test. Only Snoopy can be blissfully ignorant of life's rough truths.

All of their traits come from some part of Charles Schulz. Says Jeannie Schulz: "He's a little bit of everything in the strip. He's crabby like Lucy, diffident like Charlie Brown. There's a lot of Linus—he's philosophical and wondering about life—that's the part I really appreciate. And of course Snoopy—I wish I could be as free as he."

Schulz's real world is an island, too. In fact, Santa Rosa is the only place the cartoonist feels at ease, surrounded by familiar faces, supported by a reliable routine. He hates to travel, despises hotels, and is plagued by bouts of loneliness, panic attacks, and depression. He worries incessantly.

"He's not the hail fellow well met," says Jeannie Schulz, who satisfies her own love of travel alone. "For years he knew he didn't fit, he didn't feel comfortable in the mainstream. We may go out and laugh, but his comfort zone is where he lives. It's a narrow zone. He won't go off with a bunch of his men friends and golf for a week."

In a book of essays for the 35th anniversary of *Peanuts*, Schulz wrote: "The most terrifying loneliness is not experienced by everyone and can be understood by only a few. I compare the panic in this kind of loneliness to the dog we see running frantically down the road pursuing the family car. He is not really being left behind . . . but for that moment in his limited understanding, he is being left alone forever, and he has to run and run to survive."

Where does this anxiety come from? Schulz has often mentioned the trauma of his mother's death from cancer coming just days before he took a train eastward to join the Army. (He served in Europe near the end of World War II, working his way up to staff sergeant.) Then there was the red-haired girl who turned him down, Donna Wold, who worked at the art instruction school where Schulz taught on his return from the service. She was his first real experience with romantic love; she chose another guy.

Schulz, who married a few years later, declines to talk about his 21-year marriage to Joyce Halverson, with whom he had five children—now grown and with kids of their own—but makes clear it was not a happy union. She subsequently married the man who built the ice rink, which she had designed. And of course there were the many, many rejections from cartoon syndicates before United Feature Syndicate finally signed him to do *Peanuts.*

Still, Schulz is hardly the first artist to endure years of personal and professional failures before finally achieving success. "I honestly can't explain it; he's bitter about all kinds of things," says Lynn Johnston, creator of the strip *For Better or for Worse* and an old friend. "He's bitter about the little red-haired girl who didn't marry him, he's bitter about his divorce. He's bitter about getting old." She adds: "He's far too happy now. He needs something to be grouchy about."

Afternoon shadows fall across the cartoonist's tidy U-shaped desk. He is sketching a straightish line across a yellow legal pad, with a downward stroke at each end; a tent for Snoopy and Woodstock. The hand shakes slightly, but the uneven strokes are sure and practiced.

"This is a way of coldbloodedly taking the tablet and trying to think of an idea," Schulz is saying. Behind him hangs a large landscape in earth tones painted by a local artist and several brightly colored animal canvases by a recently deceased friend from the St. Paul art school.

A bronze statue of Lincoln, one of the cartoonist's heroes ("I bet he was fun to be with"), adorns an end table beside a couch with a "Cathy" (the cartoon) pillow. In the vestibule, where two secretaries field requests and take calls, a bronzed *Time* magazine cover of the cartoonist adorns one wall, while a photograph of Christo's wrapping of the Reichstag hangs on another. A series of tributes to Schulz drawn by fellow cartoonists lines a third.

He tries to take a visitor through the creative process. "This is a perfect example," he says. "Snoopy goes camping. He pitches a tent. I'll draw him on top of the tent, put some birds on the string. Always stay within the medium" He'll doodle and draw until something funny hits him. Sometimes it takes days.

On his desk are the three strips Schulz completed in the morning—a good day's work. "I was sitting here thinking. I scrawled some phrases on my legal pad," Schulz says, pointing at one. Here's what came out: Charlie Brown, strolling, says: "Sometimes when you're walking by the home of the girl you love, you can see her standing by the window." Next frame: "She waves at you and you wave back." Next frame: "But it's her grandmother."

You think this is easy, day after day, seven strips a week, for 56 years? "You have to keep doing something to attract attention," Schulz

says. "You always have to add new twists. Like Lucy pulling away the
football. She's done it for 40 years, and you have to find a new way for
her to do it every time. Every fall people expect it."

For Schulz, it's not a grind, no matter how many times Charlie
Brown's kite gets eaten by a tree; it's a challenge. That alone is an inspi-

ration to his younger admirers who find the strip still alive with ideas. "For those of us in the new generation, who are saying, 'I'm tired of this, I'm quitting.' I look at Sparky who is still working hard, still determined to be completely independent of any other creative help," says Johnston, who has been drawing her strip for 17 years. "When I get to the stage where I think I can give this up, I think, 'If Sparky can do it, so can I.'"

Schulz wouldn't dream of retiring or of handing his strip over to a team of assistants, as some other cartoonists have done. He does, however, think about mortality. He had bypass surgery 16 years and was supposed to live only another 10.

Schulz has decided that once he dies or becomes too ill to continue it, *Peanuts* will cease to exist. "Everything has to end," he says. "This is what I do. This is my excuse for existence. No one else will touch it."

After all, he hasn't asked for much from life, except perhaps the recognition that he did something with his talent. "I always knew what I wanted to do. If I have to brag, I'd say that I did the best that I could with the abilities that I have," he says.

Schulz doesn't have to brag, of course. But he still thinks he has to.

"For me, having made it is having thought of something funny for tomorrow. For me success is coming up with a good strip," he offers, unprompted. "I don't think that drawing a comic strip is the greatest thing in the world. But it's as good as a lot of things." He pauses to think. "You know, I'd like to be remembered with what E. B. White once said about James Thurber: 'He wrote the way a child skips rope, and the way a mouse waltzes.'"

He smiles gently. The anxiety—for once—is gone.

Schulz at 3 O'Clock in the Morning

GARY GROTH / 1997

From *Comics Journal,* No. 200
(December 1997): 3–48. Reprinted by
permission.

Charles M. Schulz was born November 25, 1922 in Minneapolis. His destiny was foreshadowed when, at the age of two days, an uncle nicknamed him Sparky (after Barney Google's racehorse Spark Plug).

"My dad was a barber," Schulz recalled. "I always admired him for the fact that he and my mother had only third grade educations and from what I remembered hearing in conversations, he worked pitching hay in Nebraska one summer to earn enough money to go to barber school, got himself a couple of jobs, and eventually bought his own barber shop. And I think he at one time owned two barber shops and a filling station, but that was either when I was not born or very small, so I don't know much about that." Except for a misguided year-and-a-half interlude spent in Needles, California ("an eerie and eternal summer" Schulz called it), he grew up in St. Paul. "We settled in a neighborhood about two blocks from my dad's barbershop and most of my playtime life revolved around the yard of the grade school across the street from our apartment."

By all accounts, Sparky Schulz led an unremarkable, albeit sheltered, childhood. He was an only child, close to both parents. His father evidently nurtured his interest in comics: according to his biography by Rheta Grimsley Johnson, his father's "one passion was the funny papers. He loved comics and read them the way some men read box scores or racing forms—with intensity and devotion. He bought four Sunday newspapers every week, for the comics, picking up the two local papers on Saturday evening hot off the presses."

His academic career was erratic. He was such an outstanding student at Richard Gordon Elementary School that he skipped two grades, but began to founder later at St. Paul's Central High School ("He became a shy, skinny kid with pimples and big ears, nearly 6 feet tall and weighing only 136 pounds")—perhaps not so coincidentally at the same time kids are going through their cruelest, most status-conscious period of socialization. The pain, bitterness, insecurity, and failures chronicled in *Peanuts* appear to have originated from this period of Schulz's life. Schulz reproduced a report card from high school in *Peanuts Jubilee* (1975), under which read the first-person caption: "This report card is printed to show my own children that I was not as dumb as everyone has said I was." (The present perfect tense Schulz chose is instructive.) His acute sense, and resentment, of small but hurtful injustices also seem to stem from this period and continue to be deeply felt to this day. "I kind of resented the whole public school system at that time," he said. "It didn't cater to the many kids who weren't big and strong. The gym teachers paid attention only to the school athletes. The rest of us were shunted aside. I really resented that." Or consider this wounded recollection: "It took me a long time to become a human being. I was regarded by many as kind of sissyfied, which I resented because I really was not a sissy. I was not a tough guy, but I was good at sports. . . . So I never regarded myself as being much and I never regarded myself as being good looking and I never had a date in high school, because I thought, who'd want to date me? So I didn't bother. And that's just the way I grew up."

Through *Peanuts*, Schulz has touched upon a truth that we are perhaps too embarrassed to acknowledge but which may paradoxically account for the strip's universal popularity: that the cruelties and slights

© by United Feature Syndicate, Inc.

we suffer as a part of growing up, regarded by adults as inconsequential, or, at any rate, ineradicable, follow us to the grave, affecting our perception and behavior in adulthood. Or, as Umberto Eco, put it: "[The *Peanuts* characters] affect us because we realize that if they are monsters, it is because we, the adults, have made them so. In them, we find everything. Freud, mass-cult, digest culture, frustrated struggle for success, craving for affection, loneliness, passive acquiescence, and neurotic protest. But all these elements do not blossom directly, as we know them, from the mouths of a group of children: they are conceived and spoken after passing through the filter of innocence."

Although Schulz enjoyed sports, he also found refuge in solitary activities: reading, drawing, watching movies. "The highlight of our lives was, of course, Saturday afternoons, going to the local theatre. We would buy a box of popcorn for a nickel from a popcorn shop a few stores down from the theatre and then we'd go to the afternoon matinee. My favorite movie, I still remember, was *Lost Patrol,* with Victor McLaglen. I loved those desert movies, which is why I like drawing Snoopy as the foreign legionnaire."

He bought comic books and big little books, poured over the newspaper strips, and copied his favorites. "Usually I tried to copy the style of *Buck Rogers,* but I was also crazy about all of the Walt Disney characters, and Popeye . . . and the characters in *Tim Tyler's Luck* . . . Clare Briggs influenced me considerably . . . I also thought there was no one who drew funnier and more warm-hearted cartoons than J. R. Williams." He was quickly becoming a connoisseur; his heroes were Milton Caniff, Roy Crane, Hal Foster, and Alex Raymond. In his senior year in high school, his mother noticed an ad in a local newspaper for Federal Schools, a "correspondence plan for aspiring artists" (now called Art Instruction Schools). "She came in one night and she said, 'Look here in the newspaper. It says, "Do you like to draw? Send for a free talent test."' So I sent in and a few weeks later, a man knocked on the door and it was a man from the correspondence school. And he sold us the course." Schulz's father paid the $170 tuition in installments. Schulz completed the course and began trying, unsuccessfully, to sell gag cartoons to magazines. (His first published drawing was of his dog, Spike, which appeared in a 1937 *Ripley's Believe It Or Not* installment.)

He was drafted in 1943 at the same time his mother was diagnosed with cancer. The timing and the circumstances made leaving home particularly excruciating for Schulz. He was home one weekend when his mother looked up at him from her bed and said, "I suppose that we should say good-bye, because we probably never will see each other again." She died the next day. His father drove him back to Fort Snelling after her funeral, from which he shipped out to Camp Campbell, Kentucky later that day. "I remember crying in my bunk that evening," he recalled. His mother's death "was a loss from which I sometimes believe I never recovered."

Schulz was discharged after the War, and started submitting gag cartoons to the various magazines of the time, but his first breakthrough came when Roman Baltes, an editor at *Timeless Topix*, a comic magazine owned by the Roman Catholic Church, hired him to letter adventure comics. Soon after that, he was hired by his alma mater, Art Instruction, to correct student lessons returned by mail. "For the next year, I lettered comic pages for *Timeless Topix*, working sometimes until past midnight, getting up early the next morning, taking a streetcar to downtown St. Paul, leaving the work outside the door of Mr. Baltes's office, and then going over to Minneapolis to work at the correspondence school."

His next break was selling 17 cartoons to the *Saturday Evening Post* between 1948 and 1950, during which time he sold a weekly comic feature called *Li'l Folks* to the local *St. Paul Pioneer Press*. It was run in the women's section and paid $10 a week. "One day Roman [Baltes] bought a page of little panel cartoons that I had drawn and titled 'Just Keep Laughing.' One of the cartoons showed a small boy who looked prophetically like Schroeder sitting on the curb with a baseball bat in his hands talking to a little girl who looked prophetically like Patty. He was saying, 'I think I could learn to love you, Judy, if your batting average was a little higher.' Frank Wing, my fellow instructor at Art Instruction, said, 'Sparky, I think you should draw more of those little kids. They are pretty good.' So I concentrated on creating a group of samples and eventually sold them as a weekly feature called *Li'l Folks* to the *St. Paul Pioneer Press.*" After writing and drawing the feature for two years, Schulz asked for a better location in the paper or for daily exposure, as well as a raise. "When he turned me down on all three counts, I suggested that perhaps I had better quit. He merely stated, 'All right.' Thus endeth my career at the *St. Paul Pioneer Press.*"

He started submitting strips to the newspaper syndicates. "I used to get on the train in St. Paul in the mornings, have breakfast on the train and make that beautiful ride to Chicago, get there about three in the afternoon, check into a hotel by myself, and the next morning I would get up and make the rounds of the syndicates. . . . At this time I was also becoming a little more gregarious and was learning how to talk with people. When I first used to board the morning Zephyr and ride it to Chicago, I would make the entire trip without talking to anyone. Little by little, however, I was getting rid of my shyness and feelings of inferiority, and learning how to strike up acquaintances on the train and talk to people."

He had a near-miss at the NEA syndicate: "I opened a . . . letter from the director of NEA in Cleveland saying he liked my work very much. Arrangements were made during the next few months for me to start drawing a Sunday feature for NEA, but at the last minute their editors changed their minds and I had to start all over again." In the Spring of 1950, Schulz received a letter from Jim Freeman, United Feature Syndicate's editorial director, announcing his interest in his submission, *Li'l Folks.* Schulz boarded a train in June for New York City to discuss drawing a strip for them. Schulz self-deprecatingly describes his successful trip thusly:

"I had brought along a new comic strip I had been working on, rather than the panel cartoons which United Feature Syndicate had seen. I simply wanted to give them a better view of my work."

"I told the receptionist that I had not had breakfast yet, so I would go out and eat and then return. When I got back to the syndicate offices they had already opened up the package I had left there and in that short time had decided they would rather publish the strip than the panel. This made me very happy, for I really preferred the strip to the panel."

"I returned to Minneapolis filled with great hope for the future and asked a certain little girl to marry me. When she turned me down and married someone else, there was no doubt that Charlie Brown was on his way. Losers get started early."

The first *Peanuts* strip appeared October 2, 1950.

Prior to *Peanuts,* the province of the comic page was that of gags, social and political observation, domestic comedy, soap opera, various adventure genres. Although *Peanuts* has changed, or evolved, over the 47 years Schulz has written and drawn it, it remains, as it began, an anomaly on the comics page—a comic strip about the interior crises of the cartoonist himself. After a painful divorce in 1973 from which he had not yet recovered, Schulz told a reporter, "Strangely, I've drawn better cartoons in the last six months—or as good as I've ever drawn. I don't know how the human mind works." Surely, it is this kind of humility in the face of profoundly irreducible human questions that makes *Peanuts* as universally moving as it is. It's worth being reminded that Charles Schulz is one of the greatest cartoonists of the 20th century, something that the global phenomenon of *Peanuts* by way of all the merchandising and licensing and media spin-offs may obscure.

* * *

Groth: In every interview I've read where you make reference to them, you've said that you sold 15 gag cartoons to the *Saturday Evening Post* in the late '40s.
Schulz: Oh, yeah.

Groth: But you actually sold 17.
Schulz: Did I?

Groth: Yeah.
Schulz: That's pretty good.

The odd thing is that the little kid ones went the best. But I remember this one [January 1, 1948] came about the morning after Harry Truman beat Thomas Dewey, I was so bitter and disgusted about the whole thing, and some old woman came in the room that day. She was one of the instructors, and she was all excited about it, and I remember turning to someone and saying, "Huh! I sleep well enough at night, it's living during the day I find so hard." And I sent the rough into the *Post* and they okayed it, and all of the sudden I realized that I didn't have any drawing style. I had to draw this thing, and I hadn't developed any style at all. Because I had been drifting into drawing the little kids, and I was working on that style, and all of the sudden I had to draw these adults. It was a very mechanical style, and I wasn't proud of it at all.

Groth: You found it difficult to stylize adults because you had gotten so used to drawing kids?
Schulz: Yeah. Uh-huh.

Taking ordinary things like the bed and turning them into a football field, and a race track was a good gimmick. Of course, since then I've drawn a million birdbaths. This was one of my favorites [Feb. 11, 1950], and they changed the word, it's a misprint, it should have been, "Oh, we got along swell." Rather than, "We get along swell." That doesn't make sense.

But my style is beginning to develop a little bit [at this point]. This one was quite successful, too, a gimmick I learned how to draw, and this was reprinted a couple of other places. I got $60 for this, and then I made $15 or $20 other dollars reprinting it someplace.

I was on the right track. That's how it all started. I was very ambitious. But I couldn't sell to any other magazine. I sent, I know, to *Collier's* and a couple of others. But I couldn't sell any other magazines.

But apparently John Bailey liked them, and he was very good to me, he must have been good, as I've talked to Mort Walker and others, he was good to cartoonists, and I sent him one batch of roughs once, and he tore out little scraps and corners of paper and attached them to each one telling me what was wrong with them, and why he didn't buy it. Which took time. But he must have felt it was important. I never met the man, but that was good.

Groth: He must have seen potential.
Schulz: Yeah, I suppose. A long time ago.

Groth: What kind of rejections did you get from other magazines?
Schulz: Just rote rejection slips.

I didn't do a lot of [submitting]. Probably *This Week,* which was another market, and *Collier's.* I don't recall sending them to the *New Yorker,* when I was at this stage, because I knew it was hopeless. So I didn't try that. A lot of amateurs do, of course. But that's a brutal business. I used to get my mail at my Dad's barber shop when I came home from Art Instruction School. We lived around the corner from the shop.

I'd open the envelope, and there'd be a little note that would say, "Here's an OK for you." The whole world suddenly became bright and cheery. But if it said, "Sorry, nothing this week," then it was so depressing. [laughs] That's why I was so glad when I finally sold the comic strip for every idea that I had thought of was used. And have a change of pace. I think a comic strip is very important to have a change of pace. That's why I have such a good group, I've got a repertory company. And I can do things that are really stupid, and give them to Snoopy, things that are really corny, kind of dumb. But they become funny because Snoopy doesn't realize how corny and dumb they are. Or else he and Woodstock will say something which is just silly and they'll laugh and laugh and they'll fall off the doghouse on their heads or something. I like to do things like that. Just slapstick. And then try to do things that are more meaningful. A really good range of ideas. And I've said that almost everything that I think of somehow can be turned into a cartoon idea. I'm not restricted in the ideas. I can go in any direction that I want to go.

Groth: And doing that also gives you a great latitude in terms of visuals.
Schulz: Oh yeah. Visuals are extremely important. I think a lot of cartoonists these days have gotten away from that. It's the basis of what

cartooning is. I've been quoted on this many times, that cartooning is still drawing funny pictures. If you don't draw funny pictures, then you might as well be writing for live television or some other form of entertainment. But visuals were extremely difficult. I think you can run out to the end very quickly. That's what worries me lately, as I turn 75 in a couple of months, that I might have done so many things with so many situations. How many funny pictures can you get out of Snoopy looking up and watching the leaf fall out of the tree? And yesterday I think I spent almost the whole afternoon trying to get something funny out of Linus sitting in a cardboard box trying to just slide down the hill. I really like drawing that, and I came up with one idea, but I still can't decide if it's funny enough or not. So I abandoned it. I finally went into a totally different direction. But there's so many things that I really liked having done, I would like to just keep playing on these themes and variations as much as I can. But sometimes I feel like I've run right out to the end and there are no more ideas any more. I'm always amazed when I haven't done something for maybe ten years on something like that and one day I think of one. And then I wonder, "Why in the world didn't I think of that ten years ago?" Why did it take me ten years? This is playing on the same theme, but this is the way it is. And I think this is one of the things you learn about after doing it for so long.

Groth: That's the way I would think the imagination would work on such an organic life's work, where you're working on variations of a handful of themes over the course of a long time.

Schulz: And so much depends upon your own life, too. [laughs] I think critics, and interviewers, forget we still have another life we live.

Groth: The demarcation between *your* life and your work is often blurred because you put so much of your life into your work.

Schulz: Well, yeah, and I find that people who don't know anything about it, friends of ours frequently say, "Oh, I know where you got that idea." And I want to say, "No, you don't." [laughs]

Groth: What you just said about the convergence of ideas and drawings reminded me of something you said about the strip: "The type of humor that I was using did not call for camera angles. I like drawing the characters from the same view all the way through, because the ideas were very brief, and I didn't want anything in the drawing to interrupt the flow of what the characters were either saying or doing."

Your respect for what you refer to as the ideas would appear to me to limit the scope of the drawings that you're able to do, and I know you take great joy in drawing. Did you ever want to draw in a way that the strip itself wouldn't allow?

Schulz: I would like to, but it's too late. I've locked myself into this drawing style, and I can't escape from it. And I think it would be a mistake of course to do it because I think for me to draw the way Hank Ketcham used to draw just wouldn't work. Hank was drawing panels from wonderful different camera angles, reflections in mirrors and things like that. Which simply would never work in my strip. For one thing, it would make everything too realistic. And *Dennis the Menace* is pretty realistic. He even said to me once on the golf course—we were playing in the AT&T together. We didn't get a chance to talk very much, but one day we were talking about the features and he said, "Your strip is really more of a fantasy, isn't it?" And I said, "Yeah, I guess maybe it is." [laughs] I didn't know he had even thought about it.

© by United Feature Syndicate, Inc.

Groth: Did you admire the *Dennis the Menace* panel?
Schulz: I admire the drawing tremendously, yeah. But I don't like annoying little kids. [laughter]

Groth: Are you friends with Hank Ketcham?
Schulz: I'd like to think so. We don't know each other that well, we've never spent a lot of time together. Those three days on the golf course at the tournament was the most we had ever spent, but even then we didn't get to talk very much. We were too busy playing.

The cartoonist whom I feel I know the best these days probably would be Lynn Johnston.

Groth: It doesn't seem like the cartooning community is very close-knit. Because Ketcham, as far as I can tell, is almost your exact contemporary.

Schulz: Yeah, yeah. Of course, he got started much quicker than I did. He and Gus Arriola both worked for Disney and so were quite accomplished before they even began [drawing strips]. Ketcham was also a successful gag cartoonist before I ever got started. Gus Arriola had worked for Disney; he was drawing *Gordo* before the war, and then he picked it up after the war. Gus is a little bit older than I am.

Groth: When you were growing up, you were a real aficionado of both comic books and newspaper strips.

Schulz: Gee, I used to buy every comic book that used to come out; I bought every Big/Little book that came out. I got the first copy of *Famous Funnies.* Some friend tore the cover off once. I lost a lot of things in a fire that took place in a big apartment building where my Dad and I lived. I had a big box of Big/Little books that was stored down in the basement in some storeroom. Lost them all. The fire department came in and flooded the basement. So I have no idea what things I even used to have.

Groth: I know that you were a big fan of comic books, but you never seemed interested in being a comic book artist as opposed to a gag panel artist or a strip cartoonist.

Schulz: Yeah, yeah. In fact, we have to skip all the early days, because they were strictly amateur days. Back before . . . it's almost as if your life goes in little sections. And I got almost no encouragement in school and high school. Drawing was almost looked down upon and cartooning really was looked down upon. I can still remember, for some strange reason in the 7th grade, it had something to do with social studies, and the teacher, amazingly enough, brought up political or editorial cartoons. She had a few people just monkey around with them. And I drew the best one, and she liked them. I don't know what she was going to do with them, maybe she was going to have them printed in some newspaper or something like that. But she actually took my cartoon and gave it to another kid in class, to have him go over the lines to make them darker. And I was appalled and insulted by this, but I didn't dare say anything. But, you know, what a dumb thing to do. [laughs] Sometimes teachers aren't very smart.

Anyway, that was my first inkling of any kind of encouragement. And then, when I got into high school, of course, high school was a total disaster for me. As was junior high school. I just failed everything. I hated the whole business. And in English once, I don't know if it was Shakespeare or what it was we were reading, but we had to do some kind of a project on what it was we were reading. And I remember thinking that I could make some drawings about this—and this may seem hard to believe, but I actually thought, "Well, this wouldn't be fair." Because the other kids in the class can't draw. So why should I take advantage of something I can do that they can't? So I didn't do it. And some other kid in the class made some nice watercolors. He must have made about ten of them, about the thing that we had been studying. And afterwards, the teacher—I don't know how she ever knew that I could draw—but she said, "Charles, why didn't you do something like that?" [laughter]

And I never explained why I didn't, either. But that was just another blow.

Groth: You learned something there.
Schulz: Oh, I learned something—I learned a lot. I learned several lessons in school, very important lessons, too, along that line. Then, of course, my greatest triumph was that book of drawings of things in threes that was reprinted in *Peanuts Jubilee.* The teacher—I guess, you know about that—she held mine up as an example. Because I batted out that whole page in about five minutes while the other kids were struggling just making three or four drawings. All the way through school, I can remember I was, if not always the best, at least one of the two or three few that could draw reasonably well. I couldn't draw *really* well, but I could draw better than most people. I was the first kid to figure out how to draw a hole in the ice. Because in Minnesota, we always had to draw something that we did at Christmas vacation, we always drew kids skating. And everybody drew a hole in the ice with the sign that said "Danger" or something like that. But the kids didn't know how to draw a hole in the ice, they just made a black spot, but I was the first one to discover how to show some thickness to the ice, because I had read it in cartoons and comic books, and the teacher looked at this one day, and she was amazed that I should've drawn something like that.

But then when I was a senior, the teacher asked me one day to draw some cartoons of things around school, which I did and I gave them to her. When the high school annual came out, I looked through it anxiously, and they hadn't printed them at all. That was a crushing blow. That was my first major rejection. During that period, I was taking the Art Instruction correspondence course, which was called Federal Schools at that time. A salesman came out to the house one cold winter night, I can still remember him coming up on the cold-storm-doored porch. So we signed up for the course, which I think cost $160, and my dad had to pay for it at a rate of $10 a month. Even at that, he struggled to make the payments. But I didn't have anything to do after graduating. I would stay home and work on the correspondence course. I never always had the right materials to draw on, either. Paper was expensive. I would sometimes go downtown to St. Paul to a big art store and I'd buy maybe two sheets of smooth-ply Strathmore. That's all I could afford. And I was experimenting with craftint double tone because of what Roy Crane was doing with it. But I could only afford maybe one sheet, because it cost 75 cents. And I could only get maybe three strips out of it. I rarely had good paper to work on. But I was always drawing something.

I used to draw a series of, like, *Believe it or Not!* panels, mostly about golf. I had become a golf fanatic, and I was drawing a lot of golf cartoons. Then when I was a senior in high school, I was also a Sherlock Holmes fanatic, and I read every Sherlock Holmes story that was ever written. I would buy a scrapbook at the dime store. And I would draw my own Sherlock Holmes stories, filled this whole scrapbook, just like it were a big comics magazine. The only person who ever read it was a friend of mine who lived up the street and around the corner named Shermy who was a violinist, and I'd go listen to him practice the violin now and then, and he would read my Sherlock Holmes stories. Nobody else ever read them.

So I filled up several books doing that. But in the meantime, I started to send in gag cartoons, mainly to *Collier's* and the *Post,* I suppose. Never sold any. My dad would take them for me in the morning to the Post Office, which was near the barber shop, with a stamped self-addressed envelope, and then they'd come back the next week. I was collecting a lot of rejection slips, never even coming close. But I studied gag cartooning very carefully. And one of my first jobs was working as a delivery boy for a direct mail advertising company in Minneapolis. And with one of my first paychecks, which was $14, I bought a collection of *Collier's* gag cartoons called *Collier's Collects Its Wits.* And I still have it. I used to read that book over and over and over, just loved looking at all the gag cartoons, and I can still remember some of the punchlines. So I was willing to be a gag cartoonist. I hadn't really decided what direction I was going to go. And I was also drawing comic strips of my own. And of course I was a great *Wash Tubbs and Captain Easy* fan, and I would send things in and get them rejected.

I became fascinated by the Foreign Legion, too. I read everything about *Beau Geste*, and the others that he had written. And I used to draw Foreign Legion strips. And then, lo and behold—I might still have been in high school, I'm not sure—my mother had read in the paper something about a cartooning class downtown in St. Paul in a great big building which was an extension of the University of Minnesota. So I went down, and I signed up for it. There was a young man teaching the class, who had a small comic strip running in our local paper. And he was pretty good, a very nice fellow, and so I signed up for it, and he told us what equipment to bring the next week, we had to bring a drawing board, and some ink, and some pencils, and pens . . . So the first night there he had some large pieces of paper tacked to the wall. And I distinctly remember that one of them was Dagwood and I don't remember what the other characters were. But he just asked each of us to copy these characters. I suppose it was a good idea just to see what level of ability each one of us had. And of course, I was used to drawing those things, because I had drawn and copied those comic characters all my life. So I just went through them like nothing. And I was done in a matter of about four or five minutes. Way ahead of everybody else. Much better than everybody else. But there was the prettiest little girl I had ever seen sitting two chairs away from me. And I wanted so much to talk to her. But there was some idiot little kid there who kept drawing Bugs Bunny and saying that it was his character. And I'd get so mad at this kid, because he had the nerve to talk to her, and I didn't. And I never did talk to her. I just didn't have the nerve.

But one time, he wanted us to each start a special project and I had drawn a Foreign Legion comic strip. And of course, having the correspondence school background, I had learned to letter very neatly and render neatly, and he showed it to her. I can still remember—isn't that something? Something that happened so many years ago—and I can remember sitting there, and he showed it to her, and she looked at it, and said, "Oh, that's so neat." [laughs] I was so flattered, but I still didn't have the nerve to talk to her.

Groth: You would have been around 16 or 17.

Schulz: I would have been 17, I guess. Six years later I had a date with her. Isn't that astounding? [laughter] After the war.

Groth: Congratulations.

Schulz: Now she's dead. Now she's dead, and it saddens me terribly. But anyway, that was the struggle I was going through, all before the War. And then the war came along, and I remembered going up to the service club one Sunday afternoon, as we used to do if we had some time off, just to have a good lunch and dinner, and upstairs in one of the rooms, they had an exhibition this one week of original gag cartoons from different magazines. And I stood there, and walked around the room and looked at them, and I was admiring so much the quality of the drawing and the rendering of these things, and I was thinking, "When in the world am I ever going to get a chance to do this?" The War is still going on, and none of us knew if we were going to return. It was so depressing. [laughs]

But after the War . . . I never got to do anything during the War. I knew I wasn't that good, and I never even tried to send in things to *Yank Magazine* or *Stars and Stripes* or anything like that. But after the War, I returned home and my Dad and I lived in this apartment with a couple of waitresses who worked in the restaurant nearby. We shared the apartment with them. I went over to Art Instruction, in Minneapolis, and showed some of my work to Frank Wing, who was a wonderful cartoonist of his day. A man named Charles Bartholomew was the head of the cartooning part of the school, and he offered me a job as a temporary replacement for one of the other men who was going on a two-week summer vacation. So I took it. There were about 10 of us in the room there. And then they ended up keeping me on permanently. And so that was the start of a whole new life. Because I was then in a room with people who were very bright, and had a lot of ability in many different directions. A couple of them had been commercial artists, Frank Wing was a good cartoonist, Walter J. Wilweding was in charge of the department. He was a fine animal painter. There was a woman named Mrs. Angelikas who was a practicing fashion artist. She did men's fashions several times a week for the local paper. She was very good. They were all quite cultured. They were all well-read, they all listened to good music. It was a good atmosphere. It was a lot like working for a newspaper, but not quite as hectic. And so I learned a lot being with them, and while I was with them, I had the chance in my off-time to work on some of my own things.

And you mentioned comic magazines. I actually drew three pages of different comic magazine samples. One was a war episode of some men in a half-track, which was autobiographical. Another one was some little characters I called Brownies, who were just cute little fanciful things, and then another jungle type page, and I sent them to some comic magazine in New York, and I got a note saying that they didn't buy freelance work like this, and that all of their work was done by hired people in New York.

I was still going around trying to get jobs. One day I was sent to downtown St. Paul to a Catholic comics magazine. They did *Catholic Digest* and some other things. I took the comic strips that I had, and a man named Roman Baltes looked at 'em and said, "Well, I think I may have something for you. I like your lettering." So I was assigned to letter the entire comics magazine. He had three or four men who were already there on the staff. Somebody else would write the stories, and they would illustrate them. Apparently, they didn't have anybody who could letter comic strips very well so they would give me the original pages, and I would take them home at night and letter all the pages. Sometimes they would give me a French or a Spanish translation, and I would have to letter the whole thing on some kind of see-through paper in these other languages. I never thought of it as being hard work, even though I was doing it in the evening after having spent the day at the correspondence school. I would do these things, and Roman liked the fact that I could do them fast. Sometimes he'd call me up in the late afternoon, and say, "Sparky, I've got five pages here; I'd sure like to have them done tomorrow morning." So I would either take the street car or my Dad's car and drive downtown. He'd leave them outside the office. I'd pick them up, take them home, sit in the kitchen and letter them. The next morning I'd get up early, drive downtown, leave them outside his office and then go on to the correspondence school. Now that may sound like Abraham Lincoln, but to me it was what I wanted to do.

And so I became very good at lettering. I could letter very fast, I got so I didn't need guidelines or spacing or anything.

That was a good training for me.

Groth: Can I ask you about ten questions based on what you've said so far?

Schulz: Please.

Groth: You mentioned going to the correspondence school and meeting all of these people who were involved in music and art and so on. Would you say that they represented an opening up of your world? Did that environment invigorate your curiosity about

© by United Feature Syndicate, Inc.

art? Was this an atmosphere you hadn't really experienced as fully before?

Schulz Oh, definitely. It was almost better than going to art school. Now most of my friends either went or graduated from the Minneapolis School of Art. Which was a fine establishment. And that was one of the first things that I did when I came back from the War—I knew that under the G.I. Bill perhaps I could finally go to a resident art school and take some actual, on-the-spot training. So I went there, and I made a few drawings, which you had to make just to demonstrate if you had any talent. Unfortunately, the administrator there said that I was about two weeks too late. The classes had already started. But then she said, "We do have some nightclasses, if you'd like to do something like that." So I signed up for a life sketching class. And I did that for one semester. I wasn't especially good at it. But that was the first real live training I had had.

So I never really did go to the Minneapolis School of Art. That was about it. The next semester I signed up for another class in just drawing. But I missed two or three classes because I had these other lettering jobs to do. And then I was told that under the G.I. Bill, if you missed three classes, you were out. So that was the end of my training.

Groth: Was that disappointing to you?

Schultz: No, not really. I knew what I wanted to do. But this Art Instruction group of instructors created an invigorating atmosphere. There was always lots of live conversations going on as the people were sitting at their desks. Some dictating responses, others just making corrections.

The only problem became a social problem, in that at the same time I still loved golf, and I had three or four friends with whom I used to caddy and play golf. So on Saturdays, sometimes Sunday afternoons, we would play golf. So that was one group of friends. Then there was a group of friends at the correspondence school, and I became very close with many of them, and that was the second group. And then at this same time, I also became very active in the Church of God movement. I went to a prayer meeting one night—we had some nice discussions—and I went to what they called a young people's meeting, and I enjoyed the discussion. They were very nice people. Now, that put me in three different social groups, and they didn't overlap. They didn't meet. I was never able to solve that.

Groth: You were never able to reconcile—or integrate—these different social strata?

Schulz: I was never able to find the right people in these things so I could concentrate on that. That caused me a lot of trouble.

Groth: In what way?

Schulz: Well, in . . . say if I liked a certain girl for instance, maybe she was with the correspondence school, but then I didn't have any girl-friends in the church group. And of course the golf kids were foreign completely to church and art and cartooning. So nothing worked. [laughs]

Groth: They didn't connect.

Schulz: Nothing connected. That made it very awkward.

Groth: It sounds like you sort of blossomed about this time. You've talked a lot about how shy you were as a kid and how you weren't really socially acclimated, but it appears as though you started traveling among three different social settings; it almost looks like you turned into a bit of a social gadabout. [laughter]

Schulz: I think shyness is an illusion. I think stupidity is a better reason. I think shyness is the overtly self-conscious, thinking that you're the only person in the world. That how you look and what you do is of any importance. Not realizing if you just get out and do something and talk to people, you don't have to be shy. It's just being overly self-conscious.

Groth: You said that when you were in high school, cartooning was looked down upon. And I wonder if you had a theory as to why that was. Was there a kind of middle class propriety involved, where cartooning was considered disreputable . . . ?

Schulz: I think it was the teachers' fault. I think . . . music teachers were the worst of all. Music teachers were the meanest. Art teachers were always pretty nice. But they weren't capable of either doing cartooning themselves, or even appreciating it. And they had to bring the whole class down to the lowest denominator. Because these weren't kids that especially were going to be artists, or even interested in it, but they had to create projects that would interest the whole class. So you ended up having to make posters, or doing watercolors of flowers or silly things like that, which just drove me out of my mind. [laughs] You never got to do any drawing, it was always some kind of project. Even linoleum cutting—which I never got into. I was glad I never had to do that. But as far as drawing goes, we rarely got to do any real drawing. It just had to have been the teacher's fault.

Groth: You referred to your stint in the army, and I think you said you didn't do much drawing in the army. You once said, "I just wasn't ready, and I think Bill Mauldin's work made me realize it." You also said, "The truth is I abandoned drawing during my years of army service." Was looking at Mauldin's work so intimidating you felt you were unprepared?

Schulz: It wasn't intimidating. I just wasn't even close to being able to do it. Plus the fact that after a while, we worked very hard at being good soldiers. I went in never having been away from home. Not knowing what it would be like to live with 200 men in the same building. And I can remember the first time I sat next to a water-cooled machine gun and heard that thing fire. Oh, man, it was so loud and shocking. And then the first time we had to dismantle a light machine gun I thought, "I'll never learn how to do this." I had no mechanical ability. I had never seen a gun in my life.

But as the months went by, and as we developed more in our training, and went on maneuvers and all that, I finally got to be squad leader of a light machine gun squad. We all worked very hard at being good soldiers. And we took great pride at being in the infantry. We were in the armored infantry. And to me at that point, even though I still loved cartooning and drawing, and I carried a sketchbook where I made some drawings of friends, I was still very interested in being a good infantryman. We were very proud of what we were.

Which is good, because I look back on it with some hateful memories, but also wonderful memories of the friends we made, and the good guys I knew and all of that. Proud of the fact that we did what we had to do. Somebody asked me just a couple months ago of all the awards you've received, what award are you the most proud of, and all of the sudden it occurred to me: the combat infantry badge. Which is over there on the wall. I'm more proud of having received the combat infantry badge than of having won the Reuben twice. [laughs]

Groth: Can I establish a context for your war experience? You were drafted in the army in 1943. Were you aware of what was at risk in that war, what you were fighting for?
Schulz: Oh yeah. Definitely.

Groth: Weren't you present at the liberation of one of the concentration camps?
Schulz: No . . . not . . . quite.

We spent the night out in a field—I don't remember if it was raining, but it was awfully cold and misty that night. I think there was a big swamp out in front of us. They said that we had to be ready because there may be a counter-attack by the SS. But it never happened. So the next morning, soon as the sun came up, we moved out. And then, that day, they told us that Dachau had been discovered. Part of our division was in on that. But we had gone on towards Munich. So we never saw it ourselves. But at least we were there.

Groth: Now, correct me if I'm wrong, but it seems that prior to your going into the army, you led a pretty sheltered life with your family in the city of St. Paul, so going to war must have been a tremendous, an almost inconceivable break from that kind of life.
Schulz: It was. It was a terrible experience.

Groth: You referred earlier to hateful memories.
Schulz: Well, just being in the army was such a desperate feeling so often. Of loneliness, and of the fear that it was never going to end. We

used to sit sometimes in the evening talking, and we'd say, "They're never going to let us out. We're in this for the rest of our lives. Where's it all going to end?" It was so depressing.

But I did make a lot of really good friends. Unfortunately, many of them have died. However, my best friend is still alive. He's 85 years old now. He was our mortar squad leader, and I was a machine gun squad leader. He was like a big brother to me. He really kept me going.

But I suppose . . . you know, the whole world was at war. It was something that had never happened before, and undoubtedly, I think, will never happen again.

Groth: When you came home from the war, did you feel transformed?
Schulz: I felt good. [laughter]

Groth: But was going through that a transformative experience?
Schulz: Yes . . . it was . . . I came home on the train. I don't know where I got discharged, from what camp it was. A duffel bag on my shoulder, the streetcar pulled up in front of my dad's barber shop. I put the duffel bag on my shoulder and got off the back of the street car. Walked around, crossed the street, into the barber shop. He was working on a customer. [laughter]

That was my homecoming. There was no party. Nothing.

© by United Feature Syndicate, Inc.

Groth: A little anti-climactic.
Schulz: Yes, it was. I look back on it, and I think, "Well, that was robbery. I didn't get to be in a parade, no one gave me a hug, or anything like that." But I felt very good about myself those days. The other friends that I had that I golfed and caddied with were all coming home at the same time. None of us had any jobs. In those days, you could join what they called a 52-20. If you didn't have a job, the government gave you $20 a week for 52 weeks. So most of us belonged to the

52-20 club, at least for a few months. We played a lot of golf. We had an early spring in Minnesota at that time. It was kind of a carefree life for a while. My cousin had just come back from the Marines, and he and I used to go bowling. Different things like that.

I still had some relatives around that I was very close to. But that all gradually just fell apart, as everybody went finding their different directions.

Groth: Was there a sense of post-War euphoria?
Schulz: No, not that I recall. Nobody even thought much about it.

Groth: You once said, "the three years I spent in the army taught me all I need to know about loneliness."
Schulz: Yes.

Groth: "And a sympathy for the loneliness that all of us experience was dropped heavily on poor Charlie Brown."
Schulz: Oh, it was terribly lonely in camp a lot of times, because you were just totally trapped. You just didn't want to be there. And I suppose I might have had an approaching agoraphobia which I still suffer from to these days in different degrees. Which made it even worse. But a lot of the truth has to do with maturity and immaturity. If a person were totally mature, and had a good outlook on life, he could make good use of experiences like that. You could have gotten a weekend pass and gone into town, done some sightseeing, or met some people. There's a thousand things you could have done. But when you're 20 years old, how do you know that? So you're not able to make use of it.

Groth: Although you made use of it later by transforming that intense feeling of loneliness into art.
Schulz: [laughs] Yeah, yeah. [pause] What a waste of time. [laughs]

Groth: How do you mean?
Schulz: To spend all of your life drawing your comic.

Groth: You don't really mean that, do you?
Schulz: Sure.

Groth: How do you mean that? I would think you'd feel exactly the opposite.
Schulz: Well, you know: what have you done? Drawn a comic strip. Who cares. [laughs] Now I'm 75 years old.

Groth: But don't you feel like you have an enormous achievement behind you, a lasting legacy because of that achievement?

Schulz: No. [laughs] Because I know that I am not Andrew Wyeth. And I will never be Andrew Wyeth. But the only thing I'm proud of is that I think I've done the best with what ability I have. I haven't wasted my ability. A lot of people wasted their ability, their talents, they don't know how to do with what they have. I'm pleased with what I have done, I haven't destroyed it, I haven't misused it in any way.

Groth: Let me try and nail you down on that, because you must be very proud of what you've done. You must know you've reached the pinnacle of your profession.

Schulz: I know, it's hard to believe. I'm amazed when I read *Cartoonists Profiles* and other magazines where young cartoonists are interviewed, and they mention my name as being one of their inspirations. That just astounds me.

Groth: Why should it?

Schulz: I don't know what it was that inspired them. I have no idea. Except that I took a unique approach, as the strip developed. I think I did things that no one else had ever done.

Groth: If I may say so, I think it's because you conveyed the depth of your humanity in the comic strip. And that's a relatively rare phenomenon in cartooning.

Schulz: You do some things that it's better you don't think about. [laughs] You can dig your own grave by thinking you're better than you really are.

Groth: I think one of the reasons *Peanuts* resonates so profoundly is because of your intense connection to your youth and to your childhood, especially that which was hurtful or painful. Your biographer wrote of you, "Schulz is capable of sitting at his drawing board and recalling, in all earnestness, a disappointment experienced in pre-school. Not just remember it, but feeling it. His own emotional jurisdiction is immense. For him personally, there are no significant boundaries between adulthood and childhood. Not in terms of what's just, what thrills, and what hurts. Especially what hurts. A man who's built a comic empire around the skeleton of his own life is not a man to look back and laugh." [Schulz laughs]

And now, of course, you're laughing. Do you agree with that?

Schulz: Oh, sure.

Rheta [Johnson] was a great lady. We got along so well, right from the moment I was introduced to her on the phone and I heard her southern accent. I think we almost fell in love right away. She came here, and sat where you are now for three days. We walked back and forth to the [ice] arena and talked. And we had a good time. We became very close friends. I think she put that very well.

But again, those are things that I don't think a creator thinks of. All you're trying to do is fill in those squares. Do something good for Monday, and then do something good for Tuesday, and then you do something for Wednesday. Where does it all come from? I think you can tell that some cartoonists have no moments of reflection at all. Or else they don't use it. You hate to say they're not sensitive. I don't think I'm more sensitive than anybody else. But I suppose I just have a knack for coining phrases that can be memorable.

Groth: You've railed against cartooning that is too hyperkinetic, and your own drawing, and the rhythms of your storytelling, had to be subtle enough to convey your experience.

Schulz: Drawing is very important. To draw, you have to have a pretty good sense of design so that the drawings are pleasant to look at. This is what made Bill Watterson so good, he drew so well. Cartooning really is just designing. It's a lot like Picasso on paintings. Take the shape of Charlie Brown's head . . . If a cartooning style is too extreme, the artist can never do or say anything that is at all sensitive. A character that is overly cartooned, cannot say anything that's very sensitive. If you look back upon all of the great comic strips down through the years, every one of them was drawn in a style that was relatively quiet. It can be outrageously funny and it can be sad, as long it's not overly cartooned. It depends on which direction you want to go.

Groth: You certainly prefer the direction of subtlety; the last panel of your strips is usually a masterpiece of understatement. You spoke very rapturously about drawing. You said, "I am still searching for that wonderful pen line that comes down when you are drawing Linus standing there, and you start with the pen up near the back of his neck, and you bring it down and bring it out, and the pen point fans a little bit, and you come down here and draw the lines this way for the marks on his sweater. This is what it's all about—to get feelings of depth and roundness, and the pen line is the best pen line you can make. That's what it's all about."

Schulz: Where'd you read that?

Groth: That's from the NCS Convention keynote speech.
Schulz: I got all done and I got a standing ovation. I couldn't figure it out. I was *stunned.* I thought, "What have I said that was so important?" They all stood and applauded. I guess nobody had ever really talked to the entire society in that manner. And somebody taped it, and they reprinted it.

© by United Feature Syndicate, Inc.

Groth: Could you elaborate on what you feel constitutes an aesthetically-pleasing line and the satisfaction you derive from creating that?
Schulz: I suppose it's as difficult as explaining what a poem is about. Look at Linus's hair, there [showing Groth a daily he'd just completed]. See? Every stroke is perfect. If it were too shiny or something, it wouldn't have that nice quality. Look at Peppermint Patty's hair. See, the lines . . . those are good lines, and that's what I'm talking about. The little fingers, the way they go that way, too. Those are nice little fingers. [laughs] And the same way, too. Those are little Picasso-like fingers, and that's important.

You can get depth from doing that, and interest. You talk about the line that comes down around the back of Linus's shirt. If it went straight down, like a lot of people would to, it loses its life. I guess in painting, you would call it its paint quality.

Groth: It has life to it. It has spontaneity.
Schulz: Life to it. Yes.

Groth: The strokes in the hair that you showed me, it looks like what you were after was a messy look, which is different from sloppiness.
Schulz: Yes, I don't pencil in. I draw it with the pen.

Groth: Is that right?
Schulz: I block in, so that I'll get them in the right place, and the right size, but I draw that face with the pen when I'm doing it. Because you want that spontaneity, you don't want to be just following the pencil line. You don't "ink in." Some people do ink in, but should be drawing with the pen while they're doing it.

Groth: You do very little underdrawing.
Schulz: I do as little as possible. Just enough to make sure that I get the heights and the space right.

Groth: I think Ralph Steadman told me the same thing. In fact, when I told him that most American comic artists actually pencil everything in and then ink it, he was at a loss as to why anyone would do that.
Schulz: Now refresh me as to who he is.

Groth: Ralph Steadman is the English illustrator, the cartoonist . . . he's illustrated a lot of Hunter S. Thompson's book. He has a very slashing style.
Schulz: The English cartoonist who draws those funny ponies and little girls is Thelwell. He can draw anything. He's really wonderful.

Groth: You once said, "I was a great student of pen techniques back when I worked at Art Instruction. The author of the original cartoon course was Charles Bartholomew, and he used to send out what he called 'Bart Pen Demonstrations,' which was a little card that had three sets of pen lines, very thin, medium, and thick, all done with the same pen. My friend and I used to practice making those when we had nothing else to do. We used to see if we could do three sets of perfect pen lines, with a space between the pen lines, narrower than the line itself."

Schulz: Yeah, like a surgeon. Uh-huh.

Groth: Could you talk a little about how much time and effort you took to master your craft so that you could express exactly what you wanted to express? I think that's very important.

Schulz: I won't say it was as calculating as it might have been if I had been going to medical school and becoming a surgeon or anything, but it was certainly something I was aware of in everything I drew. And the correspondence school did place a strong emphasis on pen technique as it did upon good lettering and things like that. And the samples that they had in their textbooks were samples of cartoonists who had a marvelous pen technique. And the man who sat in front of me when I finally started to work there and who had been one of my teachers was Frank Wing, and he had a wonderful pen technique. He drew beautifully in the cartoons that he had done. So I was a great admirer of—we always mention Percy Crosby, I can't think of anybody else right now—well, Charles Dana Gibson, the Gibson Girl. Beautiful pen. He did more than just draw with the pen, he painted with the pen, didn't he? He did more than just outline the figures. If you looked at a blowup of some of the girls' faces that he drew, he could create the features with a little tiny cross-hatches and things like that, and he molded the pen line in a marvelous way. And I've never been able to do that. But that was really, to me, the ultimate. Now, unfortunately, it doesn't mean a thing.

Groth: How do you mean that?

Schulz: Well, people are drawing comic strips that have no pen technique at all, and I think the lowest form is to draw them with a felt pen. How in the world are you going to have a good pen technique drawing with a felt pen? [Groth laughs] That's absurd. You're just missing the whole point.

Groth: Did you ever master a brush?

Schulz: Yes. Actually, I was very good with the brush when I was still working at the correspondence school. I had drawn a series of panel cartoons which were quite large, about a little girl named Judy and I remember taking about 15 of them to Chicago and I showed them around to some of the syndicates, and my brush technique was pretty good. I used a medium-surface Strathmore, but then when I sold the *Peanuts* strip, and I had to draw these four panels, I want-

ed a tighter style. My whole approach requires a tighter style of
drawing in most cases. Now and then, when I draw some violent
action or something like that, the style is a little more loose. But
that's all right. But a brush style generally from day to day wouldn't
work for me.

Groth: Peppermint Patty's hair that you just pointed out to me, was that inked with a pen or a brush?
Schulz: That's a pen.

Groth: O.K. So primarily you use a pen in the strip today.
Schulz: Yeah. Definitely.

Sometimes I go back and forth, like right in front of me now I have Charlie Brown standing with a jacket on, and he's got long winter pants on. They're going to be black. But I may scribble in some pen lines and make it black, or I may just be lazy or go for a different technique of just putting it in with a brush. I don't know what I'll do.

Groth: Talking about drawing, your biographer wrote, "He will argue that the drawing within a comic strip is more important than the writing. It is, he insists, what makes a cartoonist a cartoonist. If Schulz feels *Peanuts* is getting too wordy or if he's having trouble writing a good joke, or if he just hasn't been up to standard of late, he will deliberately return to slapstick, depicting a visual absurdity that's simply fun to look at." I was wondering if, being a cartoonist, you can really separate the writing from the drawing that easily. In a way, I think that you can forget that *Peanuts* is drawn because in an odd sort of way the drawing has become a kind of handwriting. Neither the drawing nor the writing dominate because it's such a densely conceptual strip, so it's interesting that you would say that the drawing is more important than the writing since they both work in such perfect harmony.
Schulz: Well, you really shouldn't believe anything that I've said. [Groth laughs] A lot of times, I have to say things just to explain something. I think you can look at the comic page these days and see that there's not really much interesting drawing going on. Now, the writing obviously is important. But I'm sure that the writing has placed my strip aside from a lot of others, due to the things I've written, the phrases that I've coined and all of that. But it's a mistake to eliminate drawing. There are a few collaborative efforts these days that are doing well. If the person can draw. Now Jerry Scott, has the advantage . . . he writes *Baby Blues* and the new teenage one, *Zits*, because *Zits* is beautifully drawn. Anyway, Scott can draw. If the person who is doing the creating can't draw, and even if it's an adventure strip, the creating is hampered. This is where cartooning separates itself from other mediums, because we can do things that live action can't do.

And I suppose one of the best examples of that is how it would happen now and then. I'll be sitting here trying to think of something funny, and I think of Snoopy and his troops going out on a hike. So I think, "Well, what are they going to do at night? They're going to sleep." So I draw tents like this. Now, what's the next step? Bang, all of the sudden the next step is that Snoopy is sleeping on top of the tent. Everybody else would be in the tent. There's your cartoon idea. And that's funny drawing. If you can't do that, I don't know where you're going to go. Then you can think about it again. Now the birds are sleeping on the ropes that go down from the tent. That's another idea. And you go from one thing to another.

Groth: Comics seem to me such an organic form that any strip that is written by one person and drawn by another, is going to have a severe disadvantage.

Schulz: Definitely. But you don't dare say that. You'll offend people. [laughs]

Groth: You've said in the past that you work hard not to offend people. Why is that a concern?

Schulz: I don't like to offend people. [laughs] Maybe it's a desire to be liked. Maybe that's the number one reason for not offending people. And I just don't think it's right to offend people. I could never be an editorial cartoonist, because if the governor or somebody took me out to lunch, I'd never be able to do a raunchy cartoon about him. [laughs]

Groth: You have a terrific strip from, I think, the early '60s, where Lucy wrote on the sidewalk, "Charlie Brown is a blockhead." And Charlie Brown asks her, "Why did you write that?" And she said, "Because I honestly, truly believe it. And I had to be completely honest." [Schulz laughs] And in the past panel he said something like, "You know, I kind of admire her integrity." [laughs] And I thought that was an interesting commentary on offense and honesty.

Schulz: I wouldn't do that any more.

Groth: Which wouldn't you do . . . ?

Schulz: I wouldn't even draw that cartoon.

Groth: Because it's too cruel?

Schulz: Yeah. I've gotten older. My strip is much more mild than it used to be.

Groth: It is, it is. I couldn't help but notice that the strips of the '50s and '60s, are much more barbed, more acerbic than they are now.

Schulz: One of the advertising agencies just sent in a rough idea for an animated commercial, and in the last panel, Lucy is saying "Good Grief, Charlie Brown." And I thought, "Oh boy." I haven't used "Good Grief, Charlie Brown" in 30 years. So this person is just drawing on something that I did years ago. Which is why nobody else is ever going to be able to draw the strip. The best they could do is come up, if they're lucky, to where I am now. But they'll never be able to take it into new areas. Because they're not me.

So I think the strip is much more mild. Even the insults that Marcie and Peppermint Patty go through are all done in good humor. They're serious, they get really mad at each other. But nobody ever hits anybody in my strip.

Groth: And you feel that way because you think you've changed over the years.

Schulz: Well, I'm older now. You see, I'm an old person.

Groth: I've read almost 47 years of *Peanuts*.

Schulz: Astounding.

Groth: It is.

And your creativity seems to spring not just from pain but from an intensely felt and specific recollection of pain. From what I've been able to discern, you almost seem most creatively alive when feeling pain, or musing on pain. For example, in virtually every interview I've read with you, and every biography or autobiography, you mention—and you mentioned it earlier in this interview without any prompting from me—the time when you did the drawings for that high school yearbook that were not used. So you obviously still really feel deeply about that incident.

Schulz: Oh yeah. If you're besieged with all sorts of family problems, then you have this schedule to keep up. If you have illness in the family, and you know you're going to have to draw four strips the next day, and you don't have any ideas at all, that's when it gets brutal. But what still astounds me is how you can get up in the morning, have no ideas at all, and almost dread going to the studio, and then suddenly while you're driving along, you think of something. And I can never figure out how that happens. I suppose that's what makes you what you are.

In that book up there [pointing to his bookshelf], *Caesar and Christ*, Will Durant says about the Apostle Paul, "he had to be what he was to do what he did." And I think this is the way it is with all of us. People say, "Well, how in the world can you just sit there and think of those ideas every day?" One of the reasons is that I have no desire to go anyplace else. If I was the kind that was obsessed with having to go to Australia or Nepal or Japan or something like that, then sitting here doing these things would be a real chore, wouldn't they? I'm where I want to be. I don't want to be anyplace else. So I'm perfectly content to come here. I love going to the arena in the morning, having an English muffin, a cup of coffee, reading the paper and talking to my friends there. I look forward to that every day. And I resent it when these moments out of the week are taken from me. I'm satisfied with just a five-day work week. But I'm never allowed a five-day work week. I have continual interruptions.

Groth: I'm feeling guilty right now.
Schulz: No. That's the way it is. It's been this way for 30 years.

Groth: Now, it occurs to me that part of you must enjoy engaging in those kinds of business activities. Otherwise you would turn it off.
Schulz: I don't mind the interviews. Well . . . no. A lot of it you can't turn off. I'll bet I can name you 50 people right now whose phone messages I can't turn down. You just have to. They're good, decent people. [laughs] And I have to answer the phone. Now, short interviews by newspapers and things like that are almost relaxing to me. I'm getting so I can't sit at the drawing board and draw any more hour after hour. I had a friend of mine who could do that. As long as he had a package of cigarettes sitting next to him, he could sit at the drawing table and never get up. Just draw until noon. And then we'd play pool, have a hamburger, and then he could draw all afternoon. I haven't seen him now in years. But I can't do that any more. That's why I don't mind answering the phone.

Groth: Do you almost regret, because of all the distractions, the scope of your enormous success?
Schulz: Have I had enormous success? Do you think so?

Groth: Well, it's just a shot in the dark, but I think so. Yeah [laughter]
Schulz: I suppose.

Groth: I don't know what to make of the modesty you convey in the many, many interviews I've read with you, a modesty that is almost hard to believe. [Schulz laughs] You're probably the most successful cartoonist in the world.

Schulz: The highest paid.

Groth: Well, yes, the highest paid, but also the most recognizable. The most widely-disseminated.

Schulz: Oh, there's no doubt about it. This is what amuses me, when I read about some other people, some entertainer, and they say, "Yeah, he's sold nine million books." Or nine million this or something like that. And I want to say, "Do you realize that they tell me *Peanuts* is read by an estimated 200 million people? What else has ever done that? What else . . . ? Nobody in the history of the world has ever had 200 million readers every day." [laughs]

Groth: So you are aware of your success.

Schulz: I suppose. But, success doesn't cover everything. While you're enormously successful in one area, other people don't even know you exist and regard what you do as "I don't know, I never read the funny pages." It's a low art form. It really is. In spite of people who have tried to say, "Oh no, it isn't." But to many people it really is. We don't hang in art galleries. We're not good enough. We're good if they want us to donate four originals so they can auction them off to support their art galleries. "Fine," that's what I tell them, "sure, that's great. But you would never hang my comic strips in your gallery, would you?"

"Oh, well, uh . . . I guess we've never thought about it."

"Oh, sure. Because it's not good enough." It's not art.

Groth: Do you really resent that?

Schulz: Sure.

If you take this . . . if this [pointing to a large representational painting on the wall] were just a big white canvas with a black streak through it, I'm better than that person. But I know I'm not Andrew Wyeth. I never will be Andrew Wyeth. And I wish that I were. He is what I call, what I admire . . . the perfect artist, because he can do everything that he wants. But from reading his biography a few months ago, I realize even he gets torn apart. "Oh, Andrew Wyeth is just an illustrator. He's not even an artist." I read a review of his biography. Can you imagine some reviewer, he's reviewing the book, the biogra-

phy, saying, "Of course, we know that Andrew's not a real artist."
What kind of review is that? You're supposed to be reviewing the
book, not whether Wyeth is an artist or not. Anyway, those are the
things that everybody goes through, whether you're an actress, a
singer, a violinist or a ballplayer. I suppose we're all hero worshippers of
different kinds. I've been a golfer ever since I was 16. And I would love
to have won the National Open. Or to have played in the Master's.
And I've played with a lot of the big pros, and I know people like John-
ny Miller and the others. I know them very well. I think it would have
been great to do something like that. To watch Willie Mays when he
played baseball—probably the greatest player who ever lived. To watch
some of the hockey players, or to go to a concert and see a violinist
performing, or a pianist playing a Brahms concerto or something like
that. I feel sorry for the people then, that have to live through that, but
have nothing of their own. At least I can say, "Well, I have my own
career that gives me satisfaction. I know that I've done something,
too." Now, that's something I mention very seldom because people just
don't always understand it.

So I suppose that's one of the values of success. One of the things
that helped. And I was still regarded as kind of a nothing person. To
think that I've done this, considering that everybody thought that I
would never amount to anything [laughs] that's kind of fun, too, to be
able to look back upon it.

But I know my limitations.

Groth: Let me ask you about your attitude towards comics as art. Because you've been somewhat ambivalent on the subject. And I'd like to know what your attitude was when you were still struggling with becoming a professional cartoonist. Did you think of comics as art, and if so, what was your frame of reference for art?

Schulz: I've never known much about art. I've never been a student of art. I've never found it that interesting. And to me, obtaining a comic strip was just the greatest thing in the world. To me. Because that's what I wanted, and that's what I knew I could do. I had no desire to think, "Well, a comic strip would be a good way to make a living so that someday I can be a painter" or something. I had no desire to be anything else. I supposed that would answer that. I hope.

Groth: Well, let me follow up on that. Earlier you spoke of having your range of appreciation broadened when you started hanging around your fellow instructors at Art Institute and that prior to that your conception of art was somewhat provincial or unsophisticated. Yet on the other hand, you obviously had a real appreciation for excellence in cartooning, because the people you looked up to—George Herriman, Percy Crosby, Roy Crane—they were all masters of the form.

Schulz: Yes.

Groth: So, you had an innate understanding of what constituted excellence?

Schulz: Well, at that time it would have been just standard. Those were the ones that everybody liked and admired. Now, I think the correspondence course helped. Because the textbooks that we had were very strong on pen technique and all of that sort of thing. So I began to appreciate good drawing. But art itself still doesn't interest me that much. I admire people that are good artists, I'm just astounded at what they can do. For instance, I did a whole series of lithographs where I would draw the characters in pen and ink, and then I'd have them printed on watercolor paper. Then I'd just slosh in some watercolor. And they were sold around the country. Some of 'em, I'm not too ashamed of. Some I just don't like at all, but when I see the really great watercolorists . . . I'm not going to do any more, because I just don't think they're good enough. And I hate to see somebody pay $800 for something that I did like that. [laughs] I don't mind them paying for the comic strip, because I feel that this is what I do. But I don't like to do other things.

Groth: You've downplayed the possibility that comics are capable of being a mature form of expression. And I'd like to nail your thoughts down on this. You've repeatedly said you don't regard what you're doing as "great art." And you've implied that cartooning is a second rate art. But, I felt that your phrase "great art" stacks the deck a bit.

Schulz: The comic strip artist doesn't have the total freedom, does he, to do what he wants to do because it has to be published. A pure artist can go ahead and paint whatever he wants to paint, and if no one wants to hang it in the gallery, well, who cares? At least he's painted it. But if a comic strip isn't published, then what good has it been? Unless you just want to hang it on the wall or something. So we have to cater to the subscribing newspaper editor which immediately devalues it slightly, doesn't it? Not always. This doesn't mean that some of the best things that we do don't get printed, but also I suppose I'm just being falsely modest or just protecting myself. Because the minute you start talking about what you're doing is art then you're going to get shot down. And I just like to protect myself.

Groth: Well, that was what I was going to ask you. [laughter] Because it does seem to me it does a disservice to the potential of comics because although comics have had a hard time of it, their potential seems much greater than what's been realized.

Schulz: Oh, there's no doubt about it. Unfortunately, I think that other mediums have tended to gain the spotlight on us. We had our greatest attention back in the days when our only competition was radio. And that wasn't much of a competition, really. But when movies came along, and television, then we really were in trouble, because we had to compete with live-action, we had to compete with that big screen . . . all of the things that Charlie Chaplin could do, Laurel and Hardy, and then the other great humorists, you know, it was pretty hard to compete. Not that we couldn't do it. We could. But they got all the attention and we just kind of followed along.

Groth: You just mentioned Chaplin. And I know you were a big movie buff when you were a kid.

Schulz: Oh yeah. Yeah.

Groth: And I wanted to ask you what kind of movies you grew watching. Did you watch Chaplin?

Schulz: Um . . . oddly enough, there weren't that many. We didn't see a lot of Charlie Chaplin. I never became a real Charlie Chaplin fan until I grew up. And my friends and I used to go and see his movies. As kids, I think we appreciated Laurel and Hardy more than anybody. They were really funny. So we used to go to the movies mainly on Saturday afternoon. We loved the cowboy movies, and the *Tarzan* movies, and jungle movies and things like that. They always had a serial—we followed all the serials. And of course, they hadn't started filming *Buck Rogers* at the time, and there weren't any really good animated things. I think the first *Popeye* animation that my cousin and I saw together we thought was just fantastic.

Groth: That would have been Max Fleischer.

Schulz: Yeah. They were really wonderful. So that was what I saw as a kid. Then later on, of course, I used to go to movies all the time, and I used to go a lot by myself. Where my Dad and I lived in the apartment, the theater was only half a block away. So I would see almost every movie that came out. Because I would have nothing to do some evenings, so I would just go to the movies by myself. I can still think of the feeling that I had when I walked out of the theater after having seen *Citizen Kane*. I knew that I had seen something great.

Groth: What was your exposure to art and culture like in your home?

Schulz: Both parents went only to the 3rd grade. I don't recall my Dad ever reading a book. He read the paper every night, when he came home from the barber shop after dinner. Later, I started reading a publication that came out called *Omnibook*. They abridged maybe half a dozen of the latest best-sellers; I loved *Omnibook*, I was just beginning to do a lot of reading. And I remember recommending one of these books to my mother. She read it. She really liked it. It was her first experience ever reading anything. And of course, she didn't live much longer. But, they never read anything.

Groth: If your parents weren't readers, what prompted you to become one?

Schulz: I don't know. Just started in . . . I hated the things we had to read in school. I was astounded when—I don't know if this is the 11th grade or what it was—we had to read Thomas Hardy's *Return of the Native*. And I can still remember saying to one of the other guys: "That was good, wasn't it? Yes." I think they assign things to students which are way over their heads, which destroy your love of reading, rather than leading you to it. I don't understand that. Gosh. So I started reading both the Sherlock Holmes stories and then *Beau Geste* and other Foreign Legion things. This was the time when paperbacks came along, but they were called pocketbooks. They only cost, I think, a dime. Maybe a quarter. And they fit into your pocket. During the War they gave them out for nothing. All wonderful books, all in paperback, and they would just fit in your jacket pocket. So everybody went around with one or two paperbacks in their jacket. We got into reading that way, too. And of course, by the time we went overseas, most of my friends had at least started college. So they had a better education than I had. My assistant squad leader had been a high school teacher, so he was very bright.

Groth: At what point did you start discriminating critically?

Schulz: It would have been after the war when I was working at the correspondence school. That's when I did a lot of reading. That's when I read *War and Peace,* and Scott Fitzgerald. After Joyce and I got married, we only had one car. And when she finally learned how to drive I'd leave the car home for her. And I would walk up two blocks to where the streetcar started, the end of the line, and read all the way downtown, where I had my studio. And I read all four of Thomas Wolfe's novels, riding in the streetcar back and forth. Did a lot of reading in those days. Now I probably read more than ever.

Groth: You introduced your son Monte to such writers as Flannery O'Connor and Carson McCullers and Joan Didion.

Schulz: Yes. You'd like Monte. Monte's very well read, very bright. He's working on a novel now which I have tremendous hopes for.

Groth: One paradox that I can't figure out is that you repeatedly refer to your lack of sophistication. I can't help but think this is some sort of dodge, because you seem to be enormously well-read, and in fact are sophisticated about many things.

Schulz: Up to a certain level. Have you ever been someplace and known that you were really in over your head?

Groth: Sure.

Schulz: It's an awful feeling, isn't it?

Groth: Mm-hm.

Schulz: Listening . . . I find this in listening to people and you discover that they have a bigger vocabulary than you do. Despite the fact that I read a lot, I still don't have a very good vocabulary. Fortunately, you don't have to have one drawing comics. But I have felt over my head many times.

But I also realize that among all the people we know, I am better read than any of them. And most of the guys that I talk to are interested in nothing except who's going to be in the Super Bowl. Which is all right, but now and then, I love spiritual conversation. The best friend that I have now, a new friend, is a man named Father Gary Lombardi, who's a priest in Petaluma. I'm not a Catholic, and I never will be. But he and I have a lot in common . . . we play golf every Thursday together, and we just tease him unmercifully. But I do love talking about spiritual things. I don't care who I talk with about it.

A woman minister comes to the arena now and then, and I love sitting talking with her about things. I just want to know what people think about things. Who do you think Jesus really was? What made him what he was? I want to know what people think. I think it's fascinating.

Groth: Have you read [Norman] Mailer's most recent novel?

Schulz: Monte liked it. He was surprised how much he liked it. But no, it just doesn't interest me. I don't care what Mailer thinks. [laughter] I can think of few people whose opinions interest me less than Norman Mailer. [laughs]

Groth: Now when you referred to spiritual things, you mean metaphysical . . . ?

Schulz: Oh, no, no. Definitely not. I have no interest in metaphysical things. Whatever they may be. Well, that's a whole big subject to get

into. I'd rather not even get into it. All it does is get me a bunch of
nasty letters. Oooh! Speaking of nasty letters, I like nasty letters. This is
the prized one, here [pulling an envelope out of a drawer in his desk].
Although I got a whole stack of 'em.

Groth: What in the world do you get nasty letters about? I can't imagine.

Schulz: Well, listen to this.

> Dear Sir:
>
> Received letter rejecting sending me a large signed drawing of
> Snoopy. I thought you had some caring and compassion for disabled veterans, men who fought in the war for people like you
> who did nothing but make money. What a pity. You can be sure
> that newspapers and veteran groups will be told of your lack of
> caring and lack of patriotism.
>
> God help you. You even had a woman write for you. Why?
> Mrs. Leitel, who wrote to me, says in part, you respond faithfully
> to most requests. Perhaps my Jewish name does it for you. I have
> two purple hearts serving my country. What do you have? Nothing.

[laughs] What an insulting letter, huh? Isn't that awful when you
think that there are people out there who don't know you at all and
they're so self-centered? I can't draw Snoopy for everybody in the
world.

Groth: But a person in your position has to get used to cranks.

Schulz: Oh yeah. I just think it's kind of revealing, that's all. I had a
rabbi write to me several years ago, and he says, "I have a class of
young people, and they were wondering why you did *A Charlie Brown
Christmas* and why you haven't done anything about Hanukkah or
something." And I wrote back and said, "Well, you know, I don't know
anything about Hanukkah." And [after I'd written him] he said my
answer "doesn't satisfy the young people in our class. They just wonder if there isn't a touch of anti-Semitism here." So I thought, "Well,
I'm forced to play my ace in the hole." I said, "You can accuse me of
anti-Semitism, but I was the one that spent that miserable night outside
the swamp there, the night Dachau was discovered." [laughs] And that
ended the conversation. I hated to do it. But I felt that's the only way
to put a stop to this. Because I'm not anti-Semitic or anything. And I

would love to do a Hanukkah show, but they'll never buy one. Besides, let some Jewish cartoonist do it, let Art Spiegelman do it. Or if the Mormons want to do something, let the Mormons do it. That's what Ray Bradbury says. People write to Ray and they say, "Why don't you do this or do that." He says, "Why should I do it? Do it yourself if you want to do it."

You know I did church cartoons for seven years?

Groth: Yes, I knew that.
Schulz: I was the first one to do them, I think.

Groth: Let me segue into that. You were, according to your biography, "born to casual members of the Lutheran church, the largest Protestant Denomination in the world, and one with an old, established hierarchy."
Schulz: Who said that?

Groth: Your biographer. Rheta Johnson.
Schulz: [laughs] I don't think she knows what she's talking about.

I never thought of the Lutheran church as being that enormous. But anyway, go ahead.

Groth: "Sparky found appeal in the small, fervent independent Church of God." Now could you elaborate on your upbringing in the Lutheran Church and how that differed from—
Schulz: I only went to Sunday School for one brief period one summer. With some other little neighborhood kids. Otherwise we almost never went. My dad worked very late every Saturday night, and his only recreation, his only sport, was fishing. It was the only thing—when he had Sunday off, or something to do, he would go fishing. And it never bothered him. Later on, oddly enough, after the War, and after my mother died, he remarried. His wife was Lutheran, and they attended a big church. He got involved so that he was one of the ushers and he would pass the collection plate. He was very proud of that job. And I was always pleased that he did that. I should have told him, but I never did.

But anyway, the Church of God appealed to me in its basic message. It's a non-denominational movement, and I think the message that it had, very strong, which was that—if you want to get into this—is that you did not have to join a denomination. By your belief you were already a follower of the Way. You were already a member of what the New Testament called the Church of God. Paul writes to the Church of God, which is in Corinth, and so on.

Your beliefs and your actions made you a member of the Church of God. And that's what the teaching of this movement is. We had a wonderful minister, I became very close to him. He died a few years ago. I was just wrapped up in it. I was very active. Became very close friends with some other people in it. And that's how that went.

When we moved out here, then there wasn't any [church] that I really went to. But a doctor came by our house and brought us some apples, and invited me to their Sunday School class at the Methodist Church. And like I always do, I speak up too much in those classes, and the next thing I know they invited me to teach a class, which I did for about 10 years. And I just finally figured I'd run out of things to say, let somebody else take over. I would never teach a class again. I'm not a teacher. I kind of like leading discussions, but I don't like teaching anybody.

Groth: Did you feel uncomfortable in that position?

Schulz: I don't feel that I know enough. I'm not obsessed enough with anything to be a teacher. I love the discussions, I took people through the entire Bible, chapter by chapter, three or four times. I find so many people are interested in biblical things, but they've never really studied it. They've probably never even read the Bible. And I just wanted to get them to become acquainted with it. And to make a few connections. I didn't like always having to hear, "Well it seems to me . . . I think maybe it says somewhere in the Bible such-and-such." I want them to be able to know where it says it and why it says it. That was my only purpose. As far as teaching anything, I don't care. I don't even care what they believe. I don't really care what anyone believes as long as they behave well.

Groth: Now, you drew youth-oriented cartoons from 1958 to 1964 that were consolidated into a series of books by Warner Press. Can you tell me something about those? Were they single panel gag cartoons?

Schulz: A fellow named Kenny Hall was editor of their youth magazine, and we became acquainted. He knew what I did. Her asked me to do a panel every two weeks. It took me a while to develop a style. I'm still quite proud of the way they look. But I did things that no one had ever done in church magazines before. It opened up a whole new field. Since then others have followed.

I was the first person ever to draw a nun in a protestant youth magazine. And I was the first person, I think, ever to draw a black per-

son in a cartoon like this. But nobody knows it. I just had so many things to do those days. That two weeks would come around in a hurry, and then I was doing Hallmark cards and I was doing Ford advertisements, helping them to write those commercials and drawing the storyboards. Plus the fact I was growing more and more away from youth meetings by then. I was in my 40s, and I was just going on memories.

Groth: The only time that I've known you to relinquish writing and drawing your characters was for Dell Publishing's comic book version of *Peanuts* in the '50s. I was wondering why you allowed that.
Schulz: Because it gave me a chance to have a couple friends do something.

Groth: Were you satisfied with the results?
Schulz: Only when Jim Sasseville was going them. But it gave me a chance, when we moved out here to California, to have somebody else in the studio to help run to the post office, and to take care of things. And we got, I think, $45 a page, for doing these stories, which enabled them then to earn their salary. They weren't assistants because they never did anything on the [newspaper] strip.

Groth: What did they do?
Schulz: Just things around the studio. Whatever was necessary. But they had to work hard drawing those comic books. We usually had four pages in *Nancy* comics. Eventually we got a 32-page comic book ourselves. At first, I had two men come out with me from Minneapolis. Jim Sasseville was really good. He and I did that feature called "It's Only a Game" for a while. Boy, nobody could draw better than Jim Sasseville. But his wife hated it here, and he finally had to quit because she couldn't stand living here. It was just disrupting his family life. There was never another guy who worked that good. [laughs]

Groth: You're quite adamant about not having assistants work on the strip.
Schulz: Oh, yeah.

Groth: Do you still letter the strip?
Schulz: Sure.

Groth: I heard a story that I couldn't verify, but that I thought I'd run by you. Ten, 12, 15 years ago the syndicate actually had an artist by the name of Al Plastino draw a lot of *Peanuts* strips. The story, as I recall it, was that you hit the roof when you heard this. And the syndicate did this in case you decided to drop the strip. I understood you were not happy with that. Is there any truth to that?
Schulz: That isn't quite true. I only heard it secondhand. There was a

man named Bill Payette who was head of the syndicate at the time. He took over from Larry Rutman, who was the first President when I signed up. I became very dissatisfied as the years went on, and decided more and more that I wanted ownership of the feature. No big blow-ups or anything like that, but it was getting closer and closer to it. And for some reason, now, I didn't know about this until it was all over.

Groth: Can you give me a time frame on this?
Schulz: Well, let's see . . . we were in this studio at the time. And we didn't really achieve a showdown until he finally retired. He had a vision problem. And I don't know if it forced him to retire, but when he retired Bob Metz took over. And I told Bob Metz what I wanted. And he said, "Well, that's reasonable enough." And we settled it in a five or ten minute conversation. Then he told me that he went back and he was going through some files, and he found some strips that—maybe it was Al Plastino—had drawn, that Bill Payette had asked him to draw. [chuckles] Unbelievably thinking that if I had decided to quit he would have somebody ready to take over the strip. Which was absurd. And Bob Metz was so embarrassed by the whole thing, I couldn't believe that he could do this. So he said, "I took all the strips, and I burned them." [laughs] He said, "I don't want anybody ever to see those things." So that's the story as I know about it.

Groth: How'd you feel about that when he told you?
Schulz: Well, I couldn't believe that Bill Payette would be so dumb.

Groth: It strikes me as a betrayal.
Schulz: It's disappointing that somebody thinks that it's that easy. Of course, that's been traditionally what comics have been down through the year. Just hire somebody else. Look at *Nancy* and all the others.

Groth: That's the traditional point of a businessman who doesn't respect the artist.
Schulz: And the most disappointing thing is when people say, "Oh, you're still drawing the strip?" [laughter] Here I am trying every day to draw the best I can, and doing little experiments and trying to make it better, then they ask me that. Who do they think is drawing it?

Groth: How do you feel about something like *Garfield*, which must have been drawn by assistants for something like 15 years now and it doesn't make a bit of difference.

Schulz: I don't know Jim Davis that well.

Groth: I'm interested in nailing down your attitude about—well, for the lack of a more subtle way of putting it—art and commerce.
Schulz: Oh yeah.

Groth: For example, you've had a lot of really harsh things to say about the rapacity of newspaper strip syndicates. Which surprised me.
Schulz: Do I?

Groth: Oh, yeah. I'll quote you in a moment. [Schulz laughs] In your biography, though, Johnson wrote, "One difference between Schulz and hundreds of other aspiring cartoonists, noted Harry Gilburt, United Feature Syndicate sales manager at the time, was his willingness to compromise. Syndicate executives considered such an attitude a sign of maturity and professionalism. 'He went along,' says Gilburt, 'he was smart enough to.'"

And then later she wrote, "As already mentioned, Schulz earned an early reputation around the syndicate as a reasonable, adaptable young artist. This reputation arose however not from a pliable personality, but from a calculated willingness to swallow whatever was necessary to reach his goals." Can you comment on that?
Schulz: Well, I think I've always been a reasonable person. And getting back to is this art or not, I realize that this is still a business. And for a long while, I figured that the syndicate people knew more about it than I did. They were the ones that had to go out and sell it. Harry Gilburt was a remarkable man. I don't think he knew as much about comic strips as he thought he did. We talked just a little bit last year. Very knowledgeable. He knew every editor in the world. He could go into a room and introduce you around, and say, "This is so-and-so from *The Wyoming Press* . . ." He was remarkable and very well respected in the business. As a salesman. And so I cooperated with all the different things they wanted. And just went along, until finally, as the years went on I could see that I should stand up for a few things.

Groth: That you should exercise your authority.
Schulz: No, because they knew I was right.

Groth: It took you a while to reach that point.
Schulz: Oh yeah. It took me a long time. Plus it took a long time to

achieve the power to do it. The power is either I get my way or I quit. And that's the only language they understand.

Groth: Wouldn't you have had that power by around 1960?
Schulz: No.

Groth: The strip was pretty phenomenally successful by then, wasn't it?
Schulz: Bill Payette wouldn't have had the vision. But when I finally did get my way, it was because they realized that nobody else could do it. [laughs] And they better keep me.

Groth: Did you think the contract you signed with the syndicate initially was fair?
Schulz: Um . . . at the time I thought it was. I can see now that it probably wasn't.

Groth: Do you think that was a little naive?
Schulz: Yeah. But . . . it was typical of everything. You go to Hollywood, you're going to have to take this role of the waiter, or else you're not going to get any role at all. And you have to take it, and you're going to get $40 a day for doing it. That's it. You have no choice. And if you're an athlete, and you join the ballclub, and the manager wants you to play right field, and you'd rather be pitching, you're stuck with playing right field. This is the way it is in all of these things. You have to work your way out of them. And I think you have to learn how to be cooperative. That's just the way it is.

Groth: Isn't there a sense, though, that—and I understand this is true of virtually every business relationship in America—those who are in a position of power routinely take advantage of those who are subordinate, and that at the time you signed with the syndicate you were the weaker of the two. And isn't that use of advantage wrong?
Schulz: Well, that depends on motive. Now, if you look upon these as being evil men, that distorts the whole discussion. But a syndicate invests a lot of their reputation and money when they take on a new feature. But cartoonists are notorious for not making their schedules on time, and not keeping up the quality of their work and all of that. Syndicates, as I can see, had to be firm. I suppose that the best thing they could have done would be to put a clause in there that after maybe two or three years, the contract could be renegotiated or something. There was no renegotiating those contracts at all. They had an option

for another five years, another five years, and you just took it or you were out. But if you became so good that nobody else could take your place, then you finally developed some power. I think that's the power of course that you, the cartoonist has, that the syndicate does not have. They're kind of trapped, too. They're at your mercy, the same way as the owner of a ball club is at the mercy of Willie Mays. [laughs]

Groth: Like I said, you had some pretty harsh things to say about newspaper syndicates and the businessmen who run them.

Schulz: But I always got along well with them.

© by United Feature Syndicate, Inc.

Groth: I find that . . . of course, I'm of a different generation.

Schulz: [laughs] Yeah.

Groth: And I'm interested in how your generation viewed the people for whom you were working. It seems like there was a much more compliant attitude among your generation, that there was a greater willingness to accept their authority. Or their superiority, as the case may be. But it does seem like over the years you have accepted their authority less and less. For example, you said, "the comic strip profession is a deadly serious business. And someplace up there, [corporate upstairs metaphorically]—

Schulz: Back to my NCS speech again.

Groth: Yes. [Schulz laughs]

"There are some people that you will never know existed. They don't care anything about you, so watch yourself. They don't even read the comics. They could not possibly care less what happens to you. I don't know who these people are up there, but I'm sure that every newspaper, every organization has this group of mystery people. Like the people who run the ballclub, like the man who owns the theater. He doesn't really care about the actors. He likes the bottom line." Do you question that ethos more now than you did then?

Schulz: Well, I didn't know it. Let me tell you something. The man that signed me up initially was named Larry Rutman. A very fine gentleman. He still was very narrow in his view of how it all should work. There was a certain point, after having drawn the strip clear up into the '60s, I remember saying to him, "Larry, I think I want something more."

"Oh no," he said. "We can never do that."

You see, this was beyond his scope. Nobody had ever asked for anything like this. And yet, now, two years ago, I suppose it's been, maybe a year and a half, the phone rang one day and the person said, "This is David, Larry's grandson. I just wanted to let you know that Larry died last night."

I said, "Oh gee, that's too bad." Larry after he retired moved out to Monterey, and we used to see him once a year when we'd go down for the golf tournament. Jeannie and I would always take him out to lunch or breakfast, just to renew acquaintances.

He said, "Larry died last night. I have a little list of people here that he told me to make sure, of all the people, that I call Sparky first." That is something, after all those years . . . that's what being cooperative will get you. The love and respect of a man like that. Which I'll cherish forever. To think that somebody thought that highly of me who was just another one of his cartoonists. But, he always used to tell me that he had the right to make some of these major decisions. I found out later that he didn't. That the president of the syndicate is still under the control of the board of Scripps-Howard. And up there, that's the mystery people. Yeah. So when the man came out here to discuss my eventually getting total control and everything, I said, "How old are you?" He said, "Well, I'm 57." I said, "You know, all my life I've been pushed around by your kind and told, you have to do this, you can't do that, and all that. I said, no more. From now on, I control the licensing myself and what I say goes. Either I get exactly what I want, or I quit." [laughs]

Groth: Wow.

Schulz: It worked. [laughter]

And I wasn't being nasty, but this is the truth, you see? These people, they don't care anything about you. They like all the money that you make and everything, and all of that. But if you don't produce, nice knowing you, so long, we'll get somebody else.

But it takes a long time, and as you know, only the superstars can do that. Only Tiger Woods can do it. [laughs]

Groth: What did you mean when you referred to him as "your kind"?

Schulz: The big shots, that when you're young, you have to listen to them and all their nonsense and all of that. And you don't have a chance. I went through too many interviews and talked to too many people who wouldn't even listen to me. I took some comic strips down to the *Chicago Sun* once, and the guy who was the editor, his name was Walt Ditson, nice fellow. And he looked at my *Lil' Folks* things and he said, "Boy, these are really good. I can't say no to this. But we'll take them in and show them to Harry Baker here." So Harry Baker was on a coffee break, and when he came back, he took me in and introduced me, and said, "Harry, I just want you to see the work here of this young man. I think he's really good." And [laughs] Harry looked at it, and said, "Well . . . no." And that was it. [laughs]

And my other classic story is going into a syndicate also in Chicago. I bring in the strips, and this was a nice presentation. They were well-drawn, and all of that. I always knew I was getting better all the time. And so I came in, and the guy didn't even get up when I came in. He goes, "My name is (whatever it was)." I sat there, and I handed him these things. This is the way he looked at 'em. [indifferently rustling through papers] "Not professional." And then went back to his work. I thought, "You idiot," you know. You don't even ask where I'm from. Did I have a nice trip down. All the niceties of life. So [that's what I was referring to] when I said, "I've been pushed by your kind all my life, but not any more."

Groth: Without prying unduly, may I ask you who actually owns *Peanuts*? Could you change the strip's name to *Charlie Brown* if you wanted?

Schulz: Yeah, but it's been discussed many times. But it would create so many problems with the licensees. So many products out there with the name *Peanuts* on it, and it has become so prominent. And it would cause a lot of trouble, and a lot of expense for the people that are making the products and all of that to make a change like that. And at this point, I suppose it really doesn't matter, and a lot of people think *Peanuts* is a great name. So it's just one of those things that humble you and you accept, and that's the way it goes.

Groth: So do you essentially own the strip?

Schulz: I don't own the copyright. Which is not necessary. But I have total control over everything. I can do virtually anything that I want, as

long as it doesn't damage the property. And the syndicate can't do anything with the property without my permission.

Groth: In re-reading the *Peanuts* strip, I was trying to focus on what made it as rich as it was. The central reason, it seems to me, artistically as well as commercially, is because you've created not one but several archetypes who all interact within the strip. Charlie Brown is the perpetual loser, Snoopy is the romantic, Lucy is the quintessential curmudgeon, Schroeder is the artistic conscience who cares only for his art and so on . . .

Schulz: He still plays catcher, though. [laughter]

Groth: I was going to say: none of them are one-dimensionally so. Because Snoopy's also a loser albeit a deluded one, Charlie Brown can be acerbic, and so on. I can't imagine you had all this planned out when you started the strip. Can you tell me how it developed so organically over the years?

Schulz: It depends on what ideas you have, and who in your repertory company will play the role, that's all. The characters themselves provide ideas just because of the nature that you've given them. So it works both ways. But none is consistent, as none of us is. So I think they go in all directions.

I find that coming up with ideas never ends and never gets any easier. And you find yourself going in a certain direction just to survive. Now lately, Rerun has almost taken over the strip. He's been in the strip for . . . gosh . . . 20 years.

Groth: In fact, you thought he might've been a mistake when you introduced him.

Schulz: I think he was a mistake when it first began. I was looking for something that was different. I put him on the back of his Mom's bike, and the only time he ever appeared was riding on the back of that bike. I like those. And then, we had a few grandchildren who had to start preschool and kindergarten, and I see little kids at the arena, too. I began to get some ideas and so he was the perfect one to have start kindergarten. He's different from Lucy and Linus. He's a little more outspoken. And I think he's going to be a little on the strange side . . . [laughs] the way he is already. I just had him expelled from school for another day recently, just because he spoke up. I did a strip where he's painting. And he says, "This is a border collie. See, and these are the sheep he's guarding. Suddenly a wolf comes. So the border collie gets on the phone and calls in an air strike." And a little girl says, "You're supposed to be doing watercolors of flowers." He says, "It all takes place in a meadow." He's perfect for that. The other kids are too old for this, really. So it's worked out. Which gives me an idea for another I've thought about. He's going to complain that he couldn't do watercolors any more because the fumes were overcoming him or something. [laughs] I don't know. I'll have to think about that. But you have to be careful that the strip doesn't—like I mentioned when we first sat down—run away from you. So whenever I get going on these stories, I always realize that that week is over, now I've gotta bring 'em back to the regular *Peanuts* stuff. Charlie Brown and Snoopy: they're the ones that count. So I always try to bring 'em back. I thought of one Charlie Brown idea last week, and I couldn't of any others.

And I love doing Snoopy as a World War I flying ace, but I almost feel that it's dated, that I've done it too much. So I have him doing other things. I've had him serve as a soldier at Valley Forge. I did a big Sunday page on that a couple of weeks ago. And that's kind of fun to do. But again it's quite limited. And of all the things that I've done, that probably got more attention—his flying ace adventures—than anything I've ever done.

Groth: You once said that you didn't want to portray him as the World War I flying ace because it was inappropriate during the Vietnam War.
Schulz: Yeah. I quit doing him at that point.

Groth: Can you tell me why?
Schulz: Well, because war . . . we were suddenly realizing just everybody that . . . this was such a monstrous war and everything. It just didn't seem funny. So I just stopped doing it. Then going into bookstores and seeing the revival of war books, mostly World War II, Korea, World War I books, so I thought, "It's coming back again," so then I started doing some more. But I didn't do him fighting the Red Baron. Mostly, it was just sitting in the French cafe flirting with the waitress. Then it turns out that he's not in a French cafe at all, he's in Marcie's kitchen! [laughs] Which was a real twist. He's drinking all the root beer.

Groth: Well, that brings up an interesting aspect of *Peanuts.* You've said that "the strip has become so abstract that the introduction of an adult would destroy it. You can't have an adult in a strip where a dog is sitting on a dog house pretending he's chasing the Red Baron." You've also said, "I don't know where the *Peanuts* kids live. I think that originally I thought of them living in these little veterans' developments, where Joyce and I first lived when we got married out in Colorado Springs. Now I don't think about it at all. My strip has become so abstract, and such a fantasy, that I think it would be a mistake to point out a place for them to live."
Schulz: I don't even draw houses any more [laughs]

Groth: Right. So you've really whittled it down, so that the strip can encompass almost anything. And one of the things I've noticed over the years is that the fantasy elements—I don't know if it's right to say they're taking over—but they're becoming more prominent.
Schulz: Oh, they are. No doubt about it. I never do Lynn Johnston things, and I never do *Family Circus* things. And I never do *Dennis the Menace* situations. The fantasy elements just make it much more flexible. I can do things they can't do.

Groth: And this was a gradual change.
Schulz: Oh, yeah. The strip was fairly realistic when it first began. Little

kids doing little kid things. They rode tricycles . . . of course, Charlie Brown hasn't even flown a kite for a while. Maybe I've reached the end. [Groth laughs] That's a problem. This can happen to a lot of people. You use up all of your life experiences. And you get finally to the end. And now you have to wait for new experiences, you stay alive and read a lot, and hang around with a lot of people and try to stay in tune with things. If you don't, you're going to use up all those experiences. I just read a review of Kurt Vonnegut's latest novel, and it said he has nothing left to say.

Groth: Do you fear that happening?
Schulz: Sure.

But it's a living. [laughter]

© by United Feature Syndicate, Inc.

Groth: Since we were talking about the abstract elements of *Peanuts*, let me ask you about another formal element: there's an aesthetic fragility that's an integral part of the *Peanuts* strip, by which I mean there are very clearly defined boundaries which can't be transgressed. For example, you once said, "Adults have been left out because they would intrude in a world where they could only be uncomfortable. Adults are not needed in the *Peanuts* strip. In earlier days, I experimented with offstage voices, but soon abandoned this, as it was not only impractical but actually clumsy."

Could you explain why the strip needs these boundaries? And are there any boundaries beside that of not depicting adults that you adhere to that might not be so readily apparent?

Schulz: Well, the main thing is that the kids seem to accept Snoopy's actions. Now it's totally absurd that this dog is on top of this pointed doghouse all of the time. And he's afraid to go down inside it, but the minute you see—if you go back to the earlier strips, where you see the dog house from a three-quarter view, immediately the dog house becomes too real. Snoopy can't really lie on top of that dog house because you're looking at it from the proper angle. But if we don't show it from the three-quarter view, we just keep the side view, then the reader eventually accepts that as being the dog house, but we don't care if it's the dog house any more. And he can sit there, and he can type on the typewriter and it doesn't slide off, and he can lie on his back, and all the other things, so we accept that. Then, all of the things that he thinks and does are so fanciful, the kids, again, accept it.

Now, in my strip, Snoopy never talks to the kids. You'll notice that. And the birds never talk to them. They think to each other. The animals do, but the kids somehow are aware of what he is doing without actually knowing what he is really thinking. And they accept that, because I suppose we could say children live different lives. And they probably do. The more I talk with my own children now that they've become adults, and I find out that they were doing things around the house which I never dreamed about. I never knew they did some of those things. Children, I suppose are like animals. They have to survive. And they have to keep things from the parents that they do. Nothing serious, but just things that they do that the parents never know about. Especially if you've gone away for the evening, or something like that, then they do some things that they normally wouldn't do. And I like to think that animals do the same thing. And this is what Snoopy does. He has to retreat into his fanciful world in order to survive. Otherwise, he leads kind of a dull, miserable life. I don't envy dogs the lives they have to live. They're trapped living with families that they never knew anything about [Groth laughs] and so Snoopy survives by living this extra life. Now we can go any direction with Snoopy. Woodstock, too. It's absurd to think of this dog and the bird wandering through the woods going on hikes and camping out. So as soon as an adult is in the strip, bang, the whole thing collapses. Because the adults bring everything back to reality. And it just spoils it.

Now, we have another even more practical solution or reason, and that's the fact that there's no room for adults. My strip, when it was given to me was about the size of four air-mail stamps. Well, you remember Fritzi Ritz and Nancy, Fritz Ritz could never stand in the same room as Nancy, because she was too tall. So Ernie Bushmiller always had to fake it. This is what is done in so many strips. There's just no room for adults to stay. Besides, they don't interest me. And also, it's kind of neat to have the reader create some of these characters in his or her mind. What kind of a teacher was Miss Othmar really? And what did she look like? And why did she run away and give up teaching to get married? And who are the principals that the kids are always going in and talking to? And the little red-haired girl appearing offstage. We never see her. Because it's almost too late to draw her, because I could never draw her to satisfy the readers' impression of what she's probably like. So it's good to establish a group of offstage characters.

But size is very important. I just didn't have the room to draw kids—with the result that I brought the camera right down on level with the kids. I have never drawn the kids from an adult viewpoint, looking down on them.

Groth: You just said you weren't interested in adults. Why is that?
Schulz: Well, I . . . [laughs]

Groth: Have you ever been tempted to do a strip about adults?
Schulz: Oh, I've been tempted to do a lot. I did a comic feature for three years called *It's Only a Game.* And it had adults in it. They were playing all different kinds of sports. And they played bridge all the time. And of course I did the teenage youth cartoons, which I was pretty proud of. I didn't like the drawing of them for at least a year or so. But after that, I think the drawing really came along quite nicely and I'm quite proud of the way those things appeared.

Groth: Were you as comfortable drawing teenagers and adults as you are drawing the children?
Schulz: I think they're harder to draw. [laughs]

Groth: In a peculiar way, *Peanuts* taps into the fantasy lives of children; Snoopy and Charlie Brown communicate even though the reader is never quite sure that they're aware they're communicating.
Schulz: [laughs] Yeah.

Groth: For example, when Snoopy bangs on Charlie Brown's door for a cookie in the middle of the night, Charlie Brown knows exactly what he wants and he comes out screaming at Snoopy . . .
Schulz: The theme of this business goes all the way back to . . . did you have a dog or a cat or anything like that?

Groth: Yes, I had a dog.
Schulz: And I'm sure you have done like almost all adults. We see our

dog in the morning and we say, "Good morning, Tommy. Did you sleep well at all last night?" We then kind of give a voice to Tommy, and we say, "Yeah, I slept pretty well. I wanted to bark a little bit, but I didn't want to disturb anybody." We give the dog answers, don't we?

Groth: Right.

Schulz: I think it's just a common thing that everybody does. And this is really what Snoopy's thinking is all about. This is where all of that started.

Groth: So when you did that, you were that conscious of your strategy?

Schulz: Mm-hm. But not taking it that seriously, of course. None of this is that calculated.

Groth: I guess that was my question. To what extent are these creative strategies calculated?

Schulz: Well, I think about it a lot and I consider everything carefully before I do it. But, and of course, I've made a lot of mistakes down through the years doing things I never should have done. But fortunately, in a comic strip, yesterday doesn't mean anything. The only thing that matters is today and tomorrow.

Groth: There's almost a slippery slope to the fantasy quotient of the strip where the strip started off being more realistic, and then slid more and more into fantasy. First there was Snoopy acting more and more human, and then Snoopy's fantasy life, and then the children actually entering into co-existing in Snoopy's fantasy life. Such as when Snoopy is Peppermint Patty's attorney or Marcie appears as a French lass in his World War I fantasy. Things like that. And then more recently I noticed that the inanimate objects are actually talking to the children. Sally's school building talks to her, Charlie Brown's glove and ball talk to him, etc.

Schulz: But the children don't hear them, do they? The schoolhouse used to think things all the time like Snoopy did. But Sally never heard what the schoolhouse was thinking.

Groth: Is that right? I guess I felt that was ambiguous. I wasn't sure.

Schulz: No, I don't think she ever heard what the schoolhouse was thinking. I haven't done one of those in a long time.

Groth: No, I think I read those in the late '80s. But as the strip pro-

gressed, there was less and less of a demarcation between reality and fantasy, and I was wondering why you increased the fantasy quotient.
Schulz: I suppose a lot of it is just struggle for survival, Gary. [Groth laughs] The days come and the days go, and you send in one batch, and you need another batch. And it just goes on and on and on. And what are we going to do tomorrow? And it never ends. And then you get caught up in something that works, and all of the sudden Snoopy's been pursuing the Red Baron, next thing you know, he's in the French café, and then the next thing you know his brother Spike is in the trenches. [laughs] Something works, and something doesn't work. So this is what it is, just a constant pursuit of something new.

Groth: Do you think that you would be less creatively fertile if you didn't have the pressure of a daily strip?
Schulz: Well . . .

Groth: If someone were to say, "Stop doing the strip, and just do whatever you want, whenever you want to do it," would you find that . . .
Schulz: Probably would be a handicap, wouldn't it? Because you might think about it too much. You might lose some of the spontaneity. It'd be like the argument that musicians have all of the time: should they leave in the bad notes? If you're playing a—what is it?—some very intricate violin concerto and they play as fast as they can. So they miss a note now and then. Who cares. It's the risk you take when you draw these things and you gamble on certain things. Some things work and some things don't.

Groth: You said once "I don't know which story has been my favorite, but one that worked out far beyond my expectation concerned Charlie Brown's problem when, instead of seeing the sun rise early one morning, he saw a huge baseball."
Schulz: Oh, that was great.

Groth: That was one of your most outrageous strips in terms of combining reality and fantasy. Do you have any recollection of how you came upon that idea? You'll recall his head was turning into a baseball.
Schulz: Yeah. It was kind of a head rash.

  Well, I don't know how you think of those things, but then, when you do them, I let the stories go where the daily strips take me. I discovered that if you try to plot out a story, you'll end up with some weak daily strips. And it's more important to try to make each daily strip as good as you can, no matter where the story goes. And fortunately, I sent him to camp. And there he was ashamed of it, so he put a sack over his head. And he became a leader. Nobody knew who he was. There was lesson there. [laughs]

Groth: Had you planned that?
Schulz: No.

Groth: Because it was so thematically perfect for Charlie Brown to be recognized as a leader only when he wore a bag on his head.
Schulz: [laughs] It just happened, that was all. And then, of course, I needed an ending, and that's when "What, me worry?" came up. And I called *Mad Magazine,* they said, "Well, I guess we should let you do it, because we've been parodying you for so long."

I've never understood why they mis-punctuate "What me, worry?" It should be "What, comma, me worry?" But they don't do it that way.

Groth: [laughs] Well, it was probably just a mistake the first time they did it and then they had to repeat the mistake forever.
Schulz: I think so. A lack of education.

Groth: The Sundays and the dailies have diminished in size over the years.
Schulz: The dailies haven't. They got bigger. The Sundays diminish because some of the editors won't give me a bigger size. Our local paper gives me the whole half page. But the *Chronicle*'s really insulting. They trim it down to about a sixth of a page. But it depends on the editor, how prejudiced he is.

Groth: Wasn't the size of the dailies changed around 1988?
Schulz: We made them bigger.

Groth: I see.
Because you changed your format considerably. You had a very rigid format of four square, identically-sized panels . . .
Schulz: I was given that. That was one of the things that Harry Gilburt wanted to see. That was a sales gimmick. The strip was not an instant success by any means. It took a long time.

Groth: You once referred to the format of the strip as a "space saver." Can you tell me what that was?
Schulz: It meant that an editor could buy it and put it wherever he

wanted in the paper. He could run it in the want ads, this way . . . or he could run it over on the side next to the crossword puzzle this way.

Groth: Vertically.

Schulz: Or he could run it in a square. He had three choices. It was just a sales gimmick.

Groth: So that's why you had to have a rigid four-panel format.
Schulz: Yeah. But again, I think they lied to me. It was just their sales gimmick, because about two or three years later, they came out with *Twin Earths* and *Long Sam,* which were big strips just like other ones. Of course, Long Sam was Al Capp, and he had his way about whatever he wanted. He gave them so much trouble. And *Twin Earths* was the dumbest idea for a strip there ever was. [laughter]

Groth: You really created a beautiful visual and temporal rhythm within that strict four-panel format.
Schulz: Mm-hm. But I'm glad I got rid of it.

Groth: Are you?
Schulz: It was restrictive.

Groth: It was beautiful in its way, though.
Schulz: Yeah, but . . . like this strip here . . . [shows a long, single-panel strip] which isn't quite finished. Four panels would ruin that.

Groth: So you were really very happy when you could change the size of the panels and do these large single-panel illustrations.
Schulz: I was just leaving a cartoonists meeting with Mort Walker and Mell Lazarus one evening, and I said, "You know, it's very strange. I drew my strip for years in four panels and now I can have one long panel. I can have characters talking here, here, and then finally ending up over here. And I did that, and then all of a sudden I realize, Mell, this is what you've been doing for 30 years." [laughs]

Groth: Let me ask you this: being a newspaper strip artist is unusual in the sense that most artists have a sense of completion about what they do, but strip cartoonists can't. A painter paints a painting, it's finished. A novelist writes a novel, it's finished, and he moves onto the next novel. But it seems to me like there's never a sense of completion with your work. Do you see this as one long, lifelong piece of work?
Schulz: Sure. Sure. But . . . I think there are quite a few strips that I'm very proud that I think stand absolutely on their own, and they look real good. I look at them, the worse they get. [Groth laughs] But I'm very proud of a lot. So I think each one will stand by itself.

Groth: Well, you've actually had many terrific stories. Your stories don't last more than three or four weeks as far as I can tell.
Schulz: They used to last longer. But lately I haven't been able to make

them last that long for some reason. But editors are becoming more impatient. I think there's a market for longer stories, if editors would just give us a chance.

Groth: Are you optimistic about the future of the newspaper strip?
Schulz: No, no. Not the way it's going. They're getting worse all the time.

Groth: There doesn't seem to be much room for optimism.
Schulz: And it shouldn't be that way, really.

Groth: Do you think there's something anachronistic about a strip appearing in the newspaper every day?
Schulz: Well, maybe so. Just like I imagine newspaper columnists are having trouble, too. But I think I know what has happened. Years ago, when comic strips first began to develop, the cartoonists were all newspaper people. They worked usually in newspapers, they made spot drawings and they illustrated things that were going on. Photographers weren't as prevalent as they are now, and so cartoonists all drew pretty well. Because if they didn't, they would never have gotten hired. So they had a lot of drawing to do. And then, we drifted into the '40s when gag cartooning began to become so prominent. And I think you'll find that most of the cartoonists that were drawing came from animation or gag cartooning. Walt Kelly came from animation.

Groth: Did Mort Walker come from animation?
Schulz: No, he came from gag cartooning. And I came from gag cartooning. There's a whole bunch of us who developed from gag cartooning. Then gag cartooning began to diminish as the magazines disappeared. Now where are they going to come from? They've gotta come from someplace. Newspapers don't employ cartoonists any more,

there's no gag cartoonists, so where are they going to come from? They're coming from the college. Colleges have lousy cartoonists because they'll take anything. They don't learn how to draw, and they come up with radical ideas, they're going to save the world, and all of that. And I think that's where it's falling down. Now even that's disappearing. Now housewives are becoming cartoonists. [Groth laughs]

So I don't know where it's going to end. You find so many amateur cartoon strips. Before, it took a lot of training, you had to work your way up, until you finally got a comic strip. Now they jump from nothing to drawing a comic strip. They have no training at all, no experience at it. And that's deplorable.

Groth: You just mentioned how gag cartooning became prominent in the '40s, which reminded me of something you said about the beginnings of *Peanuts*. About the early creative evolution of the strip, you said, "What has to be realized is that the characters I drew then came out of style of gag cartooning that was prevalent at the time. Tiny children looking up at huge adults and saying very sophisticated things. This was the professional school from which I graduated and which formed my style. And it took me several years to break away and develop a style of drawing that would allow the characters to do new and special things." Could you talk a little about the creative process involved in breaking away from the gag style and into a style more suited to a continuity strip? And can you define the differences between those two styles?

Schulz: I think we always have to remember that gag cartooning is different from comic strip cartooning. And it's a mistake if you don't realize that early and you never do go away from that. Now, comic strip cartooning allows you much more of a change of pace. You develop characters and from those characters you develop themes and ideas and of course, discussion too. The characters can talk to each other. You don't have to come out with one lone punch line. Now the characters also have to be drawn so that they can do different things. Gag cartoon characters don't necessarily have to be really doing anything. They only have to pose in the action that is relevant to that gag. But comic strip characters have to be a little more flexible in the way they're constructed so that they can run and talk and hold books and throw baseballs and do all sorts of different things. And do them consistently. So I think that's the difference.

I love the old gag cartoons that were back in the '40s, with the little kids with the great big heads. They were funny.

Groth: You said the characters you drew came out of a style of gag cartooning. But you were also passionately interested in comic strips at the time. Why did you choose a style from gag cartooning rather than from comic strips like *Gasoline Alley* or something like that?
Schulz: Probably because I just wanted to get started. This was what sold. I tried all sorts of different things, and could never sell anything, and it was the breakthrough to the *Saturday Evening Post* with the style, then, that I was working on. Which was little kids with great big heads saying things that were a little bit out of context. And it was just, I suppose, being commercial, that's all. Just trying to please the editors. [laughter]

Groth: You also said, "the cartooning of the characters, with their large, round heads and tiny arms, came frequently to prohibit them from doing some of the more realistic things that a more normal style of cartooning would allow."
Schulz: Yeah.

Groth: "Nevertheless, this was the direction I wanted to take. I believe it has led me to do some things that no one ever attempted in a comic strip." Now, it seems to me that *Peanuts'* intellectual status as a comic strip derives from its talkiness. The fact that there's so much conversation between the characters, so much philosophizing. Was that something that you were consciously aware of from the very beginning? Was that something you purposely wanted to do or is that something that just evolved?
Schulz: I was aware of it to a certain extent. I remember—and I don't know if I mentioned it to you before—discussing this when I first went to New York and signed the contract and I was introduced to the man who was the sales manager. His name was Harry Gilburt. Still lives in Florida. Very nice man, very knowledgeable in those days and considered one of the best sales managers in the business. And after I was introduced to him and we talked a little bit, he said, "Now, I would suggest that you don't try to make the strips and what you're doing too subtle." Being a young, wise-cracking kid, I said, "Well, if you're expecting another Nancy and Sluggo, you're not going to get it." [laughter] I've often regretted saying that, because it was a kind of a

smart-aleck thing to say. But I knew that I didn't want to draw Nancy and Sluggo. Now to me, there was nothing wrong with Ernie Bushmiller's work. He was wonderful. But that's not what I wanted to do. And so I knew that I wanted to go on what I would consider a little higher plane, but I didn't know how it was going to happen, or where, or anything like that. So a lot of it just came natural. As I've said before, what the characters say and do is really me. These are the things that I say all the time.

Groth: I think that was really something of a new direction for comic strips, where the characters were almost talking as much to the audience as they were to themselves.

Schulz: Well, I wanted to break away from the old kids' strips which were so prevalent in the earlier days, the "What are we going to do today?" sort of strips. Where the kids are just hanging around. Do you remember *Reg'lar Fellers*?

Groth: Yeah, yeah.

Schulz: And there was also *Just Kids*. You know, they were good features, but they were never very subtle, and the kids were usually just bouncing around the neighborhood, jumping over fire hydrants while they were talking and doing that kind of thing. Sort of meaningless stuff. And I just knew that it was possible to go beyond that. But there were some other wonderful strips with little kids in them at the time. Of course, *Skippy* would be the best example.

Groth: And Percy Crosby was something of an influence, wasn't he?

Schulz: Oh, yeah. Definitely. I was always appalled, I didn't know enough about the business to realize what was happening, but I was appalled at his seemingly careless attitude sometimes. And I read later on he would bat out a whole bunch of scripts in one day when he would get behind. He'd get involved in many other activities. I don't know about drinking, that's beyond me, but I would look at them when I was very young and wonder why he drew so carelessly and why he didn't even use a ruler to draw the panels [laughs]. I didn't realize he was just trying to draw as many as he could.

Groth: *Pogo* started in '48, I believe.

Schulz: Yeah.

Groth: And in a way, the two strips developed similarly, because *Pogo* is also very talky with a rich cast of characters. Were you an admirer of that strip? Did you know Walt Kelly?

Schulz: I only met Walt Kelly twice. I introduced myself to him at one of the Reuben dinners, and we only said, "hello," and that was about it. And I met him later at a meeting of cartoonists where we were doing something to raise money for war bonds or something like that. But we never had a real conversation. But I certainly thought his work was wonderful. I used to buy every *Pogo* comic book that came out, and every reprint book and all of that. And I thought they were just great. Now, unfortunately, as the years went on, I found myself buying the *Pogo* books and then not being able to read them. They became boring. He got so political and so involved in things that they just weren't funny any more.

But they were beautifully done.

Groth: I'd like to get back to your work. It occurred to me reading over all of your work that you have a lot in common, artistically, with Robert Crumb. Which is kind of an odd pairing, I'll admit, but I rather like the parallels for that very reason.

Schulz: Really?

Groth: Yeah. You're both wrestling with similar demons: Resentment from your youth, insecurity, injustices, rejection by the opposite sex. And you're doing it in very, very different ways. You went in diametrically opposite ways to deal with these issues. And I was wondering if you saw that connection or how you feel about Crumb's work, because in some ways you're so similar, and in other ways you're so radically different.

Schulz: I think he's great. I'm appalled at the vulgarity of the so-called underground cartoonists. I only met Robert once, [laughs] it was at a big convention downtown. He was just coming out of the building, and we were going in and somebody said, "Oh, there's Robert Crumb." And I said, "Hi, Robert. I'm Charles Schulz. Glad to meet you." And he was just stunned as if . . . He said, "Oh, really?" Just as if I would hate him or something. [laughs] And I really thought it was laughable that he would think that I would hate him. That I must be some kind of a wishy-washy, goody-goody two-shoes person. I think his drawing is great, he does funny things.

Groth: But he also deals with sex very overtly.

Schulz: Which is all right if it weren't so terribly vulgar. There was a young underground cartoonist, who came up to see me once here several years ago. And we sat and talked. And I said, "You know, the trouble with you guys, is that you think that you are so free in what you do, and we are inhibited." I said, "You couldn't do what I do." I said, "You guys, you all do the same thing. You all think you're free, but you all do the same jokes, the same vulgarities." And I said, "I defy you just to do what I do." I said, "You'll never be able to do it."

Because I'm not in the business to offend people or to be whatever . . .

Groth: But someone like Crumb doesn't do it to offend people, although what he does certainly can offend people, I'm sure it does offend people—but you know, in an odd way, another parallel is that you don't care if you offend people using Scripture [Schulz laughs] whereas Crumb doesn't care if he offends people with his political or sexual expression.

Schulz: No, I know.

Groth: So in a way, you both are compelled to do what you have to do. Regardless of the consequences.

Schulz: Yeah. I always wonder what made me like that. I think there is some kind of a weird connection there. I've never been able to figure it out. I've thought about it. You know, that I have never sworn in my life. And I never use vulgar phrases, and I don't know why. Now, as I get older, I find that I don't use vulgar phrases just because I'm trying to be more cultured or something. I like the niceties of language. My mother and dad were never crude, but my dad would say "damn" or "hell" or something now and then. But I never heard them tell dirty stories that way. I don't know. I went through the army, three years of the worst vulgarities imaginable. Although I think it's worse now. But I don't know whatever made me that way. Maybe there's some kind of a fatal flaw or something. I don't know what it is. [Groth laughs] But that's just the way I am.

Groth: Did it have to do with your upbringing in the Midwest?
Schulz: It was just the way we lived.

Groth: One way or the other, though, you do have an upbringing, whether it's vigorously or dogmatically imposed or if it's simply part of your environment.
Schulz: Yeah, but I was surrounded by it all the time . . .

Groth: But you never . . .
Schulz: Never. Maybe I'm competitive, that's all. I wasn't going to be dragged down.

Groth: Well apparently, you're very competitive.
Schulz: Yeah. You have to be. That's why I'm competitive in drawing the comic strip. I want to make the playoffs. [laughter]

Groth: The parallel between you and Crumb also brought to mind one other related question, which is about sex. He deals very directly with sexual impulse, and his sexual impulses. Whereas you skirt sexuality *per se* and deal with a much more romanticized or idealized version of love: Charlie Brown and the red-haired girl and his unrequited love for her, Peppermint Patty's interest in Charlie Brown is oblique and touching, Lucy's unrequited love for Schroeder, etc., but you don't deal directly with sexuality. Since the strip is one of the most personal ever done and sexuality is such an important part of one's life, I was wondering if you ever felt like you wanted to do that but couldn't because of the newspaper strip format and the restrictions of the newspaper audience.

Schulz: Well, in the first place these are just little kids. That really puts a lid on it right there.

Groth: Did you ever feel constricted by that self-limitation?
Schulz: Oh no. I never feel constricted at all. Not in the least. I can do anything that I think of.

Groth: Have you seen the Crumb documentary?
Schulz: I saw the movie. That's all I know about Robert. I admire his drawing. I think he draws beautifully. Very creative and all that. But also don't forget I raised five children. I also have 16 grandchildren which separates us, really, doesn't it?

Groth: Well, I don't know. He has two children.
Schulz: Does he?

Groth: Mm-hm.
Schulz: Well, how about a dog? [laughter]

Groth: Right. I don't think he has a dog.
Schulz: It's a difficult comparison. One that's valid, I suppose, from a journalistic state, I don't know. I'm getting too old to worry about those things.

Groth: You definitely don't feel comfortable expressing things like that.
Schulz: No.

Groth: I wonder if that's generational, or if it's simply a different world view irrespective of generational differences. Have you grown older gracefully or have you fought it?
Schulz: No, no. I'm fighting it. [laughter]

Groth: One thing I wanted to ask you is that I know your hand shakes.
Schulz: It's been shaking for a long time.

Groth: Is that getting worse, is it getting more difficult to draw the strip?
Schulz: It's just the same as always. It's leveled off now. I don't even think about it. But it bothers me if, sometimes like going back over the top of Peppermint Patty's hair or something like that . . .

Groth: Now, this is something that I became more and more curious about as I immersed myself in your life—
Schulz: [laughs] It's a boring life.

Groth: No, no, I think that's a superficial view. [Schulz laughs] One thing that fascinated me was that the shortest section of notes I have about you is on politics.
Schulz: Oh, yeah.

Groth: You don't like politics in strips. Although I might have ferreted out a little bit of political content in the early *Peanuts,* but you're very adamant about not putting political content into strips. And my impression, based on various things I've read is that your bent is somewhat conservative.
Schulz: No. I'm very liberal.

Groth: Huh. [Surprised] [Schulz laughs] You were overjoyed to have dined with Ronald Reagan.
Schulz: Well, so what? I mean, the man was governor. You get invited to have lunch with the governor, why not? [laughs]

Groth: Well, Jules Feiffer may not have been quite so eager . . .
Schulz: Well, Jules Feiffer . . . gosh. We don't want to talk about him. Feiffer and I wouldn't agree on anything.

Groth: My point is that a liberal might not be quite so eager to dine with Reagan.
Schulz: Well, there's a difference between being a liberal and being kind. By being liberal I mean being kind. Generous. I don't want to brag about it, but you'd be astounded by the amount of things that Jeannie and I do. I don't know Jules. I heard him speak once. And I thought he gave a wonderful talk. I haven't seen him since.

Groth: I mean, he's the kind of person who if Ronald Reagan invited him to dinner, he might be so opposed to Reagan's point of view that he would not do that.
Schulz: But that's . . . insulting. That's beyond politics, isn't it? One of my favorite stories is about Joanne Greenberg who wrote *I Never Promised You a Rose Garden.* She said, "I was with my father, sitting on a park bench one day, and a man came walking up. My father said, 'Stand up.' I said, 'Stand up? Why should I stand up?' And he said, 'This is Senator So-and-So coming by.' So he said, 'Good morning, Senator,' and he said 'Good morning' and walked on." Her father said that the position deserves respect. So I think to use your own personal views to say to the President of the United

States, I'm not going to come, that's childish. Again, I don't want to get into that.

I would have given anything in the world to have met General Eisenhower. What an honor. What a tremendous feat he had commanding D-Day. The decisions he had to make were just unbelievable. And a lot of other people I'd like to meet just for that . . . Reagan was a very thoughtful person.

Groth: That's hard to believe. [laughs]
Schulz: No, extremely thoughtful. Very personable, and he would never forget you. Now just in the little bit of contact I had . . . Joyce and I had lunch with him and Nancy—I didn't arrange it, he didn't arrange it—some press secretary said, "They should have a *Peanuts* day in California or something." So we went up there and had lunch with them.

Groth: Now would you have done that with a public figure with whom you completely disagreed?
Schulz: Like Barbara Boxer? [laughter]

Groth: There you go.

Schulz: I don't know, because she's never invited me. I suppose, just out of curiosity—well, I went down to see Clinton, and I've attended things for Senator Feinstein, and things like that.

But getting back to Reagan just to show what I'm talking about, several months later, after he was no longer governor, he and I and a few other people were honored as fathers of the year. We went down, and he was surrounded by some people. And I was lead over there. And he looked down and he said, "Sparky. It's good to see you." He said, "Nancy. Come over here. Look who's here. Sparky's here." Now, how many politicians and governors are going to do that? He remembers.

Groth: I don't want to sound too cynical, but couldn't that just be the kind of professional shmoozing the politicians . . .

Schulz: No, that's just the way he was. And he called me when I was in the hospital and had heart surgery.

Groth: So you think it was genuine.

Schulz: He's taken a terrible beating from the press and other people, just nastiness. [Jimmy] Carter was the same way. I was Easter Seals Chairman. We went to Washington, and had some friends that went with us, and they had to hang back, as I went in to meet Carter. We had our picture taken, with the little girl who was on the poster. And then we said thank you. He asked if there were any folks with me. And I said, "Oh, this is my wife. And her son. And some friends." And he said, "Well, I'd like to meet them." He went over, and shook hands with them. Again that was the sort of person he was. I don't think I've met any others. Shook hands with Clinton. I talked with Bush on the practice tee at the AT&T. But I'm out of that whole realm. Comic strip artists are not regarded as celebrities in that way. We don't get the medal of freedom and all of that sort of thing. They proposed it for me; I don't think we even came close. Last year on the 100th anniversary of the comics, all the cartoonists wrote to Senator Feinstein to promote it.

But that's all right. I know my place. [laughs] And it doesn't bother me.

Groth: What I mean by conservative or liberal was ideologically speaking. And it just seems like you're more on the conservative side ideologically. Of course, I could be completely wrong.

I want to ask you what you meant when you referred to that syndicate executive as "your kind." It seems to me that people of "his kind"

run the corporations, run the government, and I'm curious as to
whether you've become increasingly skeptical of that kind of arbitrary
power.

Schulz: Well, I'm out of it. I don't have any connection with it outside
of some of the licensees. Mr. Hall that runs Hallmark, seems to be a
fine gentleman. Joyce Hall was a remarkable man. Other people like
that. I've never met anybody, except the very first one when we signed
up with Metropolitan [Life Insurance]. I don't know anybody with Metropolitan. I'm just out of all of that. I don't know any of the network
people as far as television and that goes. By conservative, I think the
only definition of a conservative that I would accept would be responsible living. I live a very conservative life. I don't drink, I don't smoke, I'm
not mean to people. I built that arena, you know, cost me a fortune. I
think it costs me about $140,000 a month to keep it up. And I built this
roller hockey rink for the neighborhood kids. I saw them playing out in
the parking lot, and I thought, "They shouldn't have to play in the
parking lot. They should have a nice rink to play on." But somebody
said, "you want to put a fence around it?" Put a fence around it? It's
supposed to be for the kids. Oh well : . .

Lee Mendelson had a meeting with the CBS people a couple of
months ago, because they're going to have to do a big show about my
50th anniversary, and he said he was astounded. He said the head of
the meeting said, "Do you realize the scope of what this man has
done? The things that he has touched? Literature, music, and art and
all of these things. No comic strip has ever come close to touching all of
this." He said, "We've got to do this. We've got to put these in the
show somehow." And I hadn't even thought about it. But it's true.
Everything from Vince Gauraldi's Linus and Lucy on down to Snoopy
going to the moon.

And I love looking at the golf tournaments where Snoopy is on the
big dirigible floating over the golf tournaments. Look, it's Snoopy the
World War I flying ace. So that's, when I say, it's difficult to label somebody liberal or conservative. I think I'm very liberal in my outlook on
life and how I treat people, and all of that sort of thing.

I've always been Republican. At least up until a certain point,
because my Dad was. But . . . you see, my Dad was a Republican
because he ran his own business. And, of course, Republicans were . . .
he grew up in that era, too. Where it was Calvin Coolidge and Hoover,
until Roosevelt came along. But I think owning your own business will

turn you into a Republican in a hurry. [laughter] Because you have to start paying all the bills, and doing all the things that are required of you.

Groth: How did your father feel about Roosevelt?

Schulz: We never talked much about it, but he always voted against him. He voted for Hoover I'm sure, and I'm sure he voted Republican. Now, the odd thing was my mother's brother was a radical Democrat. In Minnesota, they were called Farmer-Laborites. He worked for a creamery, it was a cooperative creamery. So he was extremely for Roosevelt, and an extreme Democrat. But my father would never get into arguments with anybody. They saw each other as families every Friday night, but I can remember them getting into a discussion about something only once. But my dad just never got into discussions like that.

Groth: Were there discussions at home about what was going on in the world, politics . . . ?

Schulz: Not really.

Groth: So you developed your own attitudes and so forth by osmosis. By just picking things up.

Schulz: I became fascinated by Wendell Wilkie when I was young. I was downtown with my mother and I saw a little book about Wendell Wilkie. And I read it, and then I used to hear him on the radio. I used to love to listen to him speak. I have his biography and I read it every now and then. He was a remarkable man. He would have died in office, had he been elected.

Groth: Were you ever attracted to someone like Norman Thomas?

Schulz: Oh, no. No.

Groth: That would have had no appeal to you.

Schulz: No. Not at all. I think . . . well, communism has proven to be a disaster. And I think socialism, too, simply doesn't work. Not that anything ever really works. [laughter] But there was a lady who ran for governor here a couple years ago. And Jeannie and I went to a reception for her. She was a liberal. We discussed the surtax. I said, "Who is going to put a level on my income? Who is going to do that? Who is going to support Canine Companions? We built that whole building over there, and we pay to keep it going so those people in wheelchairs can have dogs. Are you going to pay for that? Is the government going to pay for it? They're not going to pay for that." And I listed all of the things that Jean and I do. Just because it's the right thing to do. And I said, "If we don't do it, don't tell me you're going to do it. Because you're not going to do it. [laughs] But you're going to take all my money, and the government is going to do it all." This is my only argument with Clinton's whole philosophy. He just thinks that government can do everything. I've never seen a president who wanted to run so many different things.

You're being hired by a newspaper editor and he buys your strip because he wants to sell his newspaper. So why should you double-cross him by putting in things that will aggravate him. That's not my job.

Groth: What do you think of Lynn Johnston's putting in the gay stories?
Schulz: [laughs] If she wants to, I don't care. But Lynn is a different person.

See, Lynn is a problem-solver. Lynn loves to get involved in all of these things. But I think I have introduced and done things that nobody else ever did, too. Who else ever did something on Amlyopia and sleep disorders? I've done a lot of medical things. I've done more theological things than anybody. And done them deeper. You never see Charlie Brown praying, saying silly things.

Groth: Your quotation of scripture could offend atheists. [Joking]
Schulz: Oh, who cares? We're going to offend somebody. But at least I know what I'm talking about there.

I always wanted to do something where Linus is going from house to house, passing out pamphlets about the Great Pumpkin, and he mentions in passing "Who are the two guys out there with the white shirts and the neckties riding those bicycles?" Because I know most of the Mormons will laugh at it. They have a pretty good sense of humor. But some of the editors are afraid of things like that. My daughter is Mormon, so we laugh about those things all the time.

I love Amy. I think her beliefs and mine have brought us even closer together—

Groth: —is that right?
Schulz: Sure. We can discuss spiritual things and our love for the gospel songs and all of that. And I really appreciate what she has done with

her life and the way she's raising her family. It's a marvel. So who am I to criticize that?

Groth: I wanted to ask you if you could comment on a couple of things that other people have said about you and your strip. There are three people specifically—Al Capp, Umberto Eco, and Bill Mauldin. [Schulz laughs] Al Capp said, "The *Peanuts* characters are good, mean little bastards. Eager to hurt each other. That's why they are so delicious. They wound each other with the greatest enthusiasm. Anybody who sees theology in them is a devil-worshipper."
Schulz: [laughs] Of course, that was a long time ago. That came from the first *Time Magazine* article, and I don't think he would say the same thing about them any more. But I think he was right on target at the time. Of course, that was typical Al Capp talking. But I don't think that would be a fair description any more.

Groth: For that very reason, he would probably not think they are so delicious now.
Schulz: You know, I knew Al quite well at one point. Until we had a falling out. Which was just a complete misunderstanding. But I liked him. I liked being around him. Because he was funny. But he and I never would have got along in the long run. We were just total opposites.

Groth: I was going to say I'm surprised you got along because in a way, he too was a mean little bastard. [laughter]
Schulz: And of course, I think real jealousy came in because I took over his number one spot at United Feature. And so when he decided to leave, Larry Rutman at United Feature was just plain glad. He didn't miss him at all, because now he had me to fill his place.

Groth: Right, right. Well, you just agreed that he wouldn't have said the same thing about the strip today. Could you tell me a little about how you think it's changed over the years? You said earlier that it's gotten less cruel.
Schulz: Well, like I probably mentioned earlier, I've simply gotten older, that's all. And I don't say sarcastic things to people any more. If I can help it. If I can catch myself. If I find myself making some kind of smart-aleck remark to somebody, now I kind of hold back, and I just don't say things like that any more. I just don't think it's a nice way to be. I think that's just the direction I've gone with the strip, too.

Groth: Well, I have to tell you that occasionally, and there was a recent example of this, you'll have a masterpiece of sarcasm in the strip. [Schulz laughs] My favorite was about seven months ago I think, and Lucy walks up to Charlie Brown on the mound and asks him something like, would I fall off the planet if I stepped far enough back in left field? And he said, "Well, the planet is actually round, just like a ball, but you

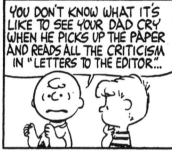

wouldn't know that because you've never touched a ball. You've never caught a ball." It was a masterpiece of sarcasm to the effect that since she's never caught a ball she wouldn't know that a ball is round, like the planet. Which leads me to believe you are really capable of incredibly sharp sarcasm.

Schulz: Oh, yeah. And I don't think it's a good quality to possess. I'm not proud of it. I have had a few incidents down through the years, you know, when I was younger, and said things that I never should have said to people. I don't think it's a good trait to have. But it's good for creativity. That's why it's nice to have a comic strip where you can have an outlet for these feelings that you have.

Groth: But it also requires a wit, which you obviously have.

Schulz: Yeah, what he was saying is funny, but it's not really mean, is it? [Groth laughs] He's not insulting her black hair, and saying "Your hair looks stupid, and you've got a funny look on your face." Or "Why do you walk funny?" Or something like that.

Groth: No, no. But he is insulting her ineptitude.

Schulz: Oh yeah. Well, she deserves it. [laughter] Totally inept. But you know, I love that relationship, because in other areas she's totally superior to him. And the same way with all the characters. I love the little relationship, which took a long time to develop, between Marcie and Peppermint Patty. They insult each other all the time, yet they still appreciate each other.

Groth: It appears in that relationship that it took a while for Marcie to screw up the courage not to be deferential. To give as good as she got.

Schulz: Oh yeah.

Groth: Was that pretty much how it happened?

Schulz: No, again, it just goes back to this search for ideas, Gary. You can't keep hitting the same note all the time. You have to try to advance. And so one thing leads to another . . .

Groth: Now another quote is from Umberto Eco. And I'm sure you read his essay about you.

Schulz: Yeah.

Groth: It was actually written as an introduction to a *Peanuts* book published in Italy, and reprinted in one of his books in English. And he said, "These children affect us because in a certain sense they are monsters. They are the monstrous, infantile reductions of all the neuroses of a modern citizen of the industrial civilization." Now that's a pretty heady observation. [Schulz laughs] I was wondering what you thought of that.

Schulz: I had breakfast with Umberto in Paris. Jeannie was there, and some other friends. We hit it off real well. And we didn't waste any time with small talk. We got into theological discussions. When I'm with somebody like that, I don't want to waste time telling him all about myself and discussing where we live and all of that. I want to find out what they think . . . who they think Jesus really was. Did Jesus have a dog, and all that sort of thing.

Groth: Exactly.

Schulz: And so we had a good time. But it didn't last very long. But I'm sure that when I'm with Umberto Eco, I'm in over my head [Groth laughs] because he's too intellectual for me, and I don't understand the things that he wrote. I like reading these things, and I'm very flattered that he should say things like that.

Groth: Do you think that he was correct in saying that your characters represented . . .

Schulz: I don't know, because I don't understand it. [laughter]

Groth: I see. O.K. Finally, Bill Mauldin said about you, "he's a preacher at heart. All good cartoonists are jack-leg preachers, reading stories, drawing morals from them."

Schulz: Mauldin's quite a guy.

Groth: Do you agree with that?

Schulz: I used to do a lot of preaching. But I'm no good at it. And I never was any good at it. And I would never do it again. I don't mind giving talks. I give talks, and I may do it again, down at Barnaby Conrad's writer's conference in Santa Barbara every year. And it's kind of fun. And I like talking about cartooning, and I love questions and answers, just talking to people about writing and all of that. But I would never want to be a preacher. Because I don't have any axes to grind or beliefs that I want to convince people of. But Mauldin's right there. Cartooning is preaching. And I think we have the right to do some preaching. I hate shallow humor. I hate shallow religious humor, I hate shallow sports humor, I hate shallowness of any kind.

Groth: It's funny, because I know what Mauldin is talking about, but in a way, you're doing the exact opposite of preaching. You're raising questions that are unanswerable.

Schulz: I suppose that's good.

Did you ever read *The Gospel According to Peanuts*?

Groth: Yeah.

Schulz: You'd like him. Robert Short. You know, wonderful guy. We didn't even know each other when he wrote the book. We didn't meet until about a year after it came out. Of course, I haven't seen him for a long time, because I think he's in Arkansas now. He's a Presbyterian minister. He finally joined the ministry after all those years. So he writes to me now and then. And sends me copies of his sermons. He loves preaching. But you'd like him. He's a very nice man.

Groth: Short once said, "Tolstoy believed love [Schulz laughs] is what it was all about, that people are capable of this, that the spirit of love was inherent in people. Culture causes people to be mean and shortsighted. So Tolstoy wanted to withdraw from culture, live very simply, work with his own hands." And he went on, "I think Sparky's religious orientation is typified by Tolstoy." [Schulz laughs] Would you agree with that?

Schulz: [laughs] I don't know. It's beyond me! That's too deep for me. [laughs]

Groth: Now, I'm not going to accept that.

Schulz: I think *War and Peace* is the greatest novel ever written. Tolstoy was a remarkable man. But he sure went through a lot of turmoil. And at one point I think, he felt that he had to give everything away, didn't he? And he also had what Scott Fitzgerald talked about once, "the dark side of the soul," didn't he? He had a terrible experience once, on a trip where he felt a darkness kind of overwhelm him. And I think perhaps a lot of us have gone through that in different ways. And I don't even know if it can be explained. But I'm just astounded that he was able to write the way he did. It's a society that I don't understand at all. I can't comprehend the whole Russian way of living, and the way he lived, did everything that he did, and was still able to write this monumental book.

I had dinner with my heart surgeon. We had played in a golf tournament, and afterwards we were talking. We only see each other about once a year, but I had bypass surgery—gosh, I think it was back around 1980 or so. He was the one who did it—and here is the man who [saved my life.] And I said, "What do you think really are the important things in the world?" He loves music, and I said, "Do you think what you do is really the greatest thing in the world . . . to be a great surgeon?" He said that writing a great symphony or a piano concerto, that's the great thing. To be able to write something that's so great that thousands, millions of people enjoy year after year. That's the real accomplishment. [laughs]

And I did a strip about that once where Charlie Brown was wondering out loud. He was sitting on a bench with Linus. [They were discussing] *War and Peace* or Beethoven's Ninth, or something like that. Then he gets up and strikes out. I think he sits down and say something like, "And I'll probably never write *War and Peace,* either."

I always think about things like that. What is of importance? I suppose the most important thing is just to do what you can do best. You have no other choice, do you? You have a certain amount of ability. And do the best with your abilities.

Groth: You made reference to something you've quoted before. It was either by Tolstoy or Fitzgerald, and it must be a favorite quote of yours. It's, "In the real dark night of the soul it is always three o'clock in the morning."

Schulz: Uh-huh. [laughs]

Groth: And that's an incredibly harsh quotation the sentiments of which fuel your strip, because in a way it's always three o'clock in the morning in *Peanuts.*

© by United Feature Syndicate, Inc.

Schulz: Well, Napoleon said you didn't have two o'clock in the morning courage: I mean unprepared courage. A military man has to have that. The attack is planned all night long, and all of the sudden, it's dawn, and you think, "What have I done?" [laughs] "I can't do this." The brave man has the courage of the early morning. And he does it anyway. I think we all have that bridge to walk and make the trip that we don't want to make, or to see somebody that we don't want to see. That takes the courage of the early morning.

Groth: Do you feel that you have that courage?

Schulz: No. [laughs] Oh, I don't think about it. I just do it because I got nothing else to do. [laughter]

Groth: Speaking of the dark night of the soul, I wanted to ask you something about your philosophical disposition, if I can put it that way, and how it manifests itself in the strip. You've said a couple of things that I thought were incredibly demoralizing or nihilistic. [Schulz laughs] And of course, the strip is very melancholy in a way. You said, "It is a virtual miracle that we've existed over these millions of years against such deplorable odds. When everything is against us." And I was wondering if you could expand on what you meant by that.

Schulz: Yeah. Well, it is astounding, isn't it, that we have survived. Just look at what's been going on over in Algeria these last couple of months. How these soldiers go into small villages and just murder everybody. Why? That's totally absurd to do that! How in the world can people become so monstrous?

You know, the kids in the strip, it's kind of a parody of the cruelty that exists among children, too. Because they are struggling to survive. How many were in your family?

Groth: I was an only child.

Schulz: I was, too, so we didn't have to go through that. But as one child comes along in a family, and another, there's a struggle just to survive and to try to make your parents like you more than they like your sister or your brother or something like that. And then, of course, the struggle in the neighborhood when you grow up is a brutal one.

Groth: You started the strip in 1950 at a time when the kinds of familial difficulties you're talking about were not acknowledged. In fact, they were, I think, hidden or disguised.

Schulz: Well, yeah. And I think I was the first one to bring them up.

Groth: Yes, yes. I mean, there was a lot of sociology from the '50s that tried to counter the widespread, post-War Eisenhower view of America, where everyone had a plot of land and a white picket fence in the suburbs and families were too busy consuming to have problems. But, pop culture is always slow to acknowledge these social realities. And what you actually came along and did at that time was say, "That's not entirely true. There's a lot of dysfunction and neuroses and problems under the veneer."

Schulz: Oh yeah. Well, I remember . . . we never could really go to a playground and have any fun. We could . . . very seldom . . . unless we took a whole baseball team over to play another baseball team on a playground, we could survive. But as far as just going to a playground to have fun, it didn't happen, because there were always other kids there that would ruin everything. And so most of our playing was done within maybe a block or two of where we lived. And there were some blocks that we never dared go to. Because we knew that they were bigger and uglier kids that lived around there. Maybe a lot of it was our own imagination. But we just didn't do that sort of thing. But we kept within our own little area. And that is one of the things I was talking about. Because I despise bullies, and I just hated them when I was a kid, and I still do. Now, I don't draw them much in the strip, because they're hard to draw and it's hard to get any humor out of it. If I was drawing a more serious strip, I think I would bring them in, but I've tried to touch on it a couple of times, but it just doesn't work. I do want to do an animated show, and I know we're going to do it, eventually, about Charlie Brown challenging this kid who is stealing everybody else's marbles, because he's a better player. And Charlie Brown ends up like Shane; he's the gunman who beats the kid.

Groth: Guns down Jack Palance, right. Well, this goes right back to what Eco said about the kids being infantile reductions of all the neuroses of a modern citizen of the industrial civilization. How conscious that this was your point of view were you in the '50s?

Schulz: Oh, I would say, virtually not conscious at all. I think once I got married and we began to raise a family, that was our whole life. And I've talked a bit about this with my son Monte, who loves talking about these things, and you know, we lived out there in that Coffee Lane, and we had our life out there. We didn't pay much attention when people talk about the '50s and '60s and '70s, I frankly don't even know what they're talking about. We lived kind of an isolated life. And that's all there was to it.

Groth: Yet the social trends, the social zeitgeist did effect you because you were aware of it if only on an unconscious or intuitive level.

Schulz: I suppose if you look back, your life goes in different sections. My most influential section of life as a child was living within about three blocks of the barber shop, down around the corner on a quiet street. But we used to play cops and robbers, and cowboys and Indians, and run around the neighborhood and go to the movies and all of that. But there were also unpleasant episodes. There were always some nasty kids around that would spoil things. But there were some good kids, too. And if everybody left us alone, we did have fun. But then later on I moved away from there and became a teenager and then my whole life was just reading comic books and drawing pictures and playing sports. You know, I loved playing baseball. And touch football. And hockey. And that sort of thing. But again, there were always invariably little incidents where nasty kids would come around and spoil things. And I just hated that. Which is, I suppose, one of the times that I loved golf. Because you were out on the golf course yourself and your struggle was with you and the course. It was a great relief.

Groth: Do you ever reflect that the kind of society we've created actually encourages the kind of cruelty and predation in adults that you see in children?
Schulz: Yeah, and I don't think it's something that can be avoided.

Groth: You don't?
Schulz: I think it will always be with us. I do feel strongly, however, that parents should watch more carefully over what is happening to their children. And I think teachers should watch more carefully. Now, a perfect example of this would be one of my grandchildren who lives in Utah came home and he was disturbed by school. He got so he was apprehensive about going to school each day. And my daughter Amy, his mother, asked him why. And he says, "Well, my fingers hurt. This so-and-so twists my fingers back. That hurts." So she said, "I wasn't going to stand for that." So she went right in and told the teacher, and I think his father told their father. "Your stupid kid [will] leave our kid alone, or I'm going to pound you myself." [laughter] And that's what you have to watch. You can't just say, "Well, let it go. It'll be all right." It won't be all right. The bully kid will keep twisting your fingers back until someday he breaks one or something. And I think we have to watch out for that all of the time. I remember my one daughter came home one day when she was in about the fourth grade or something and she says, "That stupid kid, Tom, out at recess he comes around and he pulls the girl's skirts up." And I said, "Well, has he done that to you?" And she says, "Well, not yet." And I said, "Well, if he does, kick him in the stomach." [Groth laughs] And so the next day she came home and she said, "I did what you told me to do." I said, "What was that?" She said, "He tried to pull my skirt up so I kicked him in the stomach." But Meredith was the kind you could tell that to. She wouldn't take anything from anybody. But one of the girls might not. So I think we have to be very careful with our kids and watch over them and protect them.

Groth: You said one other thing I wanted to ask you about. And it struck me as possibly revealing and terribly despairing in a way. You were referring to the animator drawing the little red-haired girl in *It's Your First Kiss, Charlie Brown*, but noting that you never drew her in the strip. And you said, "Somehow you always sell out for a cheap victory somewhere along the way."

Schulz: Yeah. It's almost inevitable when you do as many things as we have done, drawing the strip every day for all these years, and then doing all those animated shows . . . and try to attract attention, and keep them on the air, and keep getting good ratings, and keeping people at the networks interested, you have to do things that will attract some kind of attention. And there's no doubt that that was just one of those stupid stories we never should have done. But it happens. It happens all the time.

Groth: What struck me about what you said was the sense of inevitability about selling out for a cheap victory. The sense that you feel that that's impossible to avoid.

Schulz: The story I liked better was when Charlie Brown sees this girl sitting in the stands at a football game, when they used to have what they called "honey shots." They don't have them any more. The camera used to wander around until they picked out some real beautiful woman sitting in the stands. They don't do that any more. Which is kind of dumb that we should become so sensitive to things like that.

Anyway, Charlie Brown sees that girl and just falls immediately in love with her and how he tracks her down and Linus and he go to find her. That was a good little story.

But again, animation is different. It's almost impossible to talk about the characters and the feature and everything and talk about animation and the comic strip. Because it is different.

Groth: You write all of the animation material.

Schulz: And then I'm at the mercy, however, of the animators. I am not like a playwright, who can write the play, and then have it tried out in New Haven, or rehearsed and rehearsed and rehearsed until they get it just right. Once I write it, it's gone. And I don't see it until it's finished. And I'm at the mercy of the animator who's probably freelance and working at home and isn't as good an actor as I think he should be. So he blows all my scenes, because he doesn't animate the characters the way I think they should be animated. It's very aggravating.

Groth: Is that how you feel about a lot of the animation?

Schulz: Bill Melendez knows that. And he's got some good people, you know, some of them can really draw. And Bill himself is a great cartoonist. But this doesn't mean an animator is always a good actor, and that's what an animator really is, he's an actor. Or he should be.

Groth: There must have been a period where your success was just phenomenal. How did you handle that?
Schulz: No, it all happened very gradually. One thing after another, just step by step by step. While all these things were happening, I was still drawing the strip. All the time.

Groth: How did you maintain your equilibrium amidst this success that must've been growing exponentially?
Schulz: I just did it. That was all. But there did come a time, when I called a halt to some things. I was drawing the dailies, the Sundays, the youth cartoons for the Church thing. And I did some of the Hallmark cards, then we sold the advertising rights to the Ford company. So for seven years I had to help those guys write their ads and I had to draw all the Ford ads.

Groth: You didn't really like doing that, did you?
Schulz: It was hard work, yeah. I could be doing a whole Sunday page, and now I have to waste it on one of these ads.

Groth: Why did you do that?
Schulz: I thought it was just the thing to do. And there was a lot of money involved, and the syndicate was strong for it. That's when we first started making what you'd call a lot of money. And so finally I just said "No more." Also, I had done *Happiness Is a Warm Puppy*. And I did, I don't know, five or six books for Determined. And I also illustrated three books. I did two books for Art Linkletter: *Kids Say the Darndest Things*. And I did two books, *Letters to President Johnson*. Which was easy to do.

Groth: Letters to President Johnson?
Schulz: They took kids' letters and then I illustrated them with funny drawings. It was easy to do. But I didn't want to do any more. I said, "I don't want to be a book illustrator. I'm a cartoonist. I have my own work to do." I just said, "no more." [laughs] In the meantime, I was raising five kids.

Groth: It sounds like as soon as you felt you could say no, you said no.
Schulz: Yeah.

Groth: Can I ask you why you license the characters to corporations like Metropolitan Life Insurance? You obviously don't have to.
Schulz: Well, but they pay a lot of money.

Groth: But you don't need a lot of money. I mean, you already have a lot of money. Right?
Schulz: How would you like to keep this place going [gesturing at his ice skating rink] at $140,000 a month? [laughs]

Groth: But realistically, you make enough money to support this without licensing your characters to Metropolitan Life Insurance, don't you?
Schulz: Yeah, but I couldn't do all the things that we do.

Groth: Is that right?
Schulz: If you turn that off, I'll recount some of that. [The tape recorder is turned off and Schulz recounts some of his philanthropic work.]

Groth: In the course of my research, I came across what I thought was an interesting wrinkle regarding the question of licensing, which involves a complicated question about that. You did two strips, and I think they were done in the '70s, which struck a real nerve politically. One of them was a strip where Linus asks Lucy "What would happen if there were a beautiful and highly intelligent child up in heaven waiting to be born [Schulz laughs] and his parents decided that the two children they already had were enough?" And then Lucy replies, "Your ignorance of theology and medicine is appalling." And that created something of a controversy over whether that was implicitly about abortion. You got letters from both pro- and anti-abortion advocates assuming you were on both their sides. Then another strip you did was one where Sally whispers to Charlie Brown, "We prayed in school today."
Schulz: Yeah.

Groth: And you got a lot of letters from people believing that you were either pro- or anti-prayer in school.
Schulz: That one disturbed Larry Rutman of the syndicate very much. See, it disturbed him when both sides wanted to reprint the strip to promote their beliefs, so we talked about it, and he decided that we wouldn't let anybody reprint them. Now the other one, on abortion, it never even occurred to me. I don't know what I was thinking about, but there is a thought among some brands of theology that souls are

waiting up in heaven to be born. Now how in the world anybody comes up with that is beyond me, and how you can be so sure of that is also beyond me. I always like to go back to Snoopy's theological writings, which he called, "Has It Ever Occurred to You That You Might Be Wrong." And that's the way I feel. These things fascinate me, and I like to talk about them with other people, and hear what they think. But I'm always a little bit leery of people who are sure that they're right about things that nobody's ever been able to prove, and never will be able to prove.

Groth: You said that Larry Rutman decided not to let either side print the strips. Did he make that decision, or did you? Who made that decision?

Schulz: I used to do whatever Larry wanted, generally. Larry was a decent person. He and I got into, oh, a couple of discussions about things. The worst was over Franklin.

Groth: The black character?

Schulz: Yeah, when he was first introduced. Larry didn't mind the fact that Franklin was in it, but he was disturbed about the strip where I think Charlie Brown said, "Come on over to my house someday, and we'll play again" or something like that. And he wanted to make some changes. And we talked about it and talked about it. And finally, I went back to my 1950 smart-aleck mode, and said, "Well, Larry, let's put it this way. Either you print the strips exactly as I draw them, or I quit." And that ended the discussion.

But Larry and I were very close. He was a good man. He was like an uncle to me.

Groth: His objection to that strip you cited sounds racist. Do you know the basis of his objection?

Schulz: Um . . . the syndicate at that time—and maybe they still are, I don't know, maybe syndicates rightfully are—were terrified of [newspaper] editors. They never wanted to do anything that would offend an editor. Although Larry would stand up against some of them. And he told me a few stories about some editors that he just stood up against. And wouldn't let himself be pushed around, either. But it's a hard business. Salesmen are out there and they're driving around in their Dodges trying to sell these features. And I always felt sorry for the syndicate salesman who had to be out there, trying to sell a feature, and the cartoonist is doing something stupid. And he doesn't realize that if it wasn't for the salesman, he wouldn't even exist.

Groth: Do you think he was afraid that it would cause problems say in the South . . . ?

Schulz: Oh, sure. There's no doubt about it. In fact, I did get one letter from one southern editor who said something about, "I don't mind you having a black character, but please don't show them in school together." Because I had shown Franklin sitting in front of Peppermint Patty.

Groth: Good God.

Schulz: But I didn't even answer him.

Groth: Well now, this seems to be an instance where you really took a stand and said in effect you didn't care if it offended people, you thought it was the right thing to do.

Schulz: Yeah, yeah. I've done that now and then.

Groth: [laughter] I don't mean to imply you didn't.

Let me get back to my question about licensing. The strip where Sally whispered to Charlie Brown, "We prayed in school today" stirred up a little controversy.

Schulz: I don't believe in school prayer.

Groth: You don't?

Schulz: No, I think it's total nonsense.

Groth: You said that both sides wanted to use that strip in their own political campaigns, and you said the simplest solution was to deny everyone the right to reprint the strip. And you just told me you actually don't believe in school prayer. Now my question is basically this: you would allow the *Peanuts* characters to sell cars or front an insurance company, but you wouldn't allow them to be used to present a serious political point of view [Schulz laughs] that you believe in. And I was wondering why you would allow them to do one and not the other.

Schulz: Well, I think one is more personal than the other.

Groth: But, shouldn't that be why you should allow the one and not the other?

Schulz: The school prayer thing, to me, is more personal. I feel very strongly about that. Now the licensing thing has always been around. Percy Crosby did all sorts of licensing. *Buster Brown* was licensed like mad, you know. It's always been just traditional. *Lil' Abner,* Al Capp did a lot of licensing. But it comes upon you so slowly, you're not even realizing that it's happening. And also you're young, you have a family to raise, you don't know how long this is going to last. Larry Rutman was very anxious to try and promote something that would guarantee me some kind of a reasonable income for the rest of my life. The first licensing we did almost came along by accident. I was in New York one day and he said some chocolate company wanted me to draw a special strip with some kids drinking their chocolate. And they didn't want the *Peanuts* characters, but just some other little kids. So I did it. And that was our first licensing. And then the Eastman-Kodak company came and they wanted me to do a special little booklet showing the characters using the new Brownie camera. Which I did. Didn't make a lot of money, and it was hard work, but these just came along little by little by little. And then one day some company wanted to make these little rubber dolls of the characters. Well, what was wrong with that? Those were cute. And I suppose Bill Watterson came along later with his stand against licensing which is really ridiculous, but I don't know Bill, and I'm

© by United Feature Syndicate, Inc.

sure his life is different from mine. And he didn't have five kids to support and a lot of other things like that. And so it's always risky to take a stand on some things like that.

Groth: Disregarding the issues involved in licensing per se, it seems to me that the very reason you would let the *Peanuts* characters be used in a political campaign is because you personally believe in the morality of the proposition in a way you can't believe in the Ford Motor Company.

Schulz: Yeah, I suppose.

Groth: And yet you didn't. And I was wondering why . . .

Schulz: Well.

You know, Gary, I don't even remember. That was so long ago. I knew it was an issue at the time. And I just thought that this was kind of a comment on it, that's all. It wasn't even that funny, as far as I was concerned.

But I did write a letter condemning promoting school prayer to the church publication I was very active in. It was called *Vital Christianity,* published in Anderson, Indiana. And there were people writing in saying how important it was to have school prayer. I wrote a letter which was published in their letters to the editor saying how ridiculous I thought the whole thing was.

Groth: Does that belief stem from a belief in the separation of church and state?

Schulz: I just believe that it comes from an absurd use, a ridiculous use, of prayer. That . . . [laughs] this runs us off into all sort of thoughts, Gary.

Groth: Prayer should be a private act rather than a group activity . . . ?

Schulz: And all of that business. And who is the teacher there that is going to have them pray? And is the teacher going to be Catholic or Mormon or Episcopalian or what? It just causes all sorts of problems. And what are the kids praying about anyway? Does it really matter, does praying in school . . . what are you doing it for? The whole thing just opens up all sorts of elements of discussion.

I think it's crazy.

Groth: That seems like a very sensible attitude. The idea that prayer should be turned into the equivalent of an organized sport is odious.

Schulz: I do feel strongly about one other thing, though. And I think it's too late for me. But I think kids could be taught right from the very start that when the teacher comes into the room in the morning they should all stand. And I think the teacher should be referred to as whatever their name is. And I see nothing wrong with pledging allegiance to the flag and whatever it is they want to do. I think there needs to be . . . kids don't mind being polite, if they're taught that's the thing to do. And I think that they wouldn't mind. I think a proper dress . . . this business of teenagers going to school with jeans and a white t-shirt is ridiculous. So there are a lot of things that could be taught at a very early age, and kids wouldn't even mind it, as long as they were taught that this is the proper way to conduct yourself.

I remember when . . . you know, when you first go into the army, calling officers "sir" was so hard to learn to do. And saluting. Some people just thought saluting was so demeaning. But as you learn to be a good soldier, saluting is almost fun. It's a matter of dignity. "Good morning, Colonel." You salute, you're saluting the office, that's all, nothing wrong with that. We need more dignity.

Groth: Yes. That would be a good title for the interview.

Schulz: Yeah. [laughs]

Groth: Licensing has become such a ubiquitous part of our culture, that . . . I wanted to ask you if you didn't think that the public perception of your work and your strip could be transformed in the public consciousness as a result of the saturated level of licensing and merchandising that *Peanuts* achieved.

Schulz: No. I've already proved that to be wrong. This is what people were telling me 20 years ago. And I've proved that to be wrong. The strip is more popular than it's ever been. I remember back in about

1968, Al Capp said, "Well, it's just about run its course, you know. Little kids talking like adults. It's just about run its course." Well, since then, we've added about 2000 papers to our list. Al Capp was pretty jealous of me. [laughter] But I always got along well with him. He was funny.

Groth: Didn't you guys have a bit of set-to over his parody?
Schulz: Oh, yeah. That was so stupid. He just didn't understand. That's all. It was just one of those misunderstandings. Which is unfortunate. Because I always liked him. I didn't know him that well. But when I was around him, we always got along well. All of that. But he had things to be bitter about, anyway.

Groth: You're opposed to injecting politics in the strip, but have you ever thought about the political dimension of licensing? By allowing the *Peanuts* characters to promote Ford, for example, you're in a way promoting private vehicle ownership over and against public transportation [Schulz laughs] which in turn harms the environment.
Schulz: But those things happen so gradually! Larry Rutman, whom I got so close to, treated me really like a father. He had no vision, as none of them did, that this was going to last this long, and the scope of it. This had never happened to them before. The biggest thing that they had ever had was *Lil' Abner* and *Nancy,* but it never compared to this. What he wanted was to establish something for me that would last the rest of my life. He didn't want it to drift out, and then I'd be stuck when I was 45 or 50 or something.

Groth: Who was this?
Schulz: Larry Rutman. The president of United. So that's one of the reasons he took on the Ford thing. Because he thought it was a good, lasting arrangement, and it lasted for seven years. He was always looking for something, kind of . . . what he called an annuity. Something that would last the rest of my life. But it's hard to go back and realize how slowly all of this developed. One step at a time. Some things fell off, and some other things worked. And it was not . . . *Star Wars* . . . an overnight success or something like this. And you know, you look at other people. Bill Crosby does commercials. He sells things. Look at Tiger Woods! [laughs]

Groth: Is he doing it?
Schulz: Tiger Woods is the most phenomenal thing in the history of

licensing. Nothing in the world has ever compared to Tiger Woods. But if he doesn't win some golf tournaments he's in trouble. [laughter] And the fact is that I watched over it all very carefully. I always had control. There were a lot of things we turned down. I get to see everything. Make sure that it's all done properly.

But then on the other hand, we have things that the others have never been able to do. Ellen Zwilick, the most famous woman composer in the world, Pulitzer prize winner, concertos, symphonies, everything. She wrote a *Peanuts* piano concerto last year, and it was premiered in Carnegie Hall. What's wrong with that? There you are, see? That's wonderful to think that my characters can be part of a classical piano concerto. That's unbelievable. And who went to the moon? Snoopy went to the moon! [laughs]

Now, also, we must never forget that while all this is going on, who's drawing the strip? Who has thought of 16 or 17,000 ideas and has drawn all of them himself? I've been faithful to my first client. Which is the newspaper editor.

Groth: Something you just said reminded me of an observation you once made about creative inspiration: "I can almost guarantee it, if I attend a symphony concert, and see a violinist perform as a soloist in a concerto. Or if I merely watch a great conductor, my mind will begin to churn up all sorts of idea, that will have no relationship to watching a violinist or a conductor. There will be an inspiration there."
Schulz: I suppose it's the activity. Almost anything that I do will provide me with a cartoon idea. Sometimes directly applicable to what we're doing, when we're playing golf, or listening to the symphony, I'll think of something. But sometimes just the activity of what you're doing gets your mind going and kind of wakes you up and you think of things.

Groth: I like that, because there's such a subtle connection between a piece of beautiful music and the inspiration for a medium quite distant from it. I know that you used to listen to country music.
Schulz: Not any more. I just don't know where to find it any more. Of course, I never listen to the radio anyway.

Groth: You said that you don't listen to music any more. You can't enjoy music any more?
Schulz: There is no more music. [laughs]

Groth: But even if you don't like what's being done now, there's a wealth of old music.

Schulz: But I never listen to the radio. I have two stations on my car radio. One is PBS, the public radio, the other is a local classical station which most of the time I turn off because they don't play enough Brahms. I never listen to the radio at home.

Groth: You can buy Brahms on CD.

Schulz: Yeah, I bought 'em all. [laughs]

Groth: Do you derive pleasure from listening to music now? Because I got the impression you didn't.

Schulz: For a long while after my separation and my missing of the kids for a little bit, it was so depressing that I just didn't listen to any. It would make me sad. Right now, you'll be stunned to discover that the tape I've been listening to the last three days is Andy Griffith singing gospel songs. [laughs]

Groth: My God!

Schulz: I like gospel songs.

Groth: Is it good?

Schulz: Sure. I don't think he's as good as Ernie Ford. I knew Ernie Ford, but he died. Ernie Ford had a wonderful, rich voice. He used to sing those gospel songs so beautifully. And Sandi Patty was here once. We had lunch. I like her a little bit. None of it means much any more.

Groth: Why do you think that is?

Schulz: I don't know. I keep saying, "I'm getting old." And you don't believe it. But that has a lot to do with it. Things change. Your friends change, and everything else. I like Jill, who you just met. Jill is a delight.

Groth: Your daughter.

Schulz: Yeah. She was with the Ice Follies. She's a rollerblade expert. She and her husband have their production company and they produce rollerblade shows. She's really good . . . and she's fun. We have a lot of fun around her, because she's very witty. But she can't draw. None of my kids can draw! [laughter]

Groth: Is that right? That's pretty funny.

Schulz: But they all like to laugh, and they're all quite witty in their own ways. Jill is very funny. I always enjoy being around her.

Groth: Well, it sounded like you had a really good family life.

Schulz: Yeah, yeah. I really did. That's sad, too. To think you're getting old. You could die any day. That's very depressing.

Groth: [laughs] That's true. That's true.

I was interested in the authors I heard you read. I was surprised you liked Flannery O'Connor and Carson McCullers.

Schulz: They were great.

Groth: They are great. But they also deal in grotesques.

Schulz: To a certain extent. But not like some of the really grotesque writers.

Groth: I can't imagine you're a big Bukowski fan.

Schulz: Who?

Groth: Charles Bukowski.

Schulz: I don't know him at all.

Groth: Who are some of your other favorite authors?

Schulz: Well, let's see. What have I read lately? I'm just finishing John

Grisham's first novel, *A Time to Kill*. But as soon as I finish it, then I want to read *Underworld*.

Groth: By Don DeLillo.
Schulz: Yeah. I'm going to read that.

Groth: Really?
Schulz: Oh, yeah.

Groth: You like Don DeLillo?
Schulz: No, I've never read much of anything of his.

Groth: *Underworld* looks great.
Schulz: This thing has been getting rave reviews. Monte and I were talking about it the other day.

Groth: I'd be very curious to know what you think of it. Because he's not the kind of author I'd expect you to gravitate toward.
Schulz: Who knows?

There's a couple of women authors, too, from England that I like. Margaret Drabble. She's got a new one coming out. And, of course, crime novels . . . everyone likes Elmore Leonard. I've met him a few times. Oh, and I like everything Anne Tyler writes. I call her on the phone to tell her, but she never says anything. I don't think I'll call her any more. [laughter] I guess she doesn't like to talk to people on the phone. Like Fred Couples, the golfer, who says he never answers the phone because it might be somebody who wants to talk to him. [laughter]

I know a professor of English literature from South Carolina, Matthew Bruccoli, he's an expert on Scott Fitzgerald. He sends me a lot of things. I mention Fitzgerald in the strip every now and then.

Groth: I assume you like Fitzgerald a lot.
Schulz: Yes.

We did a *Great Gatsby* number here on ice. We do some things in our Christmas ice show, that nobody else ever does. It was a wonder. [laughs]

Groth: My impression is that you read a lot of dead authors.
Schulz: Not necessarily. I try to keep up on everybody.

Groth: In addition, do you also track down the Classics?
Schulz: Yeah. Oh, yeah.

Groth: So you're really very self-taught.

Schulz: I did a term paper on Katherine Anne Porter. I did one on *Pale Horse, Pale Rider.* I really enjoyed that. That's the only college I ever went to. A college course. I took a course in the novel. And I got an "A" in it. So I've never gone back. I don't want to ruin my grade average. [laughter]

Groth: Right, right. Nowhere to go but down.

It's kind of amazing that a man in your position would do that; you did that about 10 years ago?

Schulz: At least. The older I get, the most self-conscious I get about my lack of real education. But like I said before, I have a host of friends around town here who are all college graduates, and they don't know half as much as I do.

Groth: Do you find that lamentable?

Schulz: Yeah, it is. Terrible.

Groth: I feel like a fish out of water a lot of times.

Schulz: Sure.

Groth: I'll talk to my insurance adjuster or a doctor and discover they can't talk about anything but jet skiing or something.

Schulz: I know. It's terrible. [laughs]

Groth: It's hard to have a literate conversation.

Schulz: Yeah, I know. You'd like my son Monte. Monte's an expert on a lot of things. Once he gets hooked on something. Boy, he becomes an authority.

Groth: Now how old is he?

Schulz: He's just turned 45 this year. It's hard to believe he plays senior hockey now.

Groth: I can't imagine my son at 45.

Schulz: I know.

Groth: I'd have to imagine me at 85.

Schulz: [laughs] Well, I hope you make it.

Groth: I do, too. I know you watch foreign films as well as domestic ones. Do you have any favorite foreign film directors?

Schulz: I don't pay any attention to that.

Groth: People like Fellini . . .
Schulz: I knew Fellini.

Groth: Did you?
Schulz: I have a cartoon upstairs over in the other building that he drew for me.

Groth: Is that right?
Schulz: Yeah.

© by United Feature Syndicate, Inc.

Groth: Tell me how you met Fellini.
Schulz: Let me see. I was going to Rome to be given a medal by the Rome government and have a one-man show. And the lady who was in charge of it, invited lots of people. And she invited Fellini, because she said, "I heard that Fellini likes your work, and has always liked cartooning." But he couldn't make it to the opening. But he did come to the hotel. And we sat in the lobby one afternoon. And had tea, and talked. I found it difficult to talk with him, though, because here's this great man, and I just didn't know what to say to him, and we had a little language barrier. But I asked him about Charlie Chaplain and Orson Welles, and he only met them briefly, and then I had drawn a cartoon to give to him. He seemed pleased, and I said, "Would you draw something for me." He said, "Oh, no, no." He says, "I am not in your class," and all of that. But, "I will think about it." The next day, we had gone on to play golf, and he came into the hotel again and we hadn't returned yet, but Jeannie met him and had tea with him and he brought me this cartoon that he had drawn of himself and Snoopy, so it's a real collector's item. He died about a year later. But at least we can say we met him.

Groth: So that was a few years ago.
Schulz: Yeah. Not too long ago. A few years ago.

Groth: Do you like his films?
Schulz: Oh sure.
I saw one film I loved about a sculptor whose love for art finally destroyed her . . .

Groth: Camille Claudel?
Schulz: Yeah. That was a good film. I think the best movie I have ever seen about the creative process. And of course, the girl that did it . . .

Groth: Isabelle Adjani.
Schulz: She's my favorite.

Groth: I think she is one of the most stunning women in the history of film.
Schulz: She really is. I saw her in another one where she, I think, played the violin. Which was a good one. Anyway, we try almost all of those. This Japanese film is a real gem that's in town now.
Do you watch *Masterpiece Theater* at all?

Groth: No, no I don't.
Schulz: They have something on there now which ended last year called *To Play the King,* which was one of the best things I've seen anyplace, anywhere. It was three separate showings. The first one was three episodes, and then the other one is three. And they brought it back, and then they brought three more. And it is a marvelous . . . one of my girls gave me a set for a present. I never look at videos, but this has been re-run a few times on different PBS stations we have. And I always watch it. Because it's so wonderful. *To Play the King.*

Groth: Lynn Johnston wrote an introduction to one of your books, *45 Years,* and she related an anecdote. She wrote, "Last Christmas, Sparky and I wandered into a bookstore to buy a gift for his daughter. Only one of his books was on the shelf in the humor section. 'My books aren't number one any more,' he told me, 'it's hard to step aside.'"
That struck me as being very melancholy . . .
Schulz: It was.

Groth: . . . moment. I was wondering how you . . .

Schulz: I made a lot of money for a lot of bookstores. You know how many books I've sold?

Groth: I can't even conceive of how many books you've sold.
Schulz: I used to hear 300 million? Lately I've heard 400 million books.

And yet, we are still treated so shabbily. We have a new book program going now . . . but it's . . . there's no market for cartoon collections any more. No matter whose collection it is. What is appalling is to go to the airport when you're going to fly to New York, and you go into the bookstore . . . there are no cartoon books any more. There used to be all the Fawcett reprints, you had *Tumbleweeds,* and some of the ones that you normally didn't see. And they're gone. Cartoon books are just regarded as nothing.

Except, of course for Gary Larson and Bill Watterson. They were the only ones that sold. I went into one bookstore once up in the northern part of the state. And I said, "Do you have any *Peanuts* books?" "Oh no." She said, "We just don't have much call for them." I said, "Do you have any call for *War and Peace?*" [laughter] Why couldn't they order 30 copies and put them up in the front of the store. They'd sell. Nobody's going to come in and say, "Do you have any *Peanuts* books?" So that's what I was talking about there. We made a real revival last year, but that's a long story.

Groth: A cartoonist by the name of Seth, who's a big admirer of your work, wanted me to ask you a question. He wrote, "*Peanuts* may well be the last great strip of the 20th Century. Does this idea please you or sadden you?"

Schulz: Oh. Well, if it's true [laughs], I'm glad that I was the last one. But I doubt if it's true. Somebody is going to come along . . . I suppose Bill Watterson could have been it. If he hadn't quit. He certainly rose to the top in a hurry. He deserved it. And then he quit. So I don't know who will come along these days.

Groth: How did you feel about his terminating the strip?

Schulz: Didn't bother me. Because I never met him. I think that the guy who is really good these days is Patrick McDonnell. *Mutts.* He's great. We like each other . . . We're both followers of *Krazy Kat.* I think what we do is very, very similar to each other. A lot of times, we do things very, very similar. We draw differently. But he draws so funny. So I think he's the best thing around these days.

"I Hate Charlie Brown": An Appreciation

GARRY TRUDEAU/1999

From the Washington Post,
December 16, 1999, A39.
Reprinted by permission.

It was an hour before George W. Bush was to make his forensics
debut at a New Hampshire television station. At a nearby Holiday Inn,
two well-known columnists and a visiting cartoonist were sharing pre-
debate gossip over a meal of barbecue chicken. As they were finishing
up, the conversation turned unexpectedly reflective. "You know," said
the first scribe, "I wrote scores of columns condemning the Vietnam
War, and it didn't make the slightest bit of difference. With one small
exception, nothing I have ever written has remotely affected an outcome." The other columnist nodded solemnly. He too had no sense of
ever having had any meaningful effect on the course of events. Sighing
deeply, the cartoonist reached for his slice of the same humble pie. He
had made a lot of noise in his life, he admitted, but he had no preten-
sions about leaving the world a better place than he had found it. In

fact, he knew of only two people in his profession who could make such a claim—Bill Mauldin and Charles Schulz.

Schulz, of course, would have narrowed that list down to one—Mauldin. Such was Mauldin's stature in his eyes that Schulz paid him the extraordinary compliment of regularly referencing him in *Peanuts* (although as a grown-up, Mauldin could only appear off-frame). Schulz included him in full knowledge that most of his readers would have to ask their elders who Bill Mauldin was, but that was the point: If they didn't know, they should.

Mauldin had chronicled the grubby, dangerous lives of World War II soldiers, and millions of ordinary grunts like Pvt. "Sparky" Schulz had loved him for providing the balm of laughter when they needed it most. Mauldin, Schulz knew first-hand, had made a difference.

So has Schulz, profoundly, but you wouldn't know it by him. It's not that Schulz has been unmoved by the remarkable adulation that has come his way—he just never seemed to trust it much. For his colleagues, this has been perplexing, for they were among the first to appreciate how truly transformative his stripped-down little creation was. *Peanuts* was the first (and still the best) postmodern comic strip. Everything about it was different. The drawing was graphically austere but beautifully nuanced. It was populated with complicated, neurotic characters speaking smart, haiku-perfect dialogue. The stories were interwoven with allusions from religion, classical music, psychiatry and philosophy. And such was Schulz's quiet faith in the power of observational truth, he often passed up punch lines in favor of aphorisms and little throwaway codas—literary devices rarely seen in a gag-oriented medium.

On the surface, Schulz's message was filled with a uniquely American sense of optimism—"Li'l Folks" with big dreams, never giving up, always trudging out to the mound one more time. But the pain of sustaining that hope showed everywhere. Schulz subjected his clueless antihero, Charlie Brown, to the full range of childhood cruelties (it's worth noting that the very first *Peanuts* punch line was, "I hate Charlie Brown"). His strip vibrated with '50s alienation, making it, I always thought, the first Beat strip. Although Schulz would say the very notion is preposterous and grandiose, he completely revolutionized the art form, deepening it, filling it with possibility, giving permission to all who followed to write from the heart and intellect.

I sometimes tease Sparky that my career is all his fault, but I'm far from alone. Study *B.C.* or "Feiffer" or *Calvin and Hobbes* or *Bloom County* carefully, and you'll see his influence everywhere—stylistically, narratively, rhythmically. While the public at large regards *Peanuts* as a cherished part of our shared popular culture, cartoonists also see it as an irreplaceable source of purpose and pride, our gold standard for work that is both illuminating and aesthetically sublime. We can hardly imagine its absence.

For many years, Charles Schulz has celebrated Veterans Day by sending Snoopy over to Bill Mauldin's to "quaff a few root beers." Next Veterans Day, Snoopy will stay home, but his beloved master should know that he will be in the thoughts of the many colleagues to whom his work was as good as it gets.

Drawn into a Dark But Gentle World

BILL WATTERSON/1999

From the *Los Angeles Times*,
December 21, 1999.
Reprinted by permission.

Comic-strip cartooning requires such a peculiar combination of talents that there are very few people who are ever successful at it. Of those, Charles M. Schulz is in a league all his own. Schulz reconfigured the comic-strip landscape and dominated it for the last half of its history. One can scarcely overstate the importance of *Peanuts* to the comics, or overstate its influence on all of us who have followed.

By now, *Peanuts* is so thoroughly a part of the popular culture that one loses sight of how different the strip was from anything else forty and fifty years ago. We can quantify the strip's success in all its various commercial markets, but the real achievement of the strip lies inside the little boxes of funny pictures Schulz draws every day.

Back when the comics were printed large enough that they could accommodate detailed, elaborate drawings, *Peanuts* was launched with an insultingly tiny format, designed so the panels could be stacked vertically if an editor wanted to run it in a single column. Schulz somehow turned this oppressive space restriction to his advantage, and developed a brilliant graphic shorthand and stylistic economy, innovations unrecognizable now that all comics are tiny and Schulz's solutions have been universally imitated. Graphically, the strip is static and spare. Schulz gave up virtually all the "cinematic" devices that create visual drama: There are no fancy perspectives, no interesting croppings, no shadows and lighting effects, no three-dimensional modeling, few props and few settings. Schulz distilled each subject to its barest essence, and drew it straight-on or in side view, in simple outlines. But while the simplicity of Schulz's drawings made the strip stand out from the rest, it was the expressiveness within the simplicity that made Schulz's artwork so forceful.

Lucy yelling with her head tilted back so her mouth fills her entire face; Linus, horrified, with his hair standing on end; Charlie Brown radiating utter misery with a wiggly, downturned mouth; Snoopy's elastic face pulled up to show large gritted teeth as he fights the Red Baron—these were not just economical drawings, they are funny drawings.

More yet, they are beautiful. Drawn with a crow quill-type pen dipped in ink, Schulz's line work has character in its quirky velocity and pressure, unlike the slick, uniform lines of today's markers and technical pens. *Peanuts* could never be drawn by anonymous assistants, as so many other strips were and are—its line is inimitable. The strip looks simple, but Schulz's sophisticated choices reveal a deep understanding of cartooning's strengths. I studied those drawings endlessly as a kid, and they were an invaluable education in how comics worked.

Indeed, everything about the strip is a reflection of its creator's spirit. *Peanuts* is one of those magical strips that creates its own world. Its world is a distortion of our own, but we enter it on its terms and, in doing so, see our world more clearly. It may seem strange that there are no adults in the world of *Peanuts,* but in asking us to identify only with children, Schulz reminds us that our fears and insecurities are not much different when we grow up. We recognize ourselves in Schulz's vividly tragic characters: Charlie Brown's dogged determination in the face of constant defeat, Lucy's self-righteous crabbiness, Linus's need for a security blanket, Peppermint Patty's plain looks and poor grades, Rerun's baffled innocence, Spike's pathetic alienation and loneliness. For a "kid strip" with "gentle humor," it shows a pretty dark world, and I think this is what makes the strip so different from, and so much more significant than, other comics. Only with the inspired surrealism of Snoopy does the strip soar into silliness and fantasy. And even then, the Red Baron shoots the doghouse full of holes.

Over the last century, there have been only a handful of truly great comic strips, comics that pushed the boundaries of the medium and tried to do more than tell little jokes as a relief from the atrocities described in the rest of the newspaper. Schulz does it all: He draws a beautiful comic strip, a funny comic strip, and a thoughtful, serious comic strip. For that, *Peanuts* has achieved a level of commercial success the comics had never seen before. We should understand, as Schulz did, that the merchandising empire *Peanuts* created would never have worked had the strip not been so consistently good. How a cartoonist maintains this level of quality decade upon decade, I have no insight, but I'm guessing that Schulz is a driven perfectionist who truly loved drawing cartoons more than anything else.

I've never met Schulz, but long ago his work introduced me to what a comic strip could be and made me want to be a cartoonist myself. He was a hero to me as a kid, and his influence on my work and life is long and deep. I suspect most cartoonists would say something similar. Schulz has given all his readers a great gift, and my gratitude for that tempers my disappointment at the strip's cessation. May there someday be a writer-artist-philosopher-humorist who can fill even a part of the void *Peanuts* leaves behind.

Index